I0114130

Praises

General Bhopinder Singh, a thorough bred soldier and gentleman to the core has been writing in public domain for the last few years. His flair for precision and fearless expression of views, tempered by objectivity, has earned him considerable acclaim and recognition. A "must read" from an elegant man of all seasons and much distinction.

Justice TS Thakur – Former Chief Justice of India

It is very rare to come across a writer who has a wide range of interests, and can write on all issues with an amazing depth of knowledge. Lt General Bhopinder Singh's articles have been thus, invaluable and widely appreciated by The Citizen's readership, old and young. Punchy, straight to the point, packed with facts!

Seema Mustafa, Editor – The Citizen

Bayoneting with Opinions

Bhopinder Singh

ZB

ZORBA BOOKS

ZORBA BOOKS

Published in India by Zorba Books, 2017

Website: www.zorbabooks.com
Email: info@zorbabooks.com

Copyright © Bhopinder Singh

ISBN Hardcover - 978-93-86407-85-6
ISBN Print Book - 978-93-86407-83-2
ISBN eBook - 978-93-86407-84-9

All rights reserved. No part of this book may be reproduced or transmitted in any form or by any means, electronic or mechanical, including photocopying, recording, or by an information storage and retrieval system—except by a reviewer who may quote brief passages in a review to be printed in a magazine, newspaper, or on the Web—without permission in writing from the copyright owner.

Although the author and publisher have made every effort to ensure the accuracy and completeness of information contained in this book, we assume no responsibility for errors, inaccuracies, omissions, or any inconsistencies herein. Any slights on people, places, or organizations are unintentional.

Zorba Books Pvt. Ltd.(opc)
Gurgaon, INDIA

Printed at Repro Knowledgecast Limited, Thane

Foreword

Opening Fire!

Having sheathed the sabre and folded the *Olive Greens*, the Soldier in me is still 'on duty'! Baptised and bloodied into combat service at the age of 19 with the Indo-Pak war of 1965. The journey saw the Infantry soldier with his sharp bayonet in various insurgencies in the North East, as a 'Brigade Major' in Kargil, to commanding a Brigade in the Kashmir Valley.....all along with a prayer on the lip to never dishonor the name of the 'family', the *izzat* of the battalion and above all, the flag of the Nation – just another Indian soldier honouring the sacred covenant with his Nation.

The sojourns took me from the fighting fields to instructor and staff roles, international diplomatic assignment and an invaluable responsibility and exposure at the highest office of the land, Rashtrapati Bhawan, to work as the Military Secretary to two of the most illustrious son's of India, Shri KR Narayanan and Shri APJ Abdul Kalam. These many-splendored men were giants in history, scholarly intellectual and yet humble to a fault, the abiding memories and dignity of working with them can never be overstated.

Shri KR Narayanan was like a father-figure to me to whom I owe my spirit of unending enquiry. In a candid moment and conversation about the proudest moment of my career till then, led to an innocent, though wholly truthful confession of 'commanding my battalion, 17th Rajput ('Barhe Chalo')'. That same 'Soldier-in-spirit' lived on in my 'second innings' as the Civilian Administrator and the Lieutenant Governor of the 'Shining Outpost' of India, Andaman and Nicobar Islands, and later Puducherry.

From a *fauji* to a *babu,* to even a quasi-*neta,* the learning and unlearning was endless and yet the intrinsic 'Soldier' never really ebbed, as it became an integral part of DNA that came handy, yet again even in the 'third innings' of my life as a commentator and writer. The stories, perspectives and opinions were brewing for a long time and an expression was sought – the soldier to the nation, proudly apolitical, and yet deeply opinionated burst forth, this time wielding the pen. These are interesting times, challenging times and sometimes, even worrisome times, that call for the 'Soldier' to bayonet on with opinions, with utter disregard to political correctness, as the 'Soldier' only swears by the flag of the Regiment, the Army and the Nation!

These selected articles are obviously my own opinions and I do not seek to impose, appropriate or attribute the same to anybody else or that of any institution. That would defy the liberal spirit of India and its myriad perspectives and interpretations. It only seeks to 'add' to the mainstream conversations so that the eventual narrative reflects the totality of opinions, unhindered. I do believe that there is a 'siloisation' of opinions and the twain amongst the various stakeholders of the country rarely meets e.g. the common person on the street, the bureaucrat in Lutyen's Delhi, the soldier on the LoC or the fisherman in the Indian waters. They remain vulnerable and susceptible to the insularity and inadequacies of individual silos and their urgencies, necessities and instincts, as opposed to the composite Indian dream. It is this gap that I seek to address with all honesty and as fearlessly as possible.

Towards this quest of expression, I am acutely aware of my impositions that I afforded on my family, especially my wife – to her, I remain eternally grateful for her patience and support. To my children and grandchildren who remain my fiercest critics and fanatic supporters, I can never tell you how much you mean to me. Lastly, I pay my gratitude to my parents who are long gone, yet living in my dreams and aspirations. The stories have just started and there is a lot more to reflect upon, debate and comment on….. the pen will continue to fire on, no matter what!

Content

The Restive Neighbourhood

International Affairs with Geo-Political implications

**Indian Security Framework and the
Indian Defence Forces**

Governance, Administration and
Political Essays

Societal Commentary

Personal Musings

The Restive Neighbourhood

Pak Army's Journey into Unsoldierly Debasement
(ASIAN AGE/DECCAN CHRONICLE, 11 May 2017)

The military history of the Indian subcontinent is rooted in over 7,000 years of civilisation, which is replete with bloody foreign invasions, and local wars amongst kingdoms. Theories of warfare, esoteric weaponry, and chivalry in the battlefield are part of the folklore, and ingrained in the psyche and imagination of its people. References to the art and science of soldiering during the Vedic periods, in epics like the Mahabharata and Ramayana, and the subsequent ravages and wounds of aggression from distant lands, have bequeathed a unique martial tradition that made an avowed imperialist like Winston Churchill pay tribute to, "the unsurpassed bravery of Indian soldiers and officers". Nearly 150,000 soldiers from the Indian subcontinent died in the two World Wars. The raw courage of Jemadar Prakash Singh Chib (13th Frontier Force Rifles), Naik Fazal Din (10th Baluch Regiment), Rifleman Lachhiman Gurung (8th Gurkha Rifles), and the 37 others who were awarded the Victoria Cross, is a testimony to the fine soldiering traditions and instincts in the Indian subcontinent, from which nations were subsequently carved.

Modern day Armed Forces of both India and Pakistan owe their genealogical construct, and DNA, to the erstwhile British Indian Army. The shared values, ethos, and cultures of the two "partitioned" militaries, took diametrically different trajectories and narratives in their respective sovereign journeys, immediately after Partition. While India inherited a very vibrant, structured, and all-pervasive democratic culture and leadership, Pakistan was a more "sudden" reality, bed-rocked on the flawed "twin-nation" theory that hoped to unite the disparate diversities; hence, opening the space for a more assertive role for the Pakistani military in day-to-day governance. The Indian Constitution on the contrary, further ratified and legitimised the supremacy of the civilian/democratic framework, *vis-à-vis* the Defence Forces.

The Pakistani Defence Forces' baptism with "palace intrigues", and political machinations, started within days of Independence with Operation Gulmarg (involving two of the only four native lieutenant colonels of the Pakistani Army, then), a devious plan to foment and instigate a local uprising in Kashmir, by dispatching *lashkars* (tribal militias), and Pakistani regulars. Soon the patented cat and mouse game of the Pakistani establishment started, with the rocky relationship of the first Prime Minister, Liaquat Ali Khan, and the Pakistani military, culminating in the first of the many subsequent coup initiatives, with the "Rawalpindi Case" conspiracy. This led a nervous Pakistani Prime Minister to over-rule seniority, and competence, in the very first appointment of a native Pakistani Chief of Army Staff, when Gen. Ayub Khan was selected, as his name was not even in the nomination list sent for consideration. Ostensibly pliant, and the "least ambitious", Ayub would set the precedent for many more to follow, when he deposed his mentor, President Iskander Mirza, in a coup to rule till 1969, only to be replaced by Gen. Yahya Khan. However, the seeds of the Pakistani Army's interest in the civilian, political, commercial, and geopolitical domains were irreversibly planted, and an extra-constitutional role for the military, institutionalised.

In India, the Defence Forces remained disciplined in their "step", steel, and professional march. The years, 1965 and 1971, were brilliant exploits of the Indian Forces and despite the euphoria for the Indian soldier, the leadership and systems within the organisation ensured the apolitical sobriety, and the professional imperatives of honour, nobility, and dignity in the profession. In a "moral state" like India, the Armed Forces steadfastly restrained themselves to the constitutionally mandated role of the "Sword-Arm" of the nation. For sure, individual indiscretions, culpability, and mistakes have occurred. However, institutionally, the Armed Forces have no independent "will" or design of their own, other than that of the sovereign. There is no mandate for any regional, religious, or casteist bias to debar any individual from rising to the highest ranks of the three services. The Indian Armed Forces are perhaps the only breathing and thriving personification of the profound and composite concept of "India".

Whereas, the Pakistani military entertains many caveat angularities around minorities, and regional and sectarian differences, within. The formal rule of the Pakistani military for 35 out of the 70 years of Independence, and the informal "behind-the-scenes" string-pulling for the balance period, has ensured a parallel power structure in the Rawalpindi GHQ, along with the civilian government in Islamabad. The Pakistani Army is infamously known as "Army Inc." for their commercial interests, and the generosities that they bestow on themselves. Gen. Raheel Sharif was allotted 90 acres of land on retirement, apparently, "in accordance with the existing rules and purely on merit"!

Unsurprisingly, public mainstreaming of the Pakistani military has infused the larger societal decay within its veins. Unlike the "barrack-ised" Indian Forces, strains of uber-religiosity, and ideological and political affiliations afflict the Pakistani set-up. Often, reports of purges (mostly, at junior levels) are commonplace. Degradation in the soldiering ethos is an inevitable outcome of such exposure, and domain overreach. While militaries have wars, casualties, spies, and even prisoners, as part of the operational turf--there is the subscribed Geneva Convention that prohibits torture, and other cruel or inhuman treatment, and outrages upon individual dignity. In recent years, the track record of the Pakistani military has been increasingly unbecoming of a professional soldier that assumes, affords, and insists on a noble warrior's creed and conduct. The Kargil war saw the brutal and inhumane torture on Lt. Saurabh Kalia, and the return of his mutilated body was in sharp contrast to the treatment that was meted out to the 90,000 Pakistani prisoners-of-war, in 1971.

The recent mutilation and beheading of Constable Prem Sagar, and Naib Subedar Paramjit Singh, follows the similar pattern of unsoldierly and unscrupulous behaviour that happened in the Machil sector last year, in the Rajouri sector in 2013, and in the Kel sector in 2008. It is an unequivocal sign of the continuing moral debasement and ignoble soldiering sensibilities that are either encouraged or condoned, reflective of the shameful degradation of the Pakistani military culture. As a nuclear power that has never won a war, and remains vindictive, portents of increasing unprofessionalism of its Defence Forces bodes ill for the region, as indeed, for its self-combusting journey.

Pathan angst on the Durand Line

(ASIAN AGE & DECCAN CHRONICLE, 31 Mar 2017)

Festering wounds on both sides of the 2,640-km-long Durand Line, demarcating the contentious border between Afghanistan and Pakistan, have flared up again. Af-Pak relations have hit a new low in recent times, with each side accusing the other of insincerity in fighting terrorism. The Afghan President, Ashraf Ghani, is a relatively new believer in Pakistani duplicitousness, after having given Islamabad the initial long rope in the failed hope that the Pakistani state-within-the-state, the ISI, would rein in anti-Kabul terror groups, like the Afghan Taliban and the Haqqani Network. The recent attack on the Sufi shrine in Sehwan, Sindh, has led to counter-accusations by the Pakistanis that Afghanistan is soft-peddling on anti-Pakistan terror groups, like Tehreek-e-Taliban, based out of the Afghan hinterland. Each time tempers rise, the unsettled legacy of the Durand Line is invoked by the Afghans, to chafe and remind Islamabad of the historical consequences of fingering the irascible Pathans, or Pashtuns. Recently, former Afghan President, Hamid Karzai, stated, "We remind the Government of Pakistan that Afghanistan hasn't and will not recognise the Durand Line," and that Pakistan has, "no legal authority to dictate terms on the Durand Line". This outburst was fuelled by the Pakistani move to close the Af-Pak border posts indefinitely, and restrict the free flow of people and trade, ostensibly to check and control the spiralling terror attacks in Pakistan. The border was later reopened.

The "Great Game" of the 19th century, between the competing imperial powers of Russia and Britain, led to a cartographical truce, illogically knifing the lands of Pashtunistan or Pakhtunistan (land of the "Pashtuns") into two parts--between modern day Pakistan, and Afghanistan. British colonial civil servant Sir Henry Mortimer Durand, along with the then emir of Afghanistan, Abdur Rahman Khan, agreed upon territorial demarcation (Durand Line) for administrative purposes, splicing the restive Pashtun or Pathan-dominated area. Today, over 30 million Pathans are in Pakistan, while another 14 million are on the other side of the Durand Line in Afghanistan. The tribal-feudal nature of this society, and its bloody past, has seen the blood-letting of marauding conquerors--Darius I, Alexander the Great, Mahmud of Ghazni, Muhammad of Ghor, Genghis Khan, Timur, Babur, to the later-day imperial powers of the British empire, and the more recent history of the Soviets first, and now the Western forces. Violent lawlessness, leading to a constant fight for its unique independent identity, has become a way of life there. The only thing that has survived the test of time in the region is the grit of the inviolable *Pashtunwali* code that emphasises death to dishonour, as the old Afghan saying goes, "A man with the power to fight doesn't need to bargain."

What recently riled the Pathans even further were the unprecedented accusations of "Pathan profiling" in Pakistan, with the implied logic of labelling them as terror suspects by default or design. Official circulars and notifications seeking that anyone with "Pasthun attire and having Pasthun looks" be reported, willy-nilly perpetuates the negative stereotypes of the Pathans, as barbaric and lawless terrorists. The Chief Minister of Khyber-Pakhtunkhwa Pervez Khattak, himself a Pathan, had to intervene and ask, "Is the Punjab chief minister Shehbaz Sharif more Pakistani than us?" He then presciently warned, "We should not be pushed against the wall, or we become rebels."

Compounding the sense of Pathan suspicion is the ill-timed plan to merge the Federally Administered Tribal Areas (FATA) with the province of Khyber-Pakhtunkhwa. This step can be potentially volatile, if it is contextualised locally, as yet another attempt by the "Punjabis" in Islamabad to tinker with the Pashtun narrative. It potentially repeals the time-honoured tenets of the Frontier Crimes Regulation (FCR), which loosely applies as governing laws to the seven tribal agencies (districts), and six frontier regions of the FATA, and subsumes the same to come under the standard Pakistani laws that are applicable in the Khyber-Pakhtunkhwa province of Pakistan. The increasing firepower of the Pakistani military (earlier through Operation *Zarb-e-Azb*) in the region, more recently with the questionable "counter-neutralising" of over 100 terrorists in the aftermath of the terror attack in Sehwan, and the frequent cross-border firing and attack, across and into the Afghanistan border, has upped the ante of the co-Pathans on both sides of the invisible Durand Line.

While it is still early days for the immediate spectre of a return to the ghosts of a Pathan nation, or Pashtunistan--with the Afghan Taliban on the ascendancy, in Afghanistan (they too reject the Durand Line), and with an irritable Pathan populace on the other side in Pakistan, apparently suffering a "second-class" treatment, allusions to the "war of independence" in 1919 (also known as the Third Anglo-Afghan War), when Pathans on both sides of the Durand Line meshed and fought for a common cause, always lurks menacingly in the shadows. The hypothetical dissolution of the Durand Line is tantamount to questioning Pakistani sovereignty on 60 per cent of its controlled land mass. This, after the blow of Bangladesh in 1971, could be disastrous for the integrity of Pakistan, especially with other areas like Balochistan smarting under Pakistani ham-handedness. Islamabad will do anything to curb opening yet another frontier of friction, for its severely overstretched resources; therefore, it will continue playing its dangerously patented, divide and rule policy of pandering to certain specific elements/groups of terrorists in the region, who act as proxies of the Pakistan state, and continue to checkmate notional threats from Afghanistan and India, as indeed continue to keep the restive and temperamental Pashtuns divided amongst themselves.

The Afghans know that the Durand Line issue is a weak spot for Islamabad, and an emotionally uniting issue amongst Pathans on both sides, which could tie the Pakistani state into intractable knots. No technical legality of the principle of *uti possidetis juris* (honouring borders signed during/with colonial powers) will cut ice with the Pathans on either side. Similarly, Pakistanis disagree on a 100-year shelf life for the Durand Line treaty, as that makes its legality untenable. The Pathans are always prone to invoking the issue of *izzat*, which can't be transgressed, and these codes and the feudal camaraderie join them in a common cause. With a disgruntled and traditionally armed Pashtun population, not just on the Durand Line but also spread out across other Pakistani provinces (Karachi itself has over seven million), the vulnerability of the Pakistani state to control the growing Pathan angst and ire, should it escalate even further, will be severely tested.

8

Pakistan Disowns History

(STATESMAN, 9 Mar 2017)

Till very recently, Sindh or "Mehran" was an oasis within Pakistan's undeniably syncretic past, a melting pot that gently hosted the forgotten, and faceless, diversities of the ancient land. The name "Sindh" itself is etymologically derived from Sanskrit, for the river Sindhu (reference to the Indus river). Even the name "India" owes its origin to the Greek pronunciation of Sindh. This cradle of civilization that dates back to 7000 BC, and predates all modern religions of the world, has the famous Mohenjo-Daro ruins within its geographical womb.

Sindh's fabled spirit of "inclusivity" was sustained with the acceptance of Mohajirs (Muslims who migrated from India to Pakistan, after Partition), and by retaining nearly all of the remaining Hindus in Pakistan (40 per cent of Tharparkar district identifies itself as Hindus). It also played host to Balochis and Pashtuns in an occasionally uncomfortable huddle, in the tinderbox of Karachi, as well as the adherents of the Shia, Ahmadiyya, Christian, and Zoroastrian faiths. However, it was always the generous and welcoming presence of the Sufi Khanqahs, dotting the dusty arid lands of Sindh, which were symptomatic of the hope and counterpoise to the rising extremism and militant strains, and have been recently imported from the distant Arab region. The land of mystics, wanderers, and poets like Abdul Latif Bhittai, Manjhi Faqueer, Sachal Sarmast, and of the Sufi sites like the holy shrine of the great Sufi patron saint Hazrat Lal Shahbaz Qalander, has been brutally convulsed by the new reality of a terror-inspired, retrograde, and an increasingly intolerant Pakistan, which is at war with its own history, ethos, and instincts.

A major problem with Pakistan is the dangerous reworking of history--the supposition that the narrative starts with the advent of the Arab commander, Mohammad Bin Qasim (8th century CE), as the "first Pakistani". This is factually wrong, insincere, and contrary to the *Quaid-e-Azam*, Muhammad Ali Jinnah's vision of the modern state of Pakistan. The project to artificially "Arabize" itself, and deny the actual past was undertaken by the massive pumping of petro-dollars, by the Arab Sheikhdoms who generously funded the burgeoning *madrassas* that imparted regressive, sectarian, and reactionary instruction. Today, the proverbial chickens are coming home to roost.

The terror attack in Sehwan that targeted the shrine of Lal Shahbaz Qalandar, and killed nearly 100 people, was an attack on Pakistan's deep-rooted sensibilities, and future hopes. The Islamic State's Khorasan faction, which claimed responsibility for the dastardly action, represents the antithesis of the all-encompassing and pacifist school of thought, exemplified at the shrine of Syed Muhammad Usman Marwandi, generally referred to as Lal Shahbaz Qalandar of Sehwan. This revered site is for Hindus and Muslims alike, beyond the sectarian divides of Shia-Sunni-Ahmadiyya denominations, a place that willingly accepts the singing transgender community, dancing dervishes, and non-conformists who simply want to celebrate divinity without the doomsday interpretations, impositions, and rigidities of the *mullahs* and *pundits*. The *dhamaals* in these Sufi shrines, replete with philosophical questions, unanswered quests, and celebratory *qawwali* strains, are in sharp contrast to the austere, ultra-conservative, and non-questioning compliance ordained by the orthodox school of monotheistic Salafism.

Pakistan is posited at the virtual crossroads of making a choice between the original, syncretic, and profound moorings of its vibrant history, and that of the intolerant strains injected by its recent Arab benefactors, who summarily declare all non-adherents as *Takfir* (apostates) and *Kafirs* (non-believers), hence justifying the violent means of expressing dissent against them.

The outrage at the Sufi shrine was followed by the familiar political response of "eliminating terrorists with full force", and such vacuous statements as, "It is time for us to unite and fight against the internal and external terrorists". The Pakistani Army indulged in more kinetic bluster, "Every drop of the nation's blood will be revenged, and revenged immediately. No more restraint for anyone". All this was trite and meaningless. Pakistan has relentlessly persisted with the dangerous game of selectively patronizing extremist elements, as part of its "strategic depth", while pointing fingers across its borders (in this case, Afghanistan), whenever terror has struck on its soil. Directly, or indirectly, the Pakistani establishment has been a willing accomplice and catalyst in institutionalizing religious intolerance in its society, and no amount of counter-drives (apparently 100 suspected militants were "neutralised" within three days of this terror attack) will address the fundamental issue of Pakistan disowning its genealogical past, with the parallel regression of rewriting its sovereign narrative with narrow religiosity, iconography, and inspiration from the Gulf monarchies (who are paying their own price for living by the sword, and perpetuating ignorance).

The devotees of the Sehwan shrine refused to be deterred by the obvious terror threats, and immediately resumed the customary *dhamaal*--an ode to the centuries-old tradition. But the official establishment has routinely failed to confront the "terror nurseries" that breed hatred, bloodlust, and exclusivity.

One is reminded of the haunting lines of the sub-continent's poem, "Dama Dum Mast Qalandar" (originally written by Amir Khusro, and later fine-tuned by Bulleh Shah), *"Har dam peera teri khair hove, Naam-e-ali beda paar laga jhoole laalan, O naam-e-ali, O naam-e-ali beda paar laga jhoole laalan, Sindri da sehvan da sakhi Shabaz Qalandar, Dama dam mast Qalandar, Ali dam dam de andar* (O Lord, may you prevail every time, everywhere, I pray of your well-being, In the name of Ali, I pray to you to help my boat cross in safety...in the river of life)". The words ring truer today than ever before. From the voice of Runa Laila in Bangladesh, to the Wadali brothers in India, to the irrepressible Nusrat Fateh Ali Khan in Pakistan, every singer has graced and invoked the name of Shahbaz Qalandar in soulful reverence, coupled with the call for peace.

Pakistan has to reconcile itself with its own past. The creation of Bangladesh, in 1971, was an early warning of the "twin-nation" theory (a united "Muslim" nation), the non-acceptance of which is violently felt in Baluchistan, Khyber Pakhtunkhwa, and its hinterland. It is a tryst with the home-grown extremist organisations. The occasional attempts to selectively address the mushrooming terror nurseries are as cosmetic, as they are inadequate.

Pakistan must first learn to celebrate its own true history, vivid diversity and rich culture, and not suffer from any inferiority complex, as that aids the facilitation of alien sensibilities and their brutal implications.

Raheel Sharif's role to backfire on Pak

(ASIAN AGE & DECCAN CHRONICLE, 18 Jan 2017)

In the background of the bitter slugfest between the politicos and military men in Pakistan, the ease with which the former Chief of Pakistani Army Staff, Gen. Raheel Sharif, demitted office, raised many eyebrows. Earlier, rumour mills were rife of a possible extension, "field marshal-ship", to even popular support for a military takeover for the then, COAS. Defying widespread public sentiments, and the precedents of "extension" set in motion for the last 18 years, with the previous two COAS extending their terms beyond the stipulated timelines--Gen. Sharif stepped down in a civil, unhurried, and confident manner on November 29. The possible reason for the seamless "hanging up of boots" perhaps lay in the supposed Pakistani *quid pro quo*, where the Saudi Arabia-grateful government of Nawaz Sharif bought peace with the general, in return for sovereign acquiescence to the Saudi kingdom's earlier request of soliciting Gen. Sharif's services, in heading the 39-country Islamic Military Alliance to Fight Terrorism (IMAFT).

Gen. Sharif has impressive credentials when it comes to handling terrorism--he was leading the Pakistani establishment's counter-fight against its own Frankenstein monster, the Pakistani Taliban (Tehreek-e-Taliban), while on the other hand, as the overall head of the infamous ISI, he was privy to machinations of its nefarious terror networks. From spearheading Operation *Zarb-e-Azb* in the lawless North Waziristan, to his Atlas-like persona playing out on the mean streets of urban Karachi, to controlling rural banditry in the dustbowls of Sindh--being the superhero of Pakistan's fight against terror makes him a logical candidate to head such a coalition, to fight international terror. Besides, Pakistan has the largest standing Army in the Muslim world (0.6 million, sixth largest in the world), arguably the most professional within the *ummah*, and nuclear to boot--not surprisingly, Mohammad bin Salman Al Saud, Saudi Defence Minister and founder of IMAFT, had sought the additional coronation of Gen. Sharif as the head of

IMAFT, to his concurrent responsibility as Pakistani COAS. This was earlier turned down by Prime Minister Sharif owing to the impracticalities of managing dual responsibilities, and the initial scepticism of Pakistan towards the obvious "sectarian" construct of IMAFT.

IMAFT's composition is of either the "Sunni-majority" nations, or "Sunni-ruled" (Bahrain and Lebanon are not "Sunni-majority"). True to the divisions in the Islamic world, the "Shia-ruled" Iran, Iraq, and the official government of Syria are not signatories to IMAFT. Contrary to the usual ire and angst against the traditional Zionist enemy, that is Israel, or the Western world, it is the implosive sectarian Shia versus Sunni war that is bloodying West Asia--in Yemen, Shia Houthi rebels supported by Iran are fighting a violent battle against the Saudi-supported troops, in Syria and Iraq, the governmental forces, Shia militias, and the Iranian Revolutionary Guards are locked in a free-for-all bloodlust with the Gulf sheikhdom-sponsored rebels (Sunni grouping), in Lebanon the Iran-supported Shia group Hezbollah retains its independent presence, and weaponry in defiance of the National Army--the sectarian cleavage is commonly alluded to as the "Shia-Moon", with prospects of Shia-inspired rule running from the shores of Iran, and Iraq, to swathes of Syria, and Lebanon (including the pockets of Bahrain, Yemen and South Saudi Arabia, hosting the Shia enclaves).

This divide, and vitriol, got formalised by the open rift between Tehran, and Riyadh, when the Saudi Arabian embassy in Tehran was ransacked by irate protesters (following the controversial hanging of the Shia cleric Nimr al-Nimr in Saudi Arabia), and the reciprocal disallowance of Iranians to go on the annual Haj, in the holy city of Mecca, by the Saudi kingdom. The American thawing of relationship with the Iranians further riled the Saudi establishment, as it saw the move as a further enabler of its historical nemesis, Iran, in its bid to establish its alternative supremacy.

Pursuant to this obvious sectarian denomination of IMAFT, Pakistan had earlier not agreed to join Saudi Arabia's war in Yemen, against the Shia Houthi rebels. Fearing sectarian reprisals, Islamabad chose to ignore Saudi Arabia's initial request to contribute soldiers and weaponry, as it could potentially stoke anti-Shia sentiments in Pakistan's fragile fabric of Islamic diversity (Shias contribute approximately 15 per cent of the population, and are subjected to frequent clashes). Pakistani parliamentarians unanimously voted against the expansive military intervention in West Asia (even though the Pakistanis have a military presence within Saudi Arabia, ostensibly to protect the kingdom itself). However, Pakistan's presence in the proxy war in Yemen was thought to exacerbate Shia fears internally, besides risking having a disgruntled Iran.

However, Saudi Arabia has a "special" relationship with Pakistan, it routinely doles out the invaluable petro-dollars for sustenance, hosts over two million Pakistani expatriates who remit hard currency, and shelters its politicos from turmoil (PM Sharif is personally indebted to the kingdom for granting a lifeline, following the military coup in 1999). Today, international opprobrium on Pakistani duplicitousness on terror has subtly edged Islamabad towards China, and it seeks to deepen its Saudi moorings, given the lack of Western benefactors. The move to avoid joining IMAFT initially was purely driven by internal considerations. However, as it runs out of options, the spectre of a Pakistani general heading the "Muslim-NATO", is indicative of throwing caution to the winds.

IMAFT is sectarian in spirit, and the responsibility accorded to Gen. Sharif will not go unnoticed in Iran. While it is still in the formative stages, as it is headquartering in Riyadh, and its principal sponsorship is from Saudi Arabia, there is very little doubt about its definitions of "terror". This appointment has strategic import for both Pakistan, and Iran, and any official Pakistani allusion to an independent decision by Gen. Sharif would be naïve--it is a sectarian choice that is sanctified by the Pakistani establishment, and its strategic calculus.

Incorrigible Warlords

(MILLENNIUM POST, 11 Jan 2017)

Afghanistan's recent history is bloodied by various irascible and incorrigible warlords with personal militias (ethnicity or region-based), who run their geographical domains like personal fiefdoms. The non-Taliban, and non-ISIS (or *"non-Daesh"*) based Afghan warlords who are part of the loose confederation of the ruling dispensation, in Kabul, are struggling to adjust to the mandated civility, cohesiveness, and transparency of the democratic processes. While most of them view the role of Pakistan (read, ISI) suspiciously, and are extremely concerned about the rise of the phenomenon of *"Daesh"* reaching their doorsteps, and threatening their powers, yet, an unabated power struggle amongst each other ensures a meek defence against the common enemy, the Taliban, and the *"Daesh"* inspired forces.

With a history of fickle loyalties, these warlords have often changed sides with the simple incentive of suitcases filled with wads of dollars. Former US President, George Bush, admitted to the invaluable role of "a bargain" via the distribution of $70 million to these mercenary warlords, in the last few months of 2001, which proved extremely useful in "softening" the enemy, and ensuring a swift collapse of the Taliban. The ethnic diversities within Afghanistan have an uncomfortable history of bloodshed, and extreme distrust amongst each other. Therefore, retaining the logic of maintaining these militias and warlords to protect their own clansmen, or region, even though a supposed National Government exists in Kabul. So, this brings an uneasy equation for a Tajik warlord like, Atta Mohammad Nur (Governor of Balkh province), and the Uzbek warlord, General Rashid Dostum (current Vice President), making it difficult for them to coexist and fight insurgency jointly, as their own enmity goes back to the civil war that preceded the Soviet withdrawal. Today, with depleted US/NATO forces present in Afghanistan, the incumbent President, Ashraf Ghani, has no option but to punt on these strongmen to take on the resurgent Taliban, and the additional angularity of the *"Daesh"* threat.

Irrespective of their feudal ways, it is only through the counter-brutality of these warlords that Kabul controls the restive hinterland. The survival of provinces like Kandahar, and Nangarhar necessitates pandering to the likes of "Lt. Gen" Abdul Raziq, Abdul Zahir Qadir, and Gul Agha Sherzai who routinely use ham-handed and blunt tactics to suppress any dissenting voices, and thereby "control" the entry of Taliban. Routine complaints of human right violations notwithstanding, these garrulous men control the local economy, public discourse, and divert developmental funding into their domains to fatten their own purses in a virtual system of *"rentier"* economy. This challenges the effective governance, and moral position of President Ashraf Ghani, who has to walk the tightrope of indulging the "pro-government" warlords to do Kabul's bidding, ignoring their frequent oppressive instincts in the face of international opprobrium, and keep retaining their services by doling out monetary largesse, and positions in the governmental set-up.

Even the providential opportunity of a distracted ISI (dealing with its own Frankenstein monster, the Pakistan Taliban or TTP (i.e., *Tehreek-e-Taliban Pakistan*) is getting wasted in Kabul, with a rag-tag official force composed of the Afghan Defence Forces, and the unreliable private militias with vested interests. General Rashid Dostum is symptomatic of the Afghan malaise--a perennial turncoat who started out as a pro-communist general, turned into a US ally who took on the Taliban, and is now a mercurial governmental authority ("First Vice President"), who besides securing invaluable votes from his ethnic Uzbek stocks (estimated at 7-9 per cent), also muscles out any opponent, be it anti-government or even from the government. Beyond his running, and bloody feud with the Tajik warlord in the adjoining Balkh province, Atta Nur Mahmood, he has been in the news recently for having abducted his rival Ahmad Ischi, and subjecting him to extreme brutality and torture. Herein, lies the test of the rule-of-law for the President, Ashraf Ghani. He either risks prosecuting the dreaded "First Vice President", General Rashid Dostum, and earning the ire and angst of the strongman (especially when Ashraf Ghani is struggling to keep his allies in flock to meet the rising challenge of Taliban and *"Daesh"*), or he succumbs to the reality of Afghanistan, and silently overlooks the brazen violence perpetuated by these irascible warlords.

Such practical challenges impact regime survival, delay reforms, and the modernisation efforts of an instinctively democratic and committed reformist, Ashraf Ghani. In a situation, where the Western powers are selectively playing hardball against these warlords, these reckless caudillos tend to play one international power against the other, and look for new benefactors. Last year, Rashid Dostum solicited arms from Russia, ostensibly for a fight against the ISIS, and with the Russians seeking to retain a strategic foothold in the official affairs in Kabul, Rashid Dostum re-established a relationship with the Kremlin, even as Washington looked the other way. Last September, a similar agreement with the former Prime Minister, and the Pashtun warlord, Gulbuddin Hekmatyar (also known infamously as the "Butcher of Kabul"), raised a similar moral crisis. Expectedly, a lot of local Afghans were horrified at the sovereign compromise, and the Human Rights Watch called the deal, "an affront to victims of grave abuses". Such pardons afforded on the notorious history-sheeters is a debatable tactic, which divides the public opinion, and the Afghan strategists. Past experience with these warlords also points at their incorrigibility, given their unreliability and intransigence. For instance, the deal with Gulbuddin Hekmatyar was on the horizon for the longest time, due to his reluctance to sign the deal in the presence of foreign troops on Afghan soil. This was later captured, and documented as a "point of disagreement" between the two signing parties. This culture of extending impunity from prosecution warlords is fraught with risks, as proven war criminals get away scot-free, only to show their instinctive brutality whenever their individual fiefdoms are sought to be reined-in, by the national narrative of law and order.

The Hekmatyar accord was hoped to provide a template for the way forward, for other disgruntled Taliban, or *"Daesh"* supporting groups, but so far, no major group has made a similar dash for reconciliation. Ashraf Ghani is saddled with warlords who think individually, and never collectively, as Afghanistan, so this constant *impasse* ensures that the governmental alignments remain weak, and Kabul gets further enfeebled, battling its own palace intrigues.

International powers partake their choices amongst these incorrigible warlords to retain, what Pakistan calls "strategic depth", while this forced huddle of disparate warlords offers a sub-optimal opposition to the main threat to Afghanistan (i.e., the growing presence of groups like Taliban and "*Daesh*"), offering regressive, puritanical, and ultra-fundamentalist strains of governance as alternatives.

Diplomacy the only Option

(DECCAN HERALD, 24 Dec 2016)

The terror attack in Nagrota, which killed seven Army personnel, is a grim reminder of the seamless continuum of the Indo-Pak narrative, irrespective of the political *brouhaha*. Nagrota follows earlier terror patterns in Uri, Pampore, Pathankot etc., interspersed with multiple other governmental interventions, talks, and military engagements that often lead to a false sense of a national perspective, about the ground situation in Jammu and Kashmir.

The spin afforded on the recent Indian Army conducted surgical strikes, across the LoC, typifies the dangers of aggressive political appropriation and decisive supposition--of what was essentially a sub-component of the Army's ongoing means of tactical deterrence, albeit conducted with hallmark precision and guts. The "surgical strikes" were not the first time, neither will they be the last time such actions will be necessitated; but to wrap up the same as some sort of a "conclusive" deterrent would be to short-sell the complexities involved.

Similarly, the convenient allusion of the relative lull in civilian unrest and infiltration along the LoC, in Kashmir, to the economic surgical strike of demonetisation, is in the realm of a "feel-good" imperative for cadres, as it belies the blander but pertinent reality of the onset of winter, which results in the inaccessibility of mountain passes. The sombre and nuanced reality of J&K becomes a victim to comeuppance triumphalism.

Pakistan is instinctually wired towards an existential crisis, borne of the genealogical fault-lines of the "two-nation" theory, which were humiliatingly undone with the creation of Bangladesh. A certain irreconcilable angst exists in its national polity that warrants revenge against India. This inherent discomfiture with its own state sustains the diarchy of institutions that have inspired Pakistan from time to time--its military, the clergy, and the politicians.

Irrespective of the political dispensation at power in Pakistan (either civilian or military), India feeds the popular imagination, and acts as a binding agent for the otherwise irreconcilable diversities of Pakistan's sectarianism, regionalism, and conflicting religious strains. Historically, mainstream support in Pakistan has flowed towards whichever of the three institutions has offered the "best bet" to take on New Delhi.

The inglorious military defeat against India, in the 1971 war, provided legitimacy to the civilian government of Zulfikar Ali Bhutto. Later, Gen. Zia-ul-Haq built popular perceptions about his regime with trademark brinkmanship, when he professed the infamous policy of "bleeding India through a thousand cuts".

Therefore, Pakistan's belligerence towards India, and the ability to successfully espouse the proverbial "K" factor on international platforms, becomes the decisive parameter of choice between these competing institutions (the third institution of the clergy is on the back foot, post the Lal Masjid siege of 2007, and the subsequent state action against militant Islamist organisations, like Tehreek-e-Taliban, which target Pakistan, itself). The institutional cauldron of Pakistan oscillates between preference for democratic processes, and yearning for military takeover from time-to-time (as witnessed prior to Gen. Raheel Sharif's retirement).

Now, a certain formula of effective control of the Pakistani establishment, by the Pakistani military, has become visible since the time of Gen. Ashfaq Parvez Kayani, whilst still maintaining the ostensible *façade* of a civilian government in Pakistan. Persistently, this formula riles the civilian government in Islamabad, as it unsuccessfully tries to rein in the Generals.

Within Pakistan, the military is not just the "Sword-Arm" of governance (like, in India), but its role has been expanded to running vibrant and hugely successful commercial interests, defining the international policies, and postulating on matters like corruption in politics (e.g., the pointed references made at Prime Minister Nawaz Sharif, by his earlier Chief of Army Staff, Gen. Raheel Sharif).

In reality, the military calls the shots, and the politicos offer an invaluable and plausible opportunity of deniability. To keep the arrangement going, the military positions its key men in sensitive posts like the NSA, and the ISI chief. Within itself, the Pakistani military is a well-oiled organisation that protects its creatures, while in uniform, as in the case of Gen. Musharraf, even after his retirement.

The management of perceptions towards the Pakistani military are regulated by the hugely funded Inter-Services Public Relations (ISPR), which builds the alpha-male image of the likes of Gen. Raheel Sharif (and will now do so for Gen. Qamar Javed Bajwa). This is critical so as to hide institutional ignominy, and failures like the 1965 war, 1971 war, the failed race for Siachen glacier, misadventures in Kargil, and the routine bloody noses, like in the recent surgical strikes. But, the Pakistani Army still has to maintain a certain hawk-like posture, to ensure relevance and justification in the national imagination.

All talk of Gen. Bajwa's apolitical, moderate, and anti-militancy outlook is pre-mature, and has to be viewed from the operating template afforded to him by this preordained arrangement, which mandates an "active" India interfacing. Peace would be disastrous for the institution of the Pakistani military, as it destroys the existential legitimacy and commercial affluence that it offers to its incumbents, serving and retired.

Gen. Bajwa need not rearrange the formula--he is a confident Punjabi (the mess gossip in Pakistani units suggests that only the unconfident "minorities" dash into *coup d'états*--all previous coups were either by the "*Mohajir*" or "*Pathan*" Generals). The backroom control formula also insulates the military institution from domestic and international opprobrium.

All in all, India needs to recognise the existence and imperatives of this formula, and persist with the slow-burn solutions of seeking international isolation of Pakistan (diplomatically), strengthening the wherewithal of the Indian Defence Forces (militarily), and engaging in urgent rapprochement with our own Kashmiris (politically). All this, without the shenanigans of political hubris, one-upmanship, or chest thumping of which Nagrota is the unfortunate symptom.

Kathmandu's Strategic Choices

(MILLENNIUM POST, 19 Dec 2016)

Nepal is frantically getting wooed by two opposing suitors, the historical partner in India, and the proverbial "option", China. Landlocked, and geographically surrounded by these traditional foes, the dynamics within Kathmandu oscillate between flirting with one over the other, depending on the cost-benefit analysis that determines the topical preference. The recent flurry of restlessness owes its genealogical discomfiture to the view in Kathmandu, which got cemented last year, in the wake of the protests over Nepal's new Constitution--Delhi was perceived to be playing the role of an interfering spoiler, favouring the minority Madhesis. This led to mutual finger-pointing, and accusations of "big brother" attitude, which was sought to be angrily addressed by counter-courting India's nemesis, China. Except, topography and cultural context ensured the pragmatic sway in favour of India, *vis-à-vis* China, irrespective of the political shenanigans and strategic posturing, to the contrary. Since then, the freeze in the Indo-Nepalese equation has thawed with leadership visits to assuage the initial logjam that had resulted in the crippling disruption of cross-border supplies, which are critical for the Nepalese economy and polity.

The Indian intransigence of supposedly playing hardball during the crisis has inevitably left an indelible imprint within the mainstream in Kathmandu, and a frustrating sense of the need to correct the over-dependence on India has moved the popular imagination. Except, the much-bandied projects of connectivity between the Chinese mainland, and Nepal, are in the realm of strategic drawing boards, and are fundamentally prohibitive regarding investments required to overcome the geographical hurdles, and engineering complexities. This humbling realisation in Kathmandu, and the subsequent softness from Delhi, has ensured the restart of the transactional Indo-Nepalese relationship; albeit, after leaving a bitter aftertaste, and a sense of despondency that needs to be corrected, urgently. A parallel narrative is taking place in Mongolia, where akin to the trade blockade on the Indo-Nepal border last year, China has recently closed a key border crossing on the Chinese-Mongolian border. This is ostensibly in retaliation to the provocation by Mongolia of hosting Dalai Lama in its capital, Ulan Bator. Seemingly, in a repeat of what China did to India during the Indo-Nepalese stand-off, this time India has reportedly asked Mongolia to avail of a US$ 1 Billion Indian help-line, to stave off an immediate economic crisis in Mongolia.

Murmurs abound of the strategic one-upmanship by India, against China, in Mongolia, which is eerily like the scavenging role that China tried to play (and nearly succeeded in pulling off), of veering Kathmandu away from India. However, the Chinese have preferred to downplay the Indian gesture to Mongolia, smug in the comfort of the fact that over 90 per cent of Mongolian import and export is conducted with China itself (again, reminiscent of the over-indexed Indo-Nepalese trade). For China, its famed infrastructural behemoths and hyper-projects like CPEC (China-Pakistan Economic Corridor), One-Belt-One-Road, and "String-of-Pearls", entail substantial investments from Beijing to fund the same. In such an overcommitted scenario, yet another mega-infrastructural initiative to connect the Chinese mainland to Kathmandu via all-weather roads, or by rail (to connect landlocked Nepal with the Chinese ports for import-export) is realistically not feasible, economically--the "size of prize" from the Chinese perspective, simply does not add up in the immediate future, given the relatively smaller size of the Nepalese market for China to peddle their wares. The foremost Chinese priority is to ensure access to the Arabian Sea ports (hence the urgency with CPEC and the Gwadar port), and to ensure the security and safety of its sea-faring routes in the vulnerable and restive South China Sea (especially in the narrow Malacca Straits). Given the enormity of these tasks and commitments on hand, the Nepalese investments will need to be put on the back-burner. Even for Nepal itself, the convenient and historical stance of equidistance (the earlier monarchies had defined Nepal as a zone of peace), between China and India, will be tested in an increasingly black and white world, with the strategic convergence and emergence of a clear Indo-US axis on one hand, and the alternative Chinese-Pakistani axis, on the other.

Fundamentally, Nepal will have to determine the bloc that it chooses to throw its weight behind--the recent isolation and international opprobrium of Pakistan in the regional framework (SAARC summit, and during the Heart of Asia meet) will not go unnoticed in Kathmandu, as it seeks to define its future course. Even the expected ideological tilt of the incumbent Prime Minister, Pushpa Kamal Dahal "Prachanda" (also the Chairman of the Communist Party of Nepal, Maoist-Centre), towards China, was allayed when he chose to visit India, as the first port of calling, after assuming Prime Ministership in August 2016. A marked period of retrain, and acknowledgement of mutual concerns have been reinitiated. The inherent contradiction of a leftist government in Kathmandu dealing with an avowedly, rightist government in Delhi, is thankfully getting tempered with much-needed maturity, respect, and cooperation. India, too, has a task on its hand of correcting the recent perceptions of hegemonic instincts, belligerence, and unwarranted interference in the sovereign affairs of Nepal.

There is an undisputed and profound Indo-Nepalese "connect" that is civilizational, emotional, and cultural as opposed to the Chinese "connect", which is more on the rebound and tactical. The free-border and the inter-linkages of the Indian Military, owing to the outstanding service rendered by the Nepalese Gorkha soldiers in the Indian Army (providentially, both the current Chief of the Indian Army, and the Vice Chief of the Army, belong to the Gorkha Regiments), are also an integral part of the relationship shared by the two countries. The Chinese are expectedly wary of the renewed Indian moves in Nepal, and have threatened "endless trouble" if India were to perceive the Chinese largesse towards Nepal as an anti-Indian move.

Over a dozen trucks carrying basic materials like clothes, electronics, appliances, and building materials worth $2.8 million are making their difficult way towards Kathmandu. With its obvious desire to rope-in Nepal within its strategic fold, and an accompanying inability to offer an infrastructural solution, to walk the talk, the Chinese have opted for a more ostensibly pacifist and covert "cooperative" stance that would encourage Nepal to persist with its "neutrality" (read, equally friendly with China, as with India), and stand with its famed "cheque-book diplomacy" (last year, China pipped India to emerge as the largest donor of Official Development Assistance). This also enables Nepal to play the China card with India, as and when the heat from Delhi gets to Nepal. Clearly, there is a conflicting and competing flow of strategic winds in the region, and so far, Nepal has managed to utilise the conflict to its advantage. However, going forward, it will have to make a definitive choice of its preferred direction. India too has a lot to answer, and will have to make remedial amends towards Nepal to ensure that the ultimate choice made by Nepal is not one out of coercion, bluster, or necessity.

Asia's Boat People

(STATESMAN, 5 Dec 2016)

Away from the mainstream media, the tragic persecution of the forgotten Rohingyas is unfolding in neighbouring Myanmar. The recent flare-up was of a scale that prompted the UNHCR (the UN's refugee agency) to intervene, and censure the Myanmar Government, "to ensure the protection and dignity of all civilians on its territory in accordance with the rule of law and its international obligations". This purge is especially ironic as it takes place under the watch of the 1991 Nobel Peace Prize winner, Aung San Su Kyi, as the "First and incumbent State Counsellor" (a creative designation that overcomes her inability to be formally anointed as President, owing to a constitutional provision). Oddly, Suu Kyi's Nobel Peace Prize citation had mentioned, "her non-violent struggle for democracy and human rights". Today, the Muslim Indo-Aryan race of Rohingyas is facing systemic disenfranchisement in the latest democracy in the world, as indeed, violent backlash from the majority non-Muslim Rakhine people, which has led to over 100 confirmed deaths, and the displacement of 30,000 Rohingyas.

The Rohingyas have been subjected to an identity crisis for centuries, as their disputed claims of nativity to the Rakhine State (a coastal strip that is contiguous to the Chittagong division of Bangladesh), in Myanmar, are buttressed with documented records of Bengali labour imports during British rule, and by the multiple exodus warranted by the Bangladesh liberation war into the bordering Rakhine State. Their Muslim identity, separatist movements (including a failed one to join Jinnah's Pakistan in 1947), and the popular perceptions of imminent demographic changes with their burgeoning population has always posited them with suspicion and discrimination. Theravada Buddhism and Myanmar nationalism have ensured that the fractured and diverse society of Myanmar is able to close ranks against the Rohingyas, from the days of the Burmese *junta* to today's ostensibly, pacifist government of the National League for Democracy. The Bamar majority of Myanmar is openly in favour of denying the Rohingyas citizenship, with even Suu Kyi maintaining a populist and partisan stand of refuting any genocidal tendencies, and stating that there is a general "climate of fear", caused by "a worldwide perception that global Muslim power is very great".

The expected mellowing of the national narrative against the Rohingyas was short-lived, with the transition from the heavy-boots of the *junta* regime, to the freedom of participative democracy in 2016. Internationally, talk of a "democratic dictator" in new Myanmar does the rounds, as her silence on "one of the world's most persecuted minorities", is widely construed as ingenious complicity.

Even though, Myanmar hosts an uneasy and restive diversity of 135 officially recognised ethnic groups, the Rohingyas remain unrecognized under Myanmar's 1982 Citizenship Law, and are, therefore, stateless. These nowhere people, scurrying across the borders, have earned the unfortunate sobriquet of Asia's latest "boat people". Over 1 million Rohingyas reside restively in Myanmar, and an equal number are believed to have fled in exile to neighbouring Bangladesh, Indonesia, Malaysia, Thailand, some even attempting to make a desperate dash to the Indian islands of Andaman and Nicobar. Denied citizenship in Myanmar, and with the status of illegal immigrants everywhere else, the Rohingyas are closeted in squalid camps on both sides of the border. Adding to the ostensible numbers of the Rohingyas, are the fleeing Bangladeshis, who are attempting their own exodus from grinding poverty, while getting clubbed as Rohingyas, in the region.

The wave of global Pan-Islamic assertion is resulting in all Rohingyas being conveniently labelled as "Islamic Jihadists" from Bangladesh, overlooking generations of existence in the Rakhine State. But, with their own tryst of economic compulsions and unemployment levels, all countries in the vicinity like Bangladesh, Indonesia, and Thailand are pushing back the hapless Rohingyas. Deprived of civic rights, employment, or freedom of movement within Myanmar, their refugee-like status affords a ghostlike anonymity that is sought to be played down and removed from public imagination as Aung San Suu Kyi maintains an ambivalent and uncommitted attitude, "we have not tried to hide anything on Rakhine", in the face of international criticism.

There is not one nation in the region, backing the cause of the Rohingyas, and the banality of asking "both sides" to exercise restraint is widely suggested. The popular perceptions of fear and loathing against the Rohingyas, and the electoral importance of that sentiment in a participative democracy, is preventing the "champion of freedom and human rights" to come clean, and extend the equality of citizenship to the Rohingyas. The 2012 outbreak, and Rohingya riots, were attributed to the *junta-era*, but now the civilian and democratically elected government is equally failing in its first visible test of demonstrating its inclusiveness, and democratic instincts.

Today, access to the Rakhine state is tightly controlled, to-and-fro is sparse, and reportage is restricted. UN bodies, and the Human Rights Watch (HRW) are pressing for access to aid agencies, independent journalists, and humanitarian aid workers to operate freely. Equally, Bangladesh is getting pressured to provide critical humanitarian aid, as per international laws, to Rohingyas fleeing human rights violations. In such times, for Rohingyas to seek succour, relief, and protection by informing the police or the military on either side of the border is not an option. This gives rise to protectionist militant groups, like *Aqa Mul Mujahidin* (AMM), who come with the additional baggage, and regression, of promoting extremist Islamic ideology. The net result then, is the widely supported military crackdown by the Myanmar military, which results in extreme brutality, under the ostensible purpose of fighting Islamist terror.

The Rohingyas are stateless "nowhere people", who are fleeing one form of discrimination, to land in another. There are no state benefactors or mentors for their cause, caught as they are in the vortex of an apathetic regime, and an equally disinterested neighbourhood. The human crisis unfolds silently.

Game Changer or Spoiler

(STATESMAN, 18 Nov 2016)

The *pièce de résistance* at the Zhuhai air show, in Guangdong province, was the long-awaited Chinese J-20 stealth fighter jet. The 60-second fly-past, in a first ever public sneak-preview, was the cynosure of the world, as China demonstrated its claim of entering the exclusive club of countries with "fifth generation" fighter planes. Touted as the only other operation-ready answer to America's Lockheed Martin F-22 Raptor (entered service in 2005), and the Lockheed Martin F-35 (entered service earlier this year), the J-20 is a strategic statement of intent by the Chinese, which suggests the narrowing down of the critical technology gap with the US, in a fight to actualise the neologism of the "Chinese Century".

The diffusion of technology, economic output, and power has reduced the spectre of US hegemony, especially with the Chinese claiming to have overtaken the mantle of the largest economy, from the US. Earlier, it was generally accepted that the Chinese were at least two decades behind the US, in terms of military capability; especially in maritime, aerospace, and technological dimensions. Therefore, with its numerical strength (largest standing army of nearly 2.5 million *vis-à-vis* the second largest army of the US with 1.5 million), the Chinese have a robust "defensive" position. However, its hegemonic ambitions necessitate "offensive" capabilities, which call for exponential advancement in military ware, like the J-20, or a navy with "Blue-Water" capabilities. However, questions on J-20's capability, and efficacy remain.

To put it in perspective, the French Rafale (36 bought by India) is a fourth-generation fighter, whose design concepts emanated in the 1970's and 1980's, like the Eurofighter Typhoon, F/A 18 Hornet, MIG 29/35, or the Sukhoi-35. The key differentiation in the fifth-generation fighters is the emphasis on the "all-aspect stealth", highly integrated systems that enable networking with other elements, and the deployment of advanced avionics, and airframes. So far, the Russians and the Chinese are in catch-up mode, with their respective programmes of Sukhoi PAK FA, and J-20, as the contending platforms to the US F-22, or the more recent F-35. Incidentally, India has pegged its need for a "Fifth-generation" fighter, on the success of the Russian Sukhoi PAK FA (with FGFA or Fifth Generation Fighter Aircraft, envisaged to be co-developed with HAL, as an even superior platform in terms of stealth, super cruise, avionics, and sensors). India is expected to procure 144 of these two-seat versions, besides 50 original Russian single-seater versions, with the induction expected to start from 2020.

Virtually undetectable, with enhanced lethality, and the ability to operate in hostile anti-access environments, these "Fifth Generation" fighter planes are worth the extreme cost (F-35 programme is supposed to cost $1.5 trillion, making it the most expensive military weapons system in the world). The sci-fi abilities include inter-operability to share everything it can see with other aircraft and operational centres, 360-degree access to "real-time" combat information, electro-optical targeting systems that deliver laser, and GPS-guided weapons--all this, while remaining undetected!

Concerns over J-20's "stolen" technology, and inability to fully match up with the US F-22, or the F-35 abound, with questions on its radar-evading coating, design issues like poorly shielded engines, avionics on-board, or the sensor-fusion capabilities to make it a comparable "fifth-generation" competitor. It is said that data stolen, or hacked from the American contractors, contributed substantially to the development of the Chinese J-20. US Deputy Defence Secretary, Bob Work, had conceded that the Chinese "have stolen information from our defence contractors and it has helped them develop systems". The J-20 is said to proximate the F-22 platform, whereas J-31 (still under development by Shenyang Aircraft Corporation) is said to mirror F-35.

The J-20's relatively larger frame *vis-à-vis* the American fighters, ought to give it a longer reach with more internal fuel capacity, and a larger weapon carrying bay for missiles and munitions. While it may not be as stealthy, or as capable as the US platforms, it is still a quantum leap in terms of its still hard-to-detect capabilities, which could be superior to anything in the region, be it the current

Russian made Sukhois, MIGs, or the Japanese, or Indian forays (e.g., the stuttering development of Tejas-LCA). The Chinese are maintaining that the J-20 would be fully operational by 2018, and could start induction thereafter. Already the Pakistanis, who are the largest importers of Chinese arms, have evinced interest to buy the export variant of the J-20, called the FC-31.

So, while exact details on the specifications and capabilities are still patchy, and doubts over the comparable US offerings will persist, the J-20 development needs to be noted, in terms of the "reverse-engineering" feat of the Chinese, and their ability to rapidly develop, and deliver a weapons platform, ahead of schedule. Even though, it is early days to fully operationalise and functionalise the entire J-20 support system, to make it lethal, there is the threat of Indian BrahMos missiles on the Sino-Indian border, which could bring the Daocheng Yading airport in Tibet within the "first-wave" hit. We need to recalibrate our future response, with the option of accelerating the joint Indo-Russian FGFA, or even considering the American F-35s, which are on order by countries like Israel, Turkey, South Korea, and a host of European countries.

Already, tensions in Asia are rife like never before: The Middle East and the Af-Pak region are caught in a Pan-Islamic fire, the Indo-Pakistani LOC is witnessing unprecedented cross-border hostility, North Korean belligerence continues, and the Chinese have upped the ante in the restive South China Sea, with its famed bullying, and intimidation tactics that threaten the sovereignty of nations in the region. Seen in this cauldron, the J-20 threatens to unbalance the delicate security arrangement, with a fresh imperative towards a corrective arms race. The J-20 may not be a game changer in capabilities, as postured, but it surely is a dangerous spoiler.

Dubious Blasphemy Laws
(DECCAN HERALD, 21 Oct 2016)

The ongoing judicial saga in Pakistan, against the execution of Asia Bibi, has taken a curious twist with one of the three judges, Justice Iqbal Hamid-ur-Rehman, recusing himself from hearing the final appeal. This, ostensibly, since he had heard the linked case involving the former governor of Punjab, Salmaan Taseer.

Asia Bibi, who belongs to the minority Christian community, has been convicted under the notorious and dubious, blasphemy laws. In 2010, she was sentenced to death, by hanging, in a district court. This has since pricked the collective conscience of the progressive world, and some educated quarters within Pakistan, like Salman Taseer, who stood up for her, against the blasphemy laws, and paid the ultimate price of getting executed in cold blood by his own security guard.

Blasphemy, like terror, is an ambiguous and undecided issue for the Pakistani establishment. It is a political hot-potato that typifies the multitude of contradictions in the Pakistani narrative. Genealogically, Pakistan was born out of the concept of a "two-nation theory", which is premised on a separate state for Muslims. Yet, a powerful case for secularism was envisaged by the *Qaid-e-Azam* (father of the nation) Muhammad Ali Jinnah, in his policy speech on August 11, 1947, "You are free; you are free to go to your temples, you are free to go to your mosques or to any other place or worship in this state of Pakistan. You may belong to any religion or caste or creed that has nothing to do with the business of the state".

This contradictory ambiguity at birth, has retained an opportunity for the rulers of Pakistan to twist the interpretation to suit political expediency, and necessities of the times that be. While the Pakistani military (which officially ruled for 35 out of the 70 years of independence) is institutionally inclined towards secularism (but for the reign of General Zia-ul-Haq, who sowed the seeds of overt Islamisation), the civilian politicians have invariably been susceptible to pander to the religious bigotry of the *mullahs*, for electoral gratification and crowd-sourcing.

Geographical contiguity with Afghanistan had led to the massive influx of monies to support the Mujahedin movement of the 1980's. The pumping of support by the Western powers (on the last leg of the cold war), and generous doles by the Gulf monarchies, resulted in debilitating infusion of militancy, and puritanical strains of Islam within the Pakistani mainstream. Since then, the proliferation and regressive agenda of the Wahhabi-inspired *madrassas* in the Pakistani hinterland and frontiers, has changed the societal fabric from a secular and inclusive approach, towards an aggressively intolerant framework, which is at short fuse with the myriad minorities. The dangerous slide into religious extremism soon morphed into terror groups, which besides impacting the neighbourhood (India and Afghanistan), has earned Pakistan the notoriety of being the hub of global terror.

The current set of Pakistani blasphemy laws owe their form and content to Zia's Islamisation drive, which added multiple clauses and penalties (including "death, or imprisonment for life" to punish blasphemy against the Prophet Muhammad--as in the case of Asia Bibi, which if carried out, will be the first person to get executed for blasphemy, though over 50 people have been murdered by the restive populace even before the formal trial got over).

A simple accusation of blasphemy is enough to make a case against the vulnerable minorities; therefore, a disproportionately high number of minorities like the Christians, Hindus, and even Ahmediyas (declared non-Muslim, since 1973) are targets of blasphemy accusations. Basic electoral sensitivities have ensured that the political parties have not made any corrective, or protective changes for the targeted minorities.

Fundamentalist lobbies

Pressure from the powerful fundamentalist lobbies, religious parties, and wary citizenry has relegated the support for Asia Bibi to the very limited fringes of the educated classes. International support for her case is seen conspiratorially as yet another example of Western interference, compromise of Pakistani sovereignty, or as an affront to the Pakistani judicial system. No contrarian view to the blasphemy laws is allowed to be expressed or tabled, without an implied threat of accompanying violence. Soon after Taseer's murder, Shahbaz Bhatti, the Minister for Religious Minorities (a Christian himself), was shot dead in broad daylight for espousing the case of Asia Bibi.

This case is reflective of the leadership paralysis that has gripped the Pakistani establishment, and tests its resolve to effectively counter implosive tendencies. Already, murmurs of judges getting apprehensive about their personal security is doing the rounds. Earlier, the upholding of the death sentence for Mumtaz Qadri, the guard who killed Salman Taseer, had forced the Supreme Court judges to retreat shamefully from the backdoor, in order to escape public wrath, for punishing a man seen to be supporting the spirit of the blasphemy laws.

Given the current Pakistani background, the will of the law-makers, and the judiciary, to take an unbiased stand in the Asia Bibi case, is suspect. It is only the military establishment which can somehow step in, and take an unpopular position of standing up to the blasphemy laws. For all its intrigues, complicities, and murk, the Pakistani military is essentially against the *mullahs*/clergy in the battle for institutional supremacy in Pakistan. However, it is also a past-master in the duality of approach (for example, it is firm on Pakistan-facing terror groups while being supportive of the India-facing and Afghanistan-facing terror groups).

Often, the fault-lines in Pakistan are genealogical and unfixable, as they are a means of ensuring relevance to the said institutions. Tension and terror in the neighbourhood is an existential requirement for the Pakistani Army. Sectarian violence, and religious pandering is a tool of political relevance for the politicos, and the retention of poverty and ignorance an invaluable hook for the clergy.

Midnight's Children

(TRIBUNE, 31 Aug 2016)

As Prime Minister Narendra Modi invokes the Baloch people, from the Red Fort, the restive Pashtuns continue to wage their battle along the Durand Line, the Sindhis are angrily cooling their heels with the PPP in opposition, and the Punjabis are on the ascendancy with the PML(N)-led government in Islamabad. There is an almost forgotten set/race of people that is fighting its own existential crisis in Pakistan, the Mohajirs (Arabic for immigrants). The 6.5 million-odd migrants, euphemistically called "Urdu-speaking" Muslims, who chose to migrate from India to Pakistan (0.7 million went to East Pakistan, now Bangladesh), in the aftermath of the Partition, are the "Midnight's Children" who partook in the largest mass migration in history.

Like all immigrants, the "natives" looked askance at Mohajirs for doles like land grants and government job preferences. Settling mostly in Karachi and urban centres of Sindh, this hardworking lot availed of import-export opportunities, and created a cluster of small-scale industries to reach a certain affluence that became the envy of the Sindhis, Baloch, Pashtuns, and the majority Punjabis. The first open demonstration of the virulent strain came to the fore with the presidential election, in 1964, which saw General Ayub Khan (a Pathan) trounce a "Mohajir", Fatima Jinnah (the late president's sister). Soon Ayub Khan went about shifting the national capital from Karachi (Mohajir dominated) to Islamabad, and initiated a deliberate reverse-affirmation in favour of the Pathans and Punjabis to break the monopoly of the Mohajirs. This, in order to forge an unwritten and continuing alliance of the Punjabi-Pathan domination in the corridors of the government, and most importantly, the Army. The Sindhis joined in the plunder, with Zulfikar Ali Bhutto declaring Sindhi to be the sole language of Sindh, and refusing to accommodate demands of the Mohajirs (40 per cent of Sindh's population) to include Urdu, even as an additional language. This led to violent protests, and a subsequent governmental acquiescence was not without a sting in the tail, as more affirmative incentives were given to competing "natives" to retain the heat on the hapless Mohajirs.

The advent of General Zia-ul-Haq in the late 1970's, himself a Mohajir, couldn't control the societal animosity and undercurrents against the Mohajirs, as he was primarily engaged in securing and consolidating his own position by pandering to ultra-religious elements, and simultaneously doing the West's jihadist bidding during the Cold War era. This constant targeting, defencelessness, and fear among the Mohajirs led to the creation of the Muttahida Qaumi Movement (MQM, formed from the earlier Mohajir Students Organisation), with the mercurial and maverick Altaf Hussain as its head. This formation was perennially involved in gun-letting, and bloody turf wars, against the Sindhis and Pathans in Karachi. Used and abused tactically by Zia-ul-Haq, first to neutralise the PPP, then by the PPP itself, and later by the Muslim League, the MQM was involved in an unending saga of intrigues and manipulations for national electoral results. Often, the MQM was faced with unbridled brutality at the hand of the government (who outsourced the dirty job to the rival "Haqiqi" faction), and to the Rangers to reign in MQM foot soldiers.

All this led to reverse ghettoization, and reverence for the MQM and Altaf Hussain. His popularity soared even further, with the Mohajirs seeking solace and redemption against an insensitive regime, and emerging as the sole voice of the cornered Mohajirs. The second-class treatment for Mohajirs got firmly institutionalised when the term "terrorist" was apportioned on Altaf Hussain, who had to flee to London in 1992; and the term "Mohajir" itself acquired a certain pejorative implication. This set of people, who actually extracted the working concept of the "two-nation theory" used to create Pakistan, strangely faced questions of loyalty towards Pakistan, with the then Prime Minister, Benazir Bhutto, who went as far as to state, "Different blood flows in their veins", which compelled Altaf Hussain to famously state, "Though the Pakistan government sympathises with the Muslims of Kashmir and Bosnia, it has been deaf to the cries of help from these stranded Pakistanis."

Mohajirs constitute nearly 8 per cent of the population, with the MQM as the fourth largest national party. Today, the MQM and the Mohajirs, at large, are facing the latest governmental ire for the temperamental outbursts of Altaf Hussain, who on a recent diatribe against the nation, said, "Pakistan is cancer for entire world", and that, "Pakistan is headache for the entire world. Pakistan is the epicentre of terrorism for the entire world. Who says long live Pakistan...it's down with Pakistan". This was enough provocation for the Pakistani establishment to unleash an immediate clamp down, even more severely than before, while the Pakistan-based MQM leadership was left with no option but to ostensibly remove Altaf Hussain from the leadership post, and appoint a local leader, Farooq Sattar, to drown the dissonance.

Even though the Mohajirs boast of punching above their weight, in terms of contribution to Pakistan, with prominent people like presidents Pervez Musharraf, Zia-ul-Haq, nuclear scientist Dr AQ Khan, and philanthropist Abdul Sattar Edhi--they continue to fight discrimination, marginalisation, and suspicion about their societal legitimacy.

The local MQM will be tested to its limits to safeguard Mohajir interests. Altaf Hussain controlled MQM destiny (even though he has been in exile for 24 years, out of the 36 at the helm of party affairs), but the most powerful symbol of Mohajir identity, "Quaid-e-Tareek", Altaf Hussain, has been relegated to the dustbins of officialdom that will sooner than later, test the patience of the much-maligned Mohajirs. Even today, a strike call from "Altaf Bhai" could potentially bring Karachi to a grinding halt.

If Balochistan is the flavour of the month in India, it is the Mohajirs who are possibly facing the same levels of disenchantment (if not more than Baloch). Ironically, it was Altaf Hussain who led the first open rebellion against the State, when as the exiled leader of the progeny of the "two-nation theory", he confessed on Indian soil, "The division of the subcontinent was the biggest blunder...it was not the division of land, it was the division of blood."

The Mohajirs are not grabbing headlines internationally, though a bloody repression on them continues, making short shrift of the underlying rationale of Pakistan, and the "two-nation theory"--it is the same regressive and fraternal-religion based principle it seeks to invoke in Kashmir, to make its flawed point.

Chinese Checkers in Sri Lankan Waters

(TRIBUNE, 14 Jul 2016)

The recent ruling of the international tribunal in The Hague, called the Chinese bluff of claiming historical legality over the bulk of the South China Sea waters. The aggressive "nine-dash-line" approach of the Chinese swallows over 90 per cent of the disputed waters, much to the consternation of a wary neighbourhood. Behind the obvious issues of sovereignty, lies the geostrategic future and protection of the $5-trillion trade, and the very survival of the Chinese juggernaut. This survival insecurity has led to the Chinese instincts of belligerence and strategic sweeping, like the "String-of-Pearls", which encompasses active "pitching" to various countries in the vicinity. Geographically, Sri Lanka is a priceless nugget in the Chinese chessboard of strategic footprints.

In 1952, the Dudley Senanayake government in Ceylon (now, Sri Lanka), faced a dual challenge of acute shortages of the staple, rice, and limited availability of foreign exchange to source the same, from international markets. To compound the economic miseries, international commodity prices of rubber had sunk to a record low, impacting Ceylon's rubber exports and forex realisations. A masterstroke in the form of a barter-based trade agreement with China, to import the much-needed rice in exchange of rubber for the Chinese, ushered in a critical understanding and relationship of the Chinese, with the island nation.

This act of dire necessity set the backdrop of modern Sri Lankan practicality, when it came to dealing with the Chinese, thereafter. The subsequent hue and cry over the annexation of Tibet, and the plight of fellow Buddhist Tibetans, was met with a stoic silence by Colombo. This, as contrary to the language of Chapter II of the Sri Lankan constitution which mandates, "The Republic of Sri Lanka shall give to Buddhism the foremost place and accordingly it shall be the duty of the state to protect and foster the Buddha Sasana…". The Chinese paid back the Sri Lankans for their silence and acquiescence with weaponry, during the difficult days of the

Tamil wars, when neither India nor the US were forthcoming to help the Sri Lankans; then, the Chinese had readily stepped in unconditionally to bail out the Sri Lankans, this time militarily.

However, it was during the reign of the megalomaniac former President, Mahinda Rajapaksa, when the pronounced pro-China tilt took shape, and swerved dangerously to the utter discomfort of both India, and the US. This tilt manifested in murmurs of the Hambantota port emerging as another "Pearl" port (like Gwadar in Pakistan, Marao Atoll in Maldives, Sittwe in Myanmar etc.), part of the grand Chinese strategy to dominate the waters from the restive South China Sea, the vulnerable "Chicken's Neck" of the Malacca Straits, and all the way up to the African hinterlands. The alarm bells started ringing when Rajapaksa allowed Chinese submarines to dock twice in Sri Lanka, without informing New Delhi as per a long-standing agreement between the two nations. This Chinese transgression in India's backyard was against the spirit of the 1987 India-Sri Lanka accord, which binds both India and Sri Lanka, not to allow forces inimical to each other, to use the other nation's ports. However, it was the "cheque-book diplomacy" of generous doles, and infrastructure investment by way of the mega $1.4 billion land-reclamation project of the Colombo Port City (part of Beijing's One Belt, One Road and New Silk Route initiatives), which could potentially entrap Sri Lanka into a veritable vassal status due to its financial indebtedness to the Chinese. Clearly, Rajapaksa's fondness for the Chinese was not just economic but also strategic, political, and military. The end of the bloody Tamil conflict, and the victory of the Sri Lankan forces had a lot to do with the critical supplies of Chinese ammunition and ordnance, besides the timely supply of six F-7 jet fighters, scores of anti-aircraft guns, and a JY-11 radar system.

The providential electoral results spoilt the Chinese stratagem of the "String-of-Pearls" approach, with decidedly pro-India governments emerging in Myanmar (Aung San Suu Kyi's NLD replaced the *junta* rule), Bangladesh (with Sheikh Hasina's Awami League in power), and in Sri Lanka, Rajapaksa was ousted by his own former minister, Maithripala Sirisena, who promised more neutrality to correct the Chinese tilt and who stated, " (he) would not offer preferential economic or security access to any one country", besides placing several Chinese contracts on hold for audit and review of terms. Sirisena's election manifesto alluded to the impending Chinese noose by noting, "The land that the White Man took over by means of military strength is now being obtained by foreigners by paying ransom to a handful of persons. This robbery is taking place before everybody in broad daylight... If this trend continues for another six years our country would become a colony and we would become slaves".

However, a year and half down the tenure of President Sirisena, the Chinese freeze is slowly thawing, as financial considerations are forcing a climb-down from the earlier bravado, scepticism, and intransigence against the Chinese. A precarious balance-of-payment situation, falling foreign reserves, and a crippling $8-billion debt to China, has brought Sri Lanka scurrying back to the Chinese to renegotiate the repayment terms, and accept the reciprocal collateral conditions. Talk of equity swap, instead of hard currency projects to mitigate repayment term, has already been bandied.

The famed Chinese economic-statecraft via "cheque-book" diplomacy, has ensured the return of the Colombo Port City project, besides other initiatives like the expansion of the Hambantota port, and Mattala airport. Certain new projects, like the development of the Special Economic Zone, are also on the burgeoning agenda. The Sri Lankan experience with the ostensible Chinese generosity and largesse has always been smooth, and readily available (unlike the Tamil issues and conditions of India, and the tight purse strings of Western powers). Also, the Chinese are "non-judgmental", and do not allow issues like alleged human right violations during the Tamil wars, to derail stitching-up of strategic relationships.

Even though, the Sri Lankans are making meek assurances that the Chinese return to favour does not entail any ownership of land as part of the Colombo Port City project, the Sri Lankan backtracking has geopolitical ramifications. India realises the reality of the Sri Lankan financial conditions, and the resultant practicality of snuggling back to Beijing to avoid defaulting on debts. The Indians will do well to continuously forewarn, and reiterate the typical strings that come attached with Chinese doles, and partake of all possible opportunities to ensure a toehold in all development projects (as it is supposedly not exclusive to any one nation), and indulge in smarter diplomacy to "sell" the benefits of the larger picture, as an alternative "anti-Sino" bloc, which could be composed of countries like India, Japan, US, and the other ASEAN powers.

For now, the Chinese have gleefully re-entered Sri Lankan waters, by waving thick wads of hard currency.

Pakistan Plays Agent Provocateur

(MILLENNIUM POST, 13 Jul 2016)

As the Kashmir valley remained on edge, with the neutralisation of the Hizbul Mujahideen commander, Burhan Wani, the various stakeholders in the region played to the familiar script to ensure their respective relevance and positions. As expected, the moribund separatists led by the Hurriyat Conference called for a *de rigueur* strike, with the ostensibly moderate Mirwaiz Umar Farooq stating, "I think his death will definitely inspire many people to go that way. There is no denying that people feel a sense of desperation. People feel the government of India is just not ready to engage or even acknowledge the sentiments in Kashmir". Unfortunately, the state government dithered and slithered with a meek promise, to investigate any disproportionate use of force in the action, against a militant carrying a reward of Rs 10 Lakh on his head--one, that was described by the Security Forces as "the biggest-ever success" in recent times.

While there are enough regressive elements within the country to stoke fires, overtly or covertly-- Pakistan broke the unwritten code of sobriety and pacifism that usually accompanies any act of violence and bloodshed, in a neighbouring country. With tempers flying high, and over twenty deaths following clashes between protesters and the security forces, Pakistan had the opportunity to truly rewrite the standard narrative, and usher in the much-needed succour from terrorism. It had three choices--one, ideally to contribute to the much-needed efforts to denounce terrorism in the sub-continent by taking a firm stand against the terror antics of the likes of Burhan Wani; second, to avoid making any statements that could vitiate the sensitive environment, and remain aloof, while practicing non-interference in a neighbouring country; and lastly, to jump into the fray and ignite further passions, with statements that reek of blatant interference, and act as an agent provocateur of more bloodshed. Unfortunately, irrespective of its own tryst with terrorism, and the bloody price that its citizenry pays for having supported the apparatus of terrorism--Pakistan openly baited India with provocative statements, and chose to remain oblivious to a missed opportunity to truly stand against terrorism, if not for India, then for its own sake.

Ignoring the dignity to be prudent and non-judgmental at such times, without knowing the facts fully, they have already decided that the action in Anantnag district is tantamount to "extra-judicial-killings". This, in the backdrop of multiple pending enquiries pertaining to 26/11, Pathankot etc. wherein, countless dossiers of proofs submitted have never sufficed for nailing the complicity of the perpetrators of such hate crimes, by the Pakistani authorities. Unfortunately, it wasn't just the Jama'at-ud-Da'wah (JuD) Chief, and the 26/11 attack mastermind Hafiz Muhammad Saeed who cocked a snook at Muzzafarabad (in Pakistan Occupied Kashmir), by holding a prayer meeting in honour of Burhan Wani. In an instance of unprecedented brazenness, even Prime Minister Nawaz Sharif's office felt it necessary to state, "It is deplorable that excessive and unlawful force was used against the civilians who were protesting against the killing of Burhan Wani. Oppressive measures cannot deter the valiant people of Jammu and Kashmir from their demand of exercising their right to self-determination in accordance with the UN Security Council resolutions".

Pakistan's *jihadi* Frankenstein has spawned its own malignancy that is eating into Pakistan's societal equilibrium, and structure. The old strategy of treating only the Pakistan-facing terror groups like the TTP (Tehreek-e-Taliban Pakistan) as terrorists, whilst supporting and abetting the neighbour-facing terror groups as "Strategic Assets", has run its course. Afghanistan, Iran, and India are seething with rage over the duplicity of the Pakistani establishment, while the Americans are also doing some rare plain-speak about the Pakistani actions. However, they continue to stop short of pulling the support plug, owing to their own geo-strategic compulsions and necessities in Afghanistan.

The likes of Hizbul Mujahedin, Jud, Lashkar-e-Taiba etc. are the more well-known recipients of Pakistani support for anti-India terror activities, whereas the Haqqani Network (described by the former Chairman of Joint Chiefs of Staff of the US, Mike Mullen, as the "veritable arm of the Pakistani ISI.") and the Afghan Taliban are routinely blamed as Pakistani stooges, by the Afghan President, Ashraf Ghani, and even the Iranians blame the Pakistani government of being complicit with the anti-Iran *Jundallah*, or the sectarian Sipah-e-Sahaba. Now, signs of the monster acting beyond the master's control manifest with the nurseries in Pakistan accounting for 12 out of the 19 people arrested, for the three bomb attacks in Saudi Arabia, including in the holy city of Medina. However, an even more damning castigation of the Pakistani role came from the Information Minister of Bangladesh, Hasanul Huq Inu, who said that the Pakistani ISI had trained up to 8000 Bangladeshi *jihadis* in the last two years, and sent them back to launch violent attacks-- this was following the Dhaka Café attack. On a trip to Kabul, Prime Minister Narendra Modi expressed the sub-continental frustration in a veiled reference to Pakistan's terror infrastructure, by saying that Afghanistan will succeed only when terrorism stops flowing from across the border, and when nurseries and sanctuaries of terrorism are shut down.

The Americans too, have used the drone-strategy of hitting targets without necessarily involving the "leaky" Pakistani establishment--the "taking out" of Osama Bin Laden was reflective of the trust deficit between the Pakistanis, and the US government. Terrorism has cost Pakistan over $ 75 billion, and nearly 50,000 lives for itself, in the last 15 years. In many ways, it finds itself as a pariah nation with a dubious history of nurturing much of the foot soldiers, and ideologues, who have struck in the sub-continent, as indeed with traceable footprints in the US, Europe, and the Middle East.

Yet, Islamabad refuses to learn its lessons, and the instinct of pandering to its age-old politics of abetting terror and stoking fires in the neighbourhood go unchecked. By the day, the hold of self-combusting forces continue to thrive in Pakistan, and the stranglehold on its own society tightens. Nevertheless, Islamabad is content to partake of tactical interference in the Kashmir valley. But, the times are changing, terror is no longer an Asian or a Middle Eastern curse--it has reached the doorsteps of the West, and the bestiality is unravelling itself across the capitals of the world. Global patience is running woefully short, already the presumptive

Republican nominee of the US, Donald Trump, has called Pakistan "unstable", while the presumptive Democrat nominee, Hillary Clinton is known to have presciently warned the Pakistani establishment in 2011, "You can't keep snakes in your backyard and expect them only to bite your neighbours. Eventually, those snakes are going to turn on whoever has them in the backyard". Sadly, the recent events in Kashmir show that Pakistan is still acting otherwise.

Dragon focusing on Maldives

(THE PIONEER, 28 June 2016)

The fleet-footedness of the Chinese diplomacy and its strategic counter-moves is unparalleled. Less than five years ago, the Chinese had carefully plotted the dragnet of the "String-of-Pearls" strategy, by punting on establishing Chinese military presence in the pro-Chinese regimes of the *junta-ruled* Myanmar (at Sittwe port), and on the Dragon-tilting regime of Mahinda Rajapaksa in Sri Lanka (at Hambantota port).

These two "Pearl Ports", along with the Gwadar port in the "all-weather-friend" nation of Pakistan, were potentially strangulating India with the spectre of Chinese presence, floating menacingly in the Indian neighbourhood, to establish its hegemony in the region. However, the dynamics of time and tide changed everything on the global chessboard, with changes that forced a recalibration of existing bilateral equations. Within a quick span of time, democracy consumed the *junta-rule* in Myanmar, with Aung San Suu Kyi's National League for Democracy (ideologically closer to India than China) controlling the establishment in Naypyidaw, and a decidedly pro-India Government of Maithripala Sirisena, in Colombo, took over from Mahinda Rajapaksa, thereby dashing Chinese ambitions in these two envisaged "Pearl Ports", in Myanmar and Sri Lanka.

At around the same time, the traditionally pro-India Governments of Maldives, then ruled by President Mohamed Nasheed (from the Maldivian Democratic Part [MDP]) in Male paved way, initially for Mohammed Waheed Hassan, and later for the current President, Abdulla Yameen (of the Progressive Party [PP], who has been in power since November 2013). This local change of guard was accompanied with extreme bitterness and accusations between the Maldivian political parties--circumstantially, aiding a new political position to be seen as necessarily "different" from the one held by the previous political dispensations, and hence, sacrificing the steadfast "India-first" centricity that had prevailed since the Maldivian independence, in 1965.

The dragon smelt a providential opportunity to "invest" in Maldives, and immediately pounced upon the favourable turn of political events there, as opposed to the negative regime changes in Sri Lanka and Myanmar, as far as the Chinese were concerned. Suddenly, Maldives woke up as the centripetal point of the great geo-political game in the Indian Ocean, between the two competing blocs (India versus the Chinese-Pakistani combine), and the local Maldivian dispensation has since milked the tactical opportunity of extracting its pound of flesh from both.

This new reality is in sharp contrast to the historical India-Maldives equation that was bed-rocked on the interdependence of interests, and the automatic preferential treatment afforded to each other. Suddenly, a "balance" amongst the competing suitors was sought (naïvely, including the Chinese footprint in the security calculus of the region, which was earlier restricted to India). Worrisomely, President Yameen has propounded the Look East policy towards China as a major partner, in his Republic Day address, while his Vice President, Ahmed Adeeb, confirmed, "China is one of the closest friends and one of the most important development partners of Maldives". This is an unmistakable augury of the Chinese "cheque-book diplomacy" for buying new friends, à la Chinese tactics deployed in poor African countries which are seeing aggressive Chinese investments.

Like all Chinese investments, the diplomatic charm invariably sugar-coats the accompanying agenda of the steel of military might, and strategic Chinese interests. In an unprecedented show of brewing friendship and of strategic relations, Male witnessed a flurry and fury of the Chinese President, Xi Jinping, who became the first Chinese President to visit Male in 2014. This visit was immediately followed by the controversial replacement of the contract for the Indian group GMR Infrastructure, to a Chinese group, Beijing Urban Construction Group Company Ltd., to upgrade the Male airport. Recently, a $800 million contract to expand the airport further was also signed with the Chinese consortium. This is in addition to the "China-Maldives Friendship Bridge" project, which spans from Male's eastern edge to the western corner of the island of Hulhule, funded by the $126 million in grant aid from China--an unprecedented financial generosity in the Maldivian context.

The language of the Sino-Maldivian diplomatic engagement is a clear indicator of the shifting sands, with President Yameen expressing, "profound gratitude" to Xi. He added for good measure, "Today you have made our impossible dream a reality". However, India is more concerned about the strategic concessions that could have been passed to the Chinese, *in lieu* of these investments. As it is, Maldives is amongst the first signatories of the game-altering, Chinese "Maritime Silk Route" initiative. Further, murmurs are rife about a potential Chinese naval base in Marao (though, steadfastly denied by the Maldivian authorities, pursuant to the stated commitment to remain a "demilitarised zone"). In addition, in mid-last year, the shadowy and unconfirmed presence of a Chinese Yuan class 335 armed-submarine lurking in the Maldivian waters, knowingly or unknowingly, has further raised hackles in India.

India has done its bit of re-wooing with the signing of six pacts (including the "Defence cooperation plan" during President Yameen's visit to India). Last week, India gifted the Maldives, the second of the promised helicopters, with an additional commitment of a fixed wing aircraft to follow. However, this generosity has to be viewed within the context of competitive supplies of military hardware, from both Pakistan and China. The controversial Constitutional amendment that has authorised foreign freeholds in the Maldives for the first time, has also been viewed with extreme suspicion in Delhi, as a potential surrogate to allow the Chinese to develop "civil-maritime" infrastructure, which though ostensibly civilian, could double-up as military/naval bases for the Chinese Forces in times of strategic need! This move was alluded to, by the Opposition MDP as, "facilitating non-commercial logistical installations in the Maldives".

As of now, the Maldivians are literally basking in the duality of attention, and successfully playing one country against the other. It makes imminent sense for the Maldivian President, Abdulla Yameen, to ally with the Chinese, as the friendship comes without any uncomfortable strings attached--the authoritarian streak of the Maldivian Government with its inherent anti-democratic instincts is conveniently ignored--whereas, the Indians have to maintain the delicate balance of keeping the banished ex-President, Mohammed Nasheed, in good humour, with his avowedly pro-Indian, and blatantly anti-Chinese stance (he has considerable domestic popularity), *vis-à-vis* the ambivalent, though-in-chair reality of President Yameen.

China's historical track record of ultimately bearing its military fangs, after the *façade* of a civilian face, is well known, and given the imminent threat of the growing strains of militant Islam in the Maldivian society (e.g., the recent failure to arrest a family of 12 Maldivians, on their way to join the Islamic State), the long-term benefits of ditching the more liberal, progressive, and democratic hands of the India-Western bloc versus the colder and currently-convenient, Chinese-Pakistani option, is something the current political dispensation will be well aware of. However, for now, local Maldivian politics, and geopolitical realignments have shifted the glare, monies, and the "big-game" theatrics on Male; and the local establishment is giving India restless nights with its revised strategic tilt, outlook, and choice of partners.

Veering towards Anarchist Tendencies
(MILLENNIUM POST, 19 May 2016)

The cold-blooded murder of Xulhaz Mannan and his friend, Mahbub Rabbi Tonoy, by Ansar-al-Islam, an Al Qaida affiliate, in Dhaka, last month, follows a pattern of macabre killings targeting secular writers, minorities, and foreigners. In this case, "deviants" like Xulhaz, who was the editor of Bangladesh's first and only LGBT magazine, "Roopbaan", were targeted. The tragedy of illiberalism, intolerance, and extremism received international attention, in 2013, with the supposed "hit-list" of 84 bloggers, who were deemed to have committed blasphemy for their propounded "un-Islamic" thoughts and beliefs.

Today, Bangladesh is caught at a crossroads between two parallel, violently opposed, and irreconcilable strains that have split the political and social instincts of the country into two distinct parts. First, the decidedly anti-India and pro-Pakistan, "Islamist" coalition of Begum Khaleda Zia of the Bangladesh National Party (BNP) in alliance with the hard-line Jamaat-e-Islami, versus, the ruling Bangladesh Awami league, of Sheikh Hasina, who is seen to be pro-India, more "inclusive", and "Bengali" in her political identity.

It has posited the two conflicting identities--a "syncretic Bengali identity" that prides itself for the freedom struggle against the stated pogrom of 3 million Bengalis, by the Pakistani Army, versus, the other "Islamic identity" that regrets the vivisection from West Pakistan. The latter is intrinsically anti-India and covertly hand-in-glove with forces of religious extremism, which are bent on outlawing "un-Islamic" practices, institutionalizing Sharia system, and declaring Bangladesh as an "Islamic State".

Therefore, even the narrative in Bangladesh's freedom struggle is disputed by these two political belief-systems, giving rise to the violent unrest and dispiriting that has engulfed Bangladesh. There is supporting history that feeds the instincts of the two competing strains. Sheikh Hasina is the daughter of "Bangabandu", the father of the nation and the first Prime Minister of Bangladesh, Sheikh Mujibur Rehman (and therefore, she is considering the contentious "Liberation war denials crimes bill" that seeks to make questioning the Pakistani war crimes, to be an offense). Khaleda Zia is the wife of Lt. General Ziaur Rahman, the 4th President of Bangladesh, who is famous for moving away from the pro-India sentiments of Sheikh Mujibur Rehman, and initiating the re-Islamisation of politics, and rehabilitation of Jamaat-e-Islami in the national context.

The current wave of global Pan-Islamic resurgence has consumed Bangladesh, and threatened not just the 14 million or 8.5% of Hindu minorities (down from 13.5% in 1974) that live in fear; today, it is the intellectuals, professors, atheists, and other sectarian minorities like Qadianis, and the Shias, who are facing the brunt of religious extremism.

Oddly enough, constraints of participative democracy have ensured that neither parties are openly denouncing the acts of violence vigorously enough. On the contrary, while commenting on the killing of yet another blogger, Nazimuddin Samad, the Home Minister questioned incredulously, "Why are they (bloggers) using this kind of language against the religious establishment?" Such comments further embolden the Islamists to take the law into their own hands with impunity.

So, while religious intolerance is allowed to breed unchecked, the historical debate of the freedom struggle is consuming the time, attention, and actions of Sheikh Hasina's Awami League. Therefore, the Bangladesh Supreme Court's recent rejection of the final plea against the death sentence, and the subsequent hanging of Jamaat-e-Islami leader, Motiur Rahman Nizami, for war crimes during the 1971 liberation war with Pakistan, meets a strong and stoic approval from the ruling Awami League (incidentally, the judgement was made by the four-member appellate division bench, headed by the first Hindu Chief Justice, Surendra Kumar Sinha).

The streets of Bangladesh are now awash with rumours and positions, reminiscent of 2013, when the conviction of Jamaat leaders had led to the deadliest violence in years, with nearly 500 deaths. The Sheikh Hasina government is steadfastly disputing claims of the organisational presence of ISIL, or Al-Qaida. It is content to blame the opposition for trying to destabilize the country--this belies the reality of many home-grown extremist groups (e.g., Islamic Liberation Front, Ansarullah Bangla etc.), who share an ideological connect with the Pan-Islamic platforms. In other words, the government's reaction looks political rather than religious, thereby keeping some electorally relevant *mullahs* in good humour, and pussyfooting compromises on the efficacy of governmental response, which has further strengthened the brazenness of the fundamentalist elements.

More than 20 people have been killed in hate crimes since 2013; but, for the murder of blogger, Ahmed Rajib Haider, in 2013, no one has been convicted or punished for any of the subsequent attacks. On the contrary, Sheikh Hasina issued a stern warning to anyone who criticised religion, "I don't consider such writings as freethinking but filthy words. Why would anyone write such words? It's not at all acceptable if anyone writes against our prophet, or other religions", she said. However, making life difficult for Sheikh Hasina is the uncomfortable position of being seen to be supporting a BJP, or "RSS", government in India, while taking on the Islamist Jamaat-e-Islami at home. Amidst, the political wrangling and social unrest, the military is the joker in the pack that is being actively wooed by both political parties. As the largest contributor to the UN "Blue Caps", it is relatively flush with money, and is further pandered by the ruling dispensation with arms and equipment beyond its threat perceptions (e.g., nuclear submarines). Basically, Bangladesh has a history of military interventions, and there are elements within the forces who do empathise with Begum Khaleda Zia's party.

In order to avoid any such intervention, as also avoid a mutiny akin to the Bangladesh Rifles (BDR – paramilitary force guarding borders) mutiny of 2009, which led to 74 personnel dead, Sheikh Hasina is playing a dangerous high-stakes game. She is balancing electoral necessities, keeping the military on her side, and simultaneously asserting her party's legacy and role in the freedom struggle by taking on her political opponents, head-on. As a perfect example of the flawed "two-nation" theory, today, Bangladesh is struggling to reconcile with its basic and newly learned instincts that counter each other. The nation desperately seeks the poignant invocation of the syncretic Bangla spirit of Kazi Nazrul Islam, the national poet of Bangladesh. Though Nazrul used themes of Islamic renaissance to inspire, he attacked fanaticism in religion, denouncing it as evil and inherently irreligious; aptly, naming his sons with both Hindu and Muslim names, Krishna Mohammad, Arindam Khaled, Kazi Sabyasachi, and Kazi Aniruddha. It is the increasingly eerie similarities to its previous political masters from the pre-1971 history, which is driving Bangladesh towards its destructive course.

India should be Patient,
as a "Myanmar Spring" Unfolds

(NEW INDIAN EXPRESS, 21 Jan 2016)

The iron-fisted military *junta* rule in Myanmar is gently but surely tiptoeing towards a historic power-sharing transition, which envisages the reluctant Generals conceding political space to Aung San Suu Kyi's, National League for Democracy (NLD). The Nobel Prize-winner, and the daughter of Aung San (ironically, the founder of the modern Burmese Army, and negotiator of independence from the British), Aung San Suu Kyi has come a long way to establish her formal credentials with the prevailing *junta*.

From being denied her rightful political place, after winning the 1990 general elections convincingly, when the *junta* refused to honour the results, she led a valiant struggle to usher in changes despite multiple periods of detention, and other violent tribulations.

However, her peaceful means of protest, and democratic instincts were instrumental in gaining wide international support--notable visitors, included then US Secretary of State, Hillary Clinton, and Thai Prime Minister, Yingluck Shinawatra--along with support from Western powers, and pro-democracy countries like India, nudged the *junta* towards rapprochement.

The world was changing, and the economic sanctions on Myanmar for its terrible human rights record were crippling, to the extent that they remained one of the last vestiges of *junta-style* regression.

In 2008, recognising the building pressure (Buddhist monks joined the protest to give religious sanctity to the struggle), the military *junta* proposed a new constitution as part of a "roadmap to democracy". It was a sleight of hand, as it sought to cement the powers of the *junta*, whilst, ostensibly showcasing its "progressive" move. Critically, it reserved seats for the *junta* and its affiliates, and most pointedly (and damagingly), debarred anyone married to a foreign national the right to hold political office--a move aimed at cutting Aung San Suu Kyi's wings.

A farcical election, devoid of the popular party NLD followed, and ushered in the rule of the military-backed Union Solidarity and Development Party in 2010, only to have the military *junta* officially dissolved on March 30, 2011. But, the basic instincts of the *junta* remained intact, and talks about a "disciplined democracy" alluded to a quasi-military rule, as opposed to a truly free and participatory democracy.

Still, progress was made in granting general amnesty to a large number of political prisoners, the release of Aung San Suu Kyi from house arrest, establishment of a National Human Right Commission, and relaxation of curbs on the press and monetary systems.

The President, a former Army General, Thein Sein, belied a certain reformist streak which was clearly visible, and soon enough Myanmar was accepted into the ASEAN comity and, later, visits to the White House, besides other world capitals, signalled a change that culminated in the first openly contested general elections, in November 2015.

As expected, the NLD won a supermajority with 86 per cent of the open seats in the Assembly of the Union (well above the 67 per cent cut-off to ensure that the party's preferred candidate became President--albeit, with the constitutional spanner of disallowing Aung San Suu Kyi's individual accession, owing to the "foreign spouse" clause). Still, the NLD's punt in participating in the elections, with the full knowledge of the systemic issue debarring its leader, cleared the principal hurdle for the easing of the *junta* stranglehold.

The tricky jousting starts now, with Aung San Suu Kyi unambiguously declaring that she will hold the real power in the new NLD government. While the *Tatmadaw* (military) is still smarting from the election results, they have the constitutional comfort of having safeguarded themselves through reservations, of 25 per cent of seats in both national and regional parliament; thus, effectively giving the military veto power over any future changes (amending the Constitution will require the support of more than 75 per cent of MP's). So, for now the power-sharing arrangement is delicately poised, with the NLD having to tread cautiously to ensure the "Myanmar Spring" lives up to its promise.

The basic instinct of the military, and the nation, will be severely tested as the military nurses a deep-rooted distrust of civilian "party politics". Myanmar's myriad internal insurgencies, and omnipresent military deployment will also call for the retention of its firepower. Even politically, the positions of Minister of Defence, Home Affairs, and Border Affairs will remain reserved with the military, and not left to the choice of the newly-elected NLD. The ultimate ace of the military muscle thus remains with the *junta*. However, it would be acutely aware of the domestic and international consequences of any misuse of the same; therefore, necessitating a working framework of a civil-military equation to address the decades of hostility, between the two institutions. Both the civilian politicians, and the military establishment will have to tread very cautiously to build trust and not trespass on the interests of the vested powers, at least in the short to mid-term. Not succumbing to the temptations of power, and trying to accelerate the process of democratisation will be key (party and international pressures notwithstanding). The Russian Glasnost/Perestroika, and the more recent "Arab Spring", are pointers to the premature hastening from one extreme system to the other.

There ought to be a spirit of reconciliation, of avoiding questioning the established institutional interests of the military immediately, getting into witch-hunt mode, or insisting on the political coronation of Aung San Suu Kyi--this could snap the patience of the *junta*.

India, too, must play its cards sensibly. There is already a precedent of the *junta* suddenly easing ambush traps, to trapped India-centric insurgents who were allowed to escape, in the middle of a joint military operation with the Indian Army, when it learnt that the Indian government had decided to give a state honour to the then rebel leader, Aung San Suu Kyi. While the Chinese have invested for decades in building a strategic relationship with the *junta*--Myanmar could now drift towards more "balance" in favour of India, given its avowed support to Aung San Suu Kyi during her days of struggle.

As it is, there had been a gentle thawing of relationship even with the *junta*, so much so, as to allow many "operations" by the

Indian Defence Forces, to neutralise the Northeast-centric insurgent camps on the Myanmar side of the border. There needs to be a patient "wait and watch" policy towards Myanmar, as it gingerly treads towards a path of acceptance of its constituents, emotions, and contradictions. Truly, a significant experiment in democracy is occurring in the form of the "Myanmar Spring".

Erdogan's Kashmir Gambit

(STATESMAN, 13 May 2017)

On the eve of his recent visit to India, the President of Turkey, Recep Tayyip Erdogan, made an unsolicited statement about Kashmir, "We should not allow more casualties to occur (in Kashmir). By having a multilateral dialogue, we can be involved and we can seek ways to settle the issue once and for all". Implicit in the message was the hesitation to take a deliberate "position". The deeply hyphenated Indo-Pak relationship is a conundrum for any visiting dignitary-- either to Delhi or to Islamabad--to take a "side". This invariably gets wrongfully deciphered by the dignitary, who alludes to Kashmir as either a "bilateral issue" (decoded as a pro-India stance, that assumes no third party interference), or alternatively, suggests a potential solution framework of "multilateral dialogue" (tantamount to supporting Pakistan's singular quest to internationalise Kashmir). Turkey's stand was certainly unwarranted, diplomatically ungracious, and wholly avoidable, given the timing of the visit; however, it is not new.

Turkey has had an indelible imprint on the subcontinent's psyche, from Mahmud of Ghazni, who was a Turkic Mumluk, to the Khilafat movement (1919-1922) to save the Ottoman Caliphate. Turkey has held the popular imagination, especially for the *ummah*, who contextualised the country as a model Islamic state.

Logically, partition on the basis of religious identity, made Pakistan more aligned to the memories of the Ottoman Empire, although the founding father of the modern state of Turkey, Kemal Mustafa Atatürk, tried to firewall religiosity, and its Islamist heritage. Since then, the latent Islamic fissures, and strategic Cold War alignments (which put both Pakistan and Turkey on the same side, as members of the US-led Central Treaty Organization-CENTO), as the bulwark states against Soviet threat, ensured a more active Pakistan-Turkey relationship. Even from a regressive, sectarian angle, the majority in both the countries practice Sunni Hanafi Islam. Today, Turkey's swing from avowed secularism, towards its more religious moorings, has found a new champion in President Recep Tayyip Erdogan, and his ruling Justice and Development Party. This has had an impact on Turkey's domestic politics, as indeed, its international posturing and visions of a "Neo-Ottoman" regime.

Erdogan has visited Pakistan as many as seven times. There is a historical connect between the two nations, with a shared tryst, and sensibilities of military men at the helm of affairs. Unlike Pakistan, however, the military in Turkey has been neutered with Erdogan's successful Islamisation of governance. Many of Pakistan's military top brass have been part of the extensive exchange-programmes. General Musharraf spent his impressionable school years in Turkey, can speak fluent Turkish, and is an ardent admirer of Kemal Mustafa Atatürk.

With such an empathetic sense of "progressive destiny" in the global *ummah*, it is hardly surprising that Turkey routinely backs the Pakistan line in multilateral forums like OIC (on Kashmir), is a part of the "Uniting for Consensus Group", which opposes the India-backed idea of an enlarged permanent membership in the UN Security Council, and worse, has supported China in the devious, "criteria-based approach", for the "Nuclear Non-Proliferation Treaty" (NPT) states, which unsurprisingly, makes a case to accommodate Pakistan, instead of India, in the Nuclear Suppliers Group (NSG). This strategic bonhomie is reciprocated by Islamabad, which supports Turkey's stand on the ultra-sensitive issue of Cyprus, as also, converging on the battlegrounds of the Middle Eastern turmoil. Turkey, like Pakistan, is part of the 39-nation "Islamic Military Alliance to Fight Terrorism", now led by the former Pakistan Army Chief, General Raheel Sharif.

However, beyond religious, and historical convergences and impulses, both Pakistan and Turkey project themselves as "model" Islamic states. The recent tension with their principal ally, the US, has made these countries particularly brazen, and hawkish in opposing the US. Both countries boast US bases and assets. The Incirlik base in Turkey has tactical nuclear weapons, while Pakistan is nuclear armed, and dangerously flirts with China to offend the Americans. This larger geopolitical evolution lends itself to

Turkish belligerence, and support for Pakistan in the new strategic sweepstakes.

Even tactical irritants like the Afghan civil war, in which both Turkey and Pakistan are supporting opposing groups is conveniently overlooked, and Turkey props the Pakistani line, in an ode to Erdogan's comment about Pakistan being "a home away from home". Pakistan is pro-Taliban given the Pashtun composition, whereas, Turkey is pro-Northern Alliance with a *mélange* of Turkic races.

Further, the preceding visit of the President of Cyprus, Nicos Anastasiades, just before Erdogan's visit to Delhi, would not have been received very favourably by Ankara, which is hypersensitive to perceived slights on such issues as Northern Cyprus, Kurds, or more recently, the Gulen movement. With no major trade, geographical, or strategic stake involved with India (as opposed to Pakistan), it makes political sense for Erdogan to champion the Pakistani stand on Kashmir, to further bolster his own Islamic identity, and credentials.

In an unwarranted act of diplomatic provocation, the Turkish ambassador to Pakistan recently spent over a week in Muzaffarabad (in Pakistan Occupied Kashmir), to showcase his nation's sympathy with Pakistan, on Kashmir. Clearly, the optics of maintaining a "pro-Pakistan" line is politically beneficial for Erdogan, who has to contend with domestic power struggles between the forces of secularism and "alternative-politics", exemplified by the military, the Kemalist outfits like the Republican People's Party, and from cult leaders like Fethullah Gulen. This has made Erdogan's government circumspect, in the context of US-Russia relations, and yet retain his stance on the Islamist construct.

Erdogan is the new "*sultan*" on the block, and his tacit support for the Pakistani line is part of a carefully cultivated image, and global aspirations in the larger perspective.

Far from mediating on Kashmir, Ankara has its hands tied in mediating with the European Union, which is opposed to his anti-Zionism, and his autocratic streak. To that can be added Turkey's relations with Russia, and the US, the hapless Kurds and Armenians, home-grown Islamist terror groups, and the Middle East powers. Ankara's relations with Syria and Iran are far from cordial.

Erdogan's conduct in Delhi was rather undiplomatic. The ambitious semi-professional footballer-turned-conservative politician has his eyes and heart set on visions of a "Neo-Ottoman" empire, which necessitates exploiting any political opportunity, to enhance the relevance and legitimacy of the new-age *Pasha* from Turkey.

Pakistan drifts towards Isolation
(ASIAN AGE & DECCAN CHRONICLE, 3 Mar 2017)

Pakistan is furiously cobbling together alternative geostrategic tie-ups, with the prospect of a questionable future looming large with its traditional ally, the United States. Having escaped the first wave of Donald Trump's formal censure via the proposed seven-country "immigration ban", Islamabad is equally aware of the parallel risks in punting exclusively on Beijing. China is the hard-headed apostle of realpolitik, and its ostensible "all-weather friendship" with Pakistan is bereft of any cultural, civilizational, or emotional context. It is a marriage of convenience and circumstances, forever susceptible to the vicissitudes of a fickle, need-based approach. China's economic largesse, for example the China-Pakistan Economic Corridor (CPEC), and its convenient non-preachy tolerance of Pakistan's complicity in terror (often with a tacit encouragement e.g., Beijing's invaluable help in stalling the designation of the Pak-sponsored, Masood Azhar, as an "international terrorist"), is a temporary counterpoise, and relief for wary Pakistanis.

Pakistan's two other principal "blocs" of geostrategic participation--SAARC, and Organisation of Islamic Countries (OIC)--are both floundering. While the OIC is mired with its own existential, imploding, and sectarian challenges, SAARC has been less than propitious in recent times, with India giving the cold shoulder in the last SAARC meet, in Islamabad. This has led to Pakistan investing in direct bilateral relationships ("free trade" agreements with Turkey and Saudi Arabia), as well as wagering on nascent "blocs" like the Economic Cooperation Organisation (ECO). The ECO is a sub-set of the OIC as it is a "bloc" of Muslim-majority countries, which span from Turkey, Iran, Afghanistan, Pakistan, to the Central Asian countries--a geographical land mass that interconnects the landlocked, energy-rich Central Asian region with the Mediterranean ports in Turkey, to the Arabian Sea ports in Iran, and Pakistan.

However, the latest ECO summit in Islamabad too got a flavour of Pakistan's increased international and regional isolation, when

Afghanistan decided to send an unmistakable message of its displeasure to the host nation, Pakistan. Afghanistan refused to send the requisite high-level representation in the form of the President, Chief Executive, or its Foreign Minister (all other member countries were represented by the senior most officials). This open Af-Pak hostility is in the dark backdrop of the bitter innuendos, and cross-accusations, which have typified the Pakistani narrative *vis-à-vis* its neighbours--India, Iran, and Afghanistan. The tone of Afghan belligerence, and impatience towards Islamabad's duplicity and insincerity has come a long way, since the initial long rope extended to the Pakistanis by the Afghan President, Ashraf Ghani. Today, the fingerprints in most terror attacks on Afghan soil are traceable to benefactors in Pakistan, and worse, the Pakistani establishment. From the attack on the Indian consulate in Mazar-e Sharif, to the recent Pakistani shelling on the fractious Af-Pak border, the slide in the relationship is blatantly confrontational.

This build-up of fractures was evident to all when the Afghan President lambasted Pakistan in the "Heart of Asia" summit, in Amritsar, last November, with Pakistan's adviser to the Prime Minister on foreign affairs, Sartaj Aziz, in the audience, who lashed out at the Pakistani offer of aid by saying, "We need to identify cross-border terrorism and a fund to combat terrorism. Pakistan has pledged $500 million for Afghanistan's development. This amount can be spent to contain extremism," and further added, "Afghanistan suffered the highest number of casualties last year. This is unacceptable...Some still provide sanctuary for terrorists. As a Taliban figure said recently, if they had no sanctuary in Pakistan, they wouldn't last a month."

In a *quid pro quo*, the Pakistanis have upped the counter-ante on the ostensible "sanctuaries" of anti-Pakistani militants, in Afghanistan's eastern borders. The bloody attack on the shrine of the Sufi saint, Lal Shahbaz Qalandar in Sehwan, Sindh, which left nearly 100 dead, by the ISIS-"Khorasan faction", has led to a reverse accusation and finger pointing at Afghanistan. Even though the ISIS "Khorasan faction" is predominant in the Nangarhar province of Afghanistan, and is embroiled in a bitter slugfest with the Afghan National Army, this didn't stop the Pakistanis from shifting blame on its deteriorating security situation, and growing intolerance, on the footsteps of the Afghan government. The tit-for-tat that followed saw the Pakistanis brazenly asking the Afghans to hand over 76 alleged militants, while the Afghans retaliated almost immediately with their own list of 85 militants (mostly from the ISI-aided Haqqani Network) supposedly in Pakistan, along with a further list of 32 training centres!

Earlier in the year, on meeting the Pakistani Chief of Army Staff, Gen. Qamar Bajwa, the Afghan President had presciently stated, "Those who have claimed responsibility for these recent attacks freely operate, live and recruit in Pakistan, but so far there has been no action against them." After the Sehwan terror strike, a perfect role reversal ensued with Islamabad summoning Afghan officials for strong words and a dossier of names to be "neutralised".

This Pakistani blame game with Afghanistan is eerily reminiscent of the India-Pakistan equation wherein the "terror sanctuaries" get conveniently brushed under the Pakistani carpet, with a rote "non-state-actors" line. This dangerously ensures that the Pakistanis continue investing in their flawed belief of retaining "strategic depth", by supporting extremist organisations in the neighbouring countries. However, the vexatious jihadist ecosystem that the Pakistanis have singularly created, and harnessed over the years, has a dynamic of its own that often spills out of the control levers of the Pakistani establishment, and afflicts a bloody toll on its creator. This self-inflicted misery cannot be deflected onto Pakistan's already suffering neighbours. Like India, the Afghans have lost faith and patience in Pakistan's words and actions. The onus of dismantling the terror infrastructure in the Asian subcontinent resides squarely in Pakistan. Once the fundamental shift in policy and outlook is enforced by Islamabad, the parallel collapse of the terror industry in Afghanistan and India is virtually guaranteed. The latest angst in the Af-Pak relationship is an evitable, and extended, outcome of the Frankenstein project conceived by Pakistan itself.

Alarm Bells in Pakistan

(STATESMAN, 13 Dec 2016)

Pakistan's growing proximity with China, and the frustrations of the US forces in Afghanistan will ensure that Nawaz Sharif, the quintessential politician, will need more than words to thaw relations with the restless and wary US. Pakistan is nervous and faltering at every step, but its establishment: the politicos, military and clergy, have boxed itself into a corner with regressive belligerence and "selectiveness".

Since 2001, the US has supplied Pakistan with nearly $20 billion worth of invaluable military assistance and wares (the second biggest arms supplier, after China). In 2016 itself, Pakistan had substantial trade and commerce with the US (imports worth $3.5 billion and export worth $2 billion). Pakistan is among the foremost recipients of US financial aid, directly and indirectly, via multilateral organisations. The US remains unavowed in its support for Pakistan's existential "war on terror" within its borders. The much despised US drones have "neutralised" Pakistan's most wanted terrorist, Mullah Fazlullah. Pakistan was earlier conferred strategic status as a "Major Non-NATO Ally" (MNNA), in recognition of the assets committed within Pakistan, and the access that it offers to the landlocked conflict zone of Afghanistan. To put it simply, while the interdependence is vital for both countries, for Pakistan it is paramount. The sustenance stakes for Pakistan are not just military but also economic, geo-political, social and political.

In recent times, the mutual distrust between Islamabad and Washington has intensified, with incidents like the Raymond Davis fiasco, Salala incident (when the US-led NATO forces engaged with Pakistani military along the Af-Pak border), and the global embarrassment of US Forces "taking out" Osama bin Laden from the garrison town of Abbottabad. Compounding the sense of insult within Pakistan is the strategic convergence between the two "natural allies", India and the US, the continuation of drone attacks and the stalling of F-16 fighter planes. Not surprisingly, the Gallup poll within the US posited the perception for Pakistan at a 21% "favourable", to a 70% "unfavourable" (*vis-à-vis*, 75% "favourable" to an 18% "unfavourable" for India). Within Pakistan itself, perceptions about the US are even worse: a deep sense of betrayal and a need-based relationship persists (especially in the context of the Indo-Pak equation, and therefore the "all-weather-friendship", *vis-à-vis* the American nemesis, China). The wave of global Pan-Islamic resurgence and assertion has fundamentally eroded perceptions about the US, within the Pakistani mainstream.

The dichotomous dynamics of the Pak-US relationship, with the two countries struggling to bridge the conflict emanating from a "genuine need" for each other, along with the equally glaring reality, of a blatantly negative perception about each other, is increasing. Amidst this challenge for rapprochement, the news of Donald Trump taking over the White House, in Washington, has set off more alarm bells in Islamabad, than in most other capitals. Irrespective of the political talk in the Pakistani hinterland, America's support is crucial and irreplaceable for Pakistan's existence and sustenance as a modern state.

However, Donald Trump's over-simplistic appreciation of foreign affairs has been particularly severe towards Pakistan, as he has famously remarked, "They are not friends of ours". His terming Pakistan as, "probably the most dangerous" country in the world, and his counter-contextual view of India's role, "You have to get India involved...They have their own nukes and have a very powerful army. They seem to be the real check...I think we have to deal very closely with India to deal with it (Pakistan)", is worrisome for the Pakistanis. His reductionist impression further transgresses the famed Pakistani duplicity with no-holds-barred, "We've given them (Pakistan) money and they've double dealt us", leaving very little doubt about his views on the future evolution of the crucial triad of India-Pakistan-US framework. Even the recent incident during the Presidential campaign, of the very public, Democrat platform-sharing by the parents of Captain Humayun Khan (the martyred US soldier of Pakistani descent), will not be erased from Trump's famed memory soon.

As it is, Nawaz Sharif has been struggling with his own battles for survival, with the Pakistani military perennially breathing down his neck, political opponents routinely threatening clamp-downs, corruption charges of "Panamagate" flying in his face--now, he has the added pressure of having to deal with Donald Trump. Despite the initial shock of the Trump victory, the *de rigueur* diplomatic niceties of courtesy calls, by global leaders to the President-elect of the US, have exemplified the situational Pakistani nervousness with an embarrassing *gaffe* and the first public indictment by the transition team of Donald Trump.

Breaking diplomatic protocol and showing amateurish glee, the Pakistanis selectively released the supposed transcript of a conversation between the two leaders, and publicly shared Trump's ostensible statement to Nawaz Sharif, "You have a very good reputation. You are a terrific guy. You are doing amazing work which is visible in every way. I am looking forward to seeing you soon. As I am talking to you, Prime Minister, I feel I am talking to a person I have known for long. Your country is amazing with tremendous opportunities. Pakistanis are one of the most intelligent people. I am willing and ready to play any role that you want me to play, to address and find solutions to the outstanding problems...", clearly offering a counter-narrative to the established Trump impression about Pakistan, and more importantly, positioning his supposed comments to reinforce the historical dream of the Pakistani establishment, to intervene and internationalise the Indo-Pak hotspots.

The rebuttal from the Trump transition team was swift, direct and unequivocal, as they expressed their displeasure at the "flowery language" put out by Islamabad. Team Trump clearly noted the convenient and expansive approach of the Pakistanis to suggest, "more than what he (Trump) meant". The mandarins in Islamabad were soon left red-faced at the call of their bluff, and the evidence of diplomatic indiscretion and inelegant desperation shown by Pakistan. While there are good reasons for Nawaz Sharif to fake confidence in these troubled times, he has unknowingly reconfirmed the commonly-held perception of Pakistani duplicity and creative deciphering of situations.

It is true that Donald Trump will take time to evolve and concretise his thoughts about global dynamics. It will require

Pakistan to make peace with its wounded soul, and reconcile with the ill-effects of its chosen path, as no amount of phone calls can make up for institutionalised and internalised falsehoods that are perpetrated within the country, to keep the trilogy of its institutions going.

Chinese reminder of 'history' – a crude allusion to its defeat of India in 1962 war – is too clever by half

(TIMES OF INDIA, 4 July 2017)

Deploying theatrics, hyperbole, and implied threats are part of standard Chinese diplomacy, reflecting an authoritarian state. For a structurally insecure regime, maintaining national positions, aspirations, and narratives requires consistency of pre-planned belligerence, manufactured fears, and indoctrination to support the imagined state of affairs.

Facilitating this sovereign effort is the economic success of China, which has fuelled dreams of the 21st century as the Chinese century. This also legitimises its questionable international relationships with countries with dubious track records, like Pakistan or North Korea, in its quest to realise it's widely believed "Chinese Dream".

Therefore, checkmating potential competition from countries like India, by blocking its entry into NSG, or its rightful permanent seat in the UNSC, tactically supporting terrorists like Hafiz Saeed, or even keeping the Sino-Indian border "active", is part of a calibrated game-plan to keep India on its toes.

China regularly invokes its conveniently assumed, and often manufactured "history", to buttress its claims of sovereignty. Last year, the International Court of Justice, in The Hague, had adjudicated in favour of Philippines, declaring that China had "no historical rights", as claimed by Beijing via its creative interpretation of the "nine-dash-line" approach, in the South China Sea arbitration case.

Similarly, Vietnam has called the bluff on the disputed Paracel and Spratly Islands, which the Chinese readily traced back to its Ming dynasty (overlooking subsequent treaties). The latest stand-off, involving the tri-junction of India-Bhutan-China at Doklam, is yet again conveniently cherry-picked from the pages of history; citing the ostensible convention between China and Britain, relating to Sikkim and Tibet (in 1890).

Amidst these ongoing disputes, and expected differences of history, was a loaded statement that was too clever by half. The spokesperson of the Chinese People's Liberation Army, Col. Wu Qian, suggested, "Indian army could learn from historical lessons", an unmistakable allusion to the 1962 China-India war. Such classic Chinese one-upmanship hides as much as it suggests; the reality of 2017 is that the nuclear power status of both countries brings its own strategic equanimity.

Unlike China, or Pakistan, where Armed Forces command an extra-constitutional position, the Defence Forces in India are proudly apolitical, and serve as the "Sword-Arm" of the nation, at the behest of the democratically elected dispensation of the day. Structurally, this often results in inadequate appreciation of the security imperatives, investments, and strategic planning (as exemplified in the 1962 war). Yet, this insulation from governance and mass politics (unlike China and Pakistan) has afforded unmatched professionalism, potency, and efficacy to the Indian Armed Forces, who have since repeatedly overcome the 1962 experience against multiple challenges, including those emanating from China.

Couched between the drive to Lahore, in 1965, and the brilliant dismemberment of Pakistan, in 1971, are the lesser known exploits of the Nathu La and Cho La clashes with China, in 1967. This limited "war" resulted in an estimated 400 Chinese casualties, as against around 70 for India. Clearly, the "historical lessons" of 1962 were not forgotten by the still numerically, and materially inferior Indian Defence Forces in 1967, when they defeated the Chinese forces. The exemplary military leadership of Lt. General Sagat Singh, the steel and resolve of infantry battalions like 18 Rajput, 2 Grenadiers, 7/11 Gorkha, etc., had indeed defied conventional wisdom, and rewritten history for posterity.

Like any other Defence Force, the PLA too has its own share of history that it needs to internalise and introspect on, from the disastrous performance in the Korean War (1950-53), which resulted in 4,00,000 confirmed fatalities, and over 2,00,000 missing PLA soldiers, to the first, second, and third "Taiwan Strait Crisis", where the numerically overwhelming PLA's efforts to "liberate" Taiwan, came a cropper.

On the contrary, the Indian Armed Forces have routinely proved themselves in multiple insurgencies, besides external involvements in places like Maldives, IPKF, etc., and delivering during the Kargil war.

Perhaps unknown to the PLA spokesperson, the Indian Armed Forces don't disown "history". On the contrary, they internalise celebrations and tribulations equally. Battles are studied rigorously and dispassionately; sand models and war games are not exercises in hagiographic glory.

In that context, the Indian Army Chief's statement that India is fully ready for a two and a half front war is not idle sabre rattling, but a cold fact that needs to be appreciated without any expansionist import implied--because neither is it the grain of the institution to overstep, nor is it in the history of India, to disrespect its own or anyone else's sovereignty.

International Affairs
with Geo-Political implications

In Mideast Spat, Pot calls the Kettle Black
(ASIAN AGE/DECCAN CHRONICLE 16 June, 2017)

The Saudi-led combine of Sunni-Arab states (including the UAE, Bahrain, Yemen, and Egypt) has stunned the international community with a coordinated severing of ties, with its fellow GCC (Gulf Cooperation Council) member and co-sectarian, the Sunni-ruled sheikhdom of Qatar. The timing of the move was surprising, as all the nations in the Middle East (irrespective of their deep intra-regional divides) were in the midst of reclaiming vast swathes of land from the principal enemy in the region, Islamic State or *Daesh*. Undoubtedly, parallel sectarian struggles like the one between the Tehran-led "Shia Crescent" of Iran, Iraq, Syria, and its proxies like the Hezbollah and Houthis, were embroiled in a parallel power struggle against the combined forces of Sunni-ruled nations, and their sponsored Sunni militias. The international powers in the region like the United States, Russia, or Turkey have their own national or geopolitical agendas that further muddied the waters, with their own interventions and alliances. Disentangling the genealogical roots of the unrest in the Middle East is an endless saga of intrigues, complicities, and "terror-sponsorships" that can be traced to all regimes in the region without exception, as indeed, to the policies, secret agencies, and militaries of other regional players (such as Israel and Turkey) that are traceable directly to Western capitals. Every nation has blood on their hands, and has contributed to the bloody quagmire in the Middle East.

A WikiLeaks email that was purportedly sent from Hillary Clinton, to John Podesta, reads,"We need to use our diplomatic and more traditional intelligence assets to bring pressure on the governments of Qatar and Saudi Arabia, which are providing clandestine financial and logistic support to ISIL (*Daesh*) and other radical Sunni groups in the region". Indisputably, the rise of extremist militias like "Al-Nusra Front" (also known as "Al-Qaeda in the Levant"), owe its sustenance and fighting abilities to the generous financial doles from Qatar. While initially the Qatari support was more overt and public via various "social" or "religious" charities, international pressure forced it to adopt a more a covert way of facilitating "ransom monies", in exchange for kidnapped prisoners by organisations like Al-Nusra Front. From managing prisoner swaps in Lebanon to the more high-profile release of American writer Peter Theo Curtis (where the mediation was done by Ghanim Khalifa al-Kubaisi, head of Qatar state security), "petro-dollars" and hydrocarbon-fuelled coffers have allowed Qatar to pick its own independent choice of regional organisations, which it wishes to support, even if the Qatari choice rails against the instincts of its other Arab neighbours, such as Doha who have been openly courting the Palestinian Hamas, as opposed to the more Riyadh-friendly PLO, and in Egypt, the ousted Muslim Brotherhood.

Similarly, Qatar is hosting Taliban elements to push reconciliation between Taliban, Afghanistan, and the US government--though importantly, the move to allow the Taliban to open an "office" in Doha was done after a specific request was made to this effect, by the US.

However, the obvious hypocrisy in this latest Arab spat emanates from the supposed Saudi indignation against "terror sponsorship", which is oblivious to its own role in spreading the extremist, and violent strains of puritanical religiosity globally. The released portions of the congressional investigation into the 9/11 terror attack on the United States (in which 15 of the 19 hijackers were Saudis), has some discomforting statements that suggest Saudi linkages, such as this reference on Page 415, "While in the United States, some of the September 11 hijackers were in contact with, and received support and assistance from, individuals who may be connected to the Saudi government... [At least] two of those individuals were alleged by some to be Saudi intelligence officers." Earlier still, the Saudis had matched the US contributions towards arming and abetting the Mujahedin in Afghanistan, in the 1980-90's; the progenitors of Osama bin Laden, Taliban, and suchlike mutations.

The acquiescence of the Western powers in allowing the Al Saud family to infuse Wahhabism as an antidote to the Cold War challenges, and energy considerations, facilitated the global export of Salafist tendencies that gave birth and inspiration to organisations like ISIS, Boko Haram, and Taliban. Beyond sovereign funding, the concept of raising funds through private individuals and institutions, towards causes that impacted the *"ummah"*, was afforded by the affluence of Saudi society. Later, the same energy-related wealth in countries like Qatar allowed a similar fundraising initiative. Today, both Qatar and Saudi Arabia claim to have tightened the screws on private fundraising for terrorist organisations. However, the survival of various organisations in the Middle East like Al Nusra, ISIS, Hezbollah, or Hamas without sovereign support, directly or indirectly, is hardly plausible. So even if Saudi Arabia is not directly involved in funding terror organisations any longer, its role in creating the infrastructure, ideological framework, and societal justifications is undeniable.

Therefore, the Qatar-Saudi spat is a perfect case of the pot calling the kettle black, and is more likely due to the fears emanating from the "independent streak", originating in Doha, which threatens the status quo in the Arab world. The Arab monarchies are pathologically petrified of an "Arab Spring" redux; hence, the aversion to the likes of the Muslim Brotherhood, which Qatar supports. Further, the convenient illiberalism of the region gets threatened by the relative independence of Al Jazeera. The unkindest cut, however, was the unpardonable act of legitimising Iran as an "Islamic power", and forcing the Saudis to accuse Qatar of supporting "Iran-backed terror groups" (even though, Qatar deployed over 1,000 troops in Yemen to support the Saudi-led drive against the Iran-supported Houthi rebels).

The unwarranted tilt of US President, Donald Trump, in the Saudi-Qatar *fracas*, has demonstrated the curse of perpetuating selective truths that ensures the dominance of certain regional, and international powers.

Beyond fighting ISIS, local conflicts (such as Turks versus Kurds), sectarian conflicts (Shia-Sunni), and geopolitical conflicts (Russians versus Americans), a fifth internecine dimension of intra-GCC conflict has emerged to diminish prospects for peace.

In Biblical Lands

(STATESMAN, 28 Apr 2017)

Given strategic stakes and political symbolism, Narendra Modi's first prime ministerial visit to Israel is logically overdue, though he had visited the country as the Chief Minister of Gujarat. On the contrary, he has charmingly courted the Arab states by visiting and signing major deals with Saudi Arabia, Qatar, and the UAE. The Crown Prince of Abu Dhabi, Mohammed bin Zayed Al Nahyan, was the Chief Guest at this year's Republic Day parade. All this, is in addition to the sectarian "other" in the region, Iran, with whom the geopolitical alignment on the Chabahar port, energy, and Afghanistan, were deftly managed with some tightrope diplomacy, without offending Arab or Israeli sensibilities.

Considering the relatively recent "formal" friendship of the Indo-Israeli framework (full-fledged Embassies opened in 1992), the 25-year journey has witnessed a frenetic pace of mutually-beneficial transactions, which were artificially stifled owing to India's moral and genealogical conundrum of reconciling with a state, created on the basis of a religion. Israel describes itself as a "Jewish and democratic state". The other factor is the political and psychological impact on the Indian Muslims, given the sensitive issue of Palestine.

Civilian trade with Israel is now $5 billion annually, and in the ultra-sensitive defence sector, India is the largest purchaser of Israeli weaponry and wares. The implicit trust in the Indo-Israeli equation affords itself to strategic cooperation in intelligence, technology-sharing, and joint development of military platforms. Recently, a Rs 17,000 crore deal between DRDO, and IAI, for joint development of medium-range surface-to-air missile, MR-SAM, was cleared by the Cabinet Committee on Security. Clearly, there is a certain acceptance and understanding of India's occasional ambivalence towards Israel, and the same is counter-rationalised and contextualized in Tel Aviv, as India's own domestic and historical compulsions. Realpolitik ensures the continuum of expansion in the

Indo-Israeli equation. A healthy and logical geopolitical alignment in the Indo-Israeli framework, overrides India's historical and moral commitment towards Palestine.

However, for all its hard-nosed realpolitik, Israel is not beyond the sensitivities of symbolism. From permanently downgrading its diplomatic ties with New Zealand, and Senegal, for co-sponsoring anti-settlement resolutions in the United Nations Security Council, to chiding President Obama for a "gang-up" in abstaining from the voting at the UN, to vociferously supporting the ultra-divisive move of shifting the US Embassy from Tel Aviv, to Jerusalem-- Israel reacts ferociously against sovereign moves that signify anti-Israeli intent, even if it is without any punitive bite, or impact, by attaching a huge value to these symbolic moves. This has been the typical Israeli-Palestinian narrative, where the moves of third countries are keenly watched, analysed, and decoded for a "for" or "against" verdict.

Thus, India is among the rare countries that has managed a certain ambiguous balance, and sensitivity towards both Israeli and Palestinian causes, without offending the other. Against this backdrop, the scheduled summer visit of Prime Minister Modi to Israel--but not to Palestine-- ostensibly to "de-hyphenate" the equation is either naïve, or brazen. In a deeply hyphenated relationship (Indo-Pak), a visit by the US President to either Delhi or Islamabad, but not to the other, acquires adjectives beyond naivety and innocence. It is clearly tantamount to deliberate political messaging. Similarly, the equally hyphenated Israeli-Palestinian reality was historically respected, and the accompanying dignity of affording dual "visits" to both countries, ensured visits to the region of the Biblical lands.

Diplomacy ought to be dynamic, and not confined to the ghosts of the past. Yet, it needs a simple "net gain or net loss" calculation to ascertain the prudence of either changing or retaining the historical narrative and tradition. Just as the reason to visit both Israel and Palestine simultaneously on a visit to the region was essentially "political", now the reason to abstain from visiting one country, would similarly be deciphered to be even more "political", and not just administrative. The delicate counterpoise of subsequently hosting the Palestinian President, Mahmoud Abbas, would be a post-facto balm, and perhaps inadequate, especially given the hyper-sensitivity of the polarised times.

The Indian government's existing formula in the Middle East has been successful. The trick has been to engage equally with all regional stakeholders (i.e., Arabs, Israelis, and the Iranians) separately, without offending any "other". However, Palestine goes beyond a territorial dispute, it is an emotional and strictly hyphenated issue with Israel, as far as the global *ummah* is concerned. It goes beyond sovereign insularities. By de-hyphenating Palestine during this visit, the net gains of playing to the extreme right-wing in the Zionist galleries, or even domestically, just does not add up to the potential counter-reaction; both domestically, and externally.

Palestine has been relegated to the relative backbenches of the Middle Eastern saga, with the other self-imploding instincts, and sectarian angularities dominating the modern narrative. Yet, Palestine is probably the only issue that all warring factions in the *ummah* agree upon, as it overcomes the sectarian, theological, and political divides that are otherwise tearing apart the region. India, with its own moral high-ground of respecting the Palestinian cause, and yet "normalising" relations with Israel is ensuring a judicious middle-path that works to our commercial, security, and moral advantage. Linking Palestinian de-hyphenation with the questionable and duplicitous antecedents of the OIC resolutions, on Kashmir, will invariably prop up justification of the move, as yet another show of diplomatic muscularity of the incumbent government. However, this does not work to our advantage in the long run. India needs to mesh dignified morality with prudent necessity.

The quintessential "Indian moment", was the Republic Day parade, on 26 January, 2017, when an Arab leader poignantly applauded the late Havildar Hangpan Dada for fighting terrorists in Kashmir, and later clapping simultaneously at the ironical sight of the Arab military contingent walking down Rajpath, only to be followed by weaponry and wares on display, some of them manufactured by Israel. This is the ideal normal that works to India's advantage, without the unnecessary shenanigans and posturing of choosing one over the other. India's own pluralistic, moralistic, and diplomatic instincts will be severely tested in the forthcoming years, as it works towards achieving a permanent seat in the Security Council. This will call for persisting with the winning formula, and not succumbing to the internal and political temptations of looking more "decisive".

Shift in Power Levers

(DECCAN HERALD, 25 Mar 2017)

There has been an undeniable increase in the Chinese strategic capabilities, while those of the other "superpowers"--USA and Russia--have diminished. This shift in power levers has resulted in the new-found confidence, proactivity, and assertion of the Chinese roadmap that has threatened established global equations.

China was historically shy of voting in the UN on international issues; but, recently it has modulated its response by jettisoning the move to designate Masood Azhar as a "global terrorist" (even though, his group Jaish-e-Mohammed is already a UN designated terrorist group). Beijing has expressed "limited support" for US strikes against the terror group Islamic State (IS)--nuancing its response to suit its own national narrative, pursuant to its fancied image as a "responsible stakeholder" in the international arena.

Flush with financials coughed up by its economic juggernaut, China blatantly practices "cheque-book diplomacy" and "infrastructure diplomacy" to win over new friends. In a world fractured by past mistakes, humiliation, and perceptions--China emerges as the perfect antidote for various disgruntled regimes.

While it retains a relationship with isolated (or increasingly isolated) countries like North Korea or Pakistan, its proposition is equally seductive for historical foes like Philippines (with whom they have had a bitter territorial dispute that got escalated to the International Tribunal in The Hague). The Philippines President, Rodrigo Duterte, has made a complete U-turn in its foreign policy by ditching the US, and unabashedly courting the Chinese, as a counterpoise.

Expectedly, all these "converts" are rewarded with generous Chinese largesse in the form of "developmental aid". Masked behind the nobility of the "developmental aid" is the invisible benefit that invariably accrues back to the Chinese mainland: the

CPEC (China Pakistan Economic Corridor), or the tectonically transforming OBOR (One Belt, One Road) for the landlocked, and energy-rich Central Asian countries.

This is an irresistible economic *manna* for the participating countries, as indeed for the Chinese, which ensures an uninterrupted supply chain, market for its wares, and the critical reduction in dependence on the hostile West. However, perhaps the most convenient aspect of cosying up to the Chinese is their deliberate lack of concern about the internal affairs, and governance style of the friendly regimes. It seldom criticises the means and methods of quelling internal dissent, human rights, or other "preachy issues" propagated by the Western powers.

The lure of an alternative benign power, which doles out *moolah* to cash-starved nations without any "strings attached", is a welcome alternative to the much-conditional "ifs and buts" of the Western powers.

China is the veritable high church of cold realpolitik, it is behaviourally driven by what serves its interests best, without injecting the moral, democratic, or ideological angularities in its bilateral relations. So, elegance in diplomacy is a complete non-consideration, and China never hesitates from flexing its military muscle to protect its geostrategic ambitions.

On the contentious South China Sea issue, Chinese Foreign Minister Wang Yi bluntly called for "elimination of interference" by the US, and merrily deployed the still "sub-Blue Water" capability naval elements to intimidate the wary neighbourhood. It went on to brazenly create artificial islands with offensive capabilities--like, landing airstrips for fighter planes and missile systems.

The Sino-USSR relationship offers an insight into the famed Chinese fleet-footedness that is based on tactical requirements, and a need-based approach, shorn of any emotions ("*Hindi-Cheeni-Bhai-Bhai*").

The Chinese relationship with the Soviets was borne of an ideological convergence, economic dependence, and fears of regime change (Mao feared a US invasion to re-establish Chiang Kai-shek). Expectedly, the Soviets lent aid and diplomatic support

(USSR singularly supported China on Taiwan and jointly supported North Korea in the Korean War etc.).

Soon, the Chinese outlived their dependence on the Soviets and started to chart their independent course. The Soviets retaliated by supplying weapons to India in the Sino-India war of 1962-- but, it climaxed in 1969 with unprecedented border clashes, and both countries reconfiguring their nuclear missiles at each other, as opposed to the US. Since then, the ties have seen ups and downs, but essentially China has emerged from the shadows, and is posited to fructify the neologism of the "Chinese Century".

Global conflicts

Interestingly, the Chinese strategy of remaining "non-committal" in most of the recent global conflicts like West Asia, Balkans, Somalia, Afghanistan, Libya etc., has ensured that while the coffers of the Western powers have bled profusely with the outreach (US spending on West Asian wars and Homeland Security is expected to reach $4.79 trillion in 2017), the Chinese have gingerly stepped aside, and conserved their energy, and resources, towards strengthening themselves.

Today, it would be naïve to presume that the Chinese are not convinced of the antecedents of elements like Masood Azhar and their ilk, yet they play hardball with India to score a larger geopolitical goal of retaining its equations with its "all-weather-friend" Pakistan. Clearly, the Chinese are aware of the dangers of pandering to Islamist hardliners, as it fights Islamic separatist groups like East Turkestan Islamic Movement, in its restive Xinjiang province.

The Muslim Uighurs in Xinjiang are routinely subjected to ruthless clampdowns, ban on protests, and disallowance of religious rituals and observances. However, the Chinese realpolitik mandates the parallel thwarting of Masood Azhar as a global terrorist, as it ostensibly seeks "solid evidence". The Chinese are adept at compartmentalising issues without a linear or consistent logic, as that could trip its own narrative, internally and externally.

The way to approach the Dragon is without the shenanigans of a holistic charm offensive. Instead, it should be a piece-meal discussion based on individual issues like the border issue, NSG entry, Arunachal, or even Masood Azhar; this, without necessarily hoping for inter-linkages of common logics across all sore points.

China offers a simpler, and modular opportunity, of negotiating issues that can be addressed, given the hand of cards on the specific issues, without attaching the usual notions and romance of civilizational-connect, statesmanship, or even joint-destiny.

Trump Policy against Iran set to Dilute Gains against ISIS

(THE CITIZEN, 16 Feb 2017)

National narratives are matters of time-invested truths, partial-truths and untruths.

The period between 2010 and 2013, saw the lightening emergence of the brutal Salafi-jihadist and Sunni supremacist, ISIS, who rebelled against the Shia-ruled governments of Iraq and Syria, whilst, integrating splinter remnants of the co-sectarian, Al Qaida and Al Nusra.

The period also witnessed the re-emergence of other Wahhabi-inspired VEO's (Violent Extremist Organisations) like the Taliban in the Af-Pak region, Boko Haram in Nigeria, and the continuing mayhem in Libya which saw the killing of the American Ambassador to Libya, J. Christopher Stevens.

The implosive tendencies in the Middle East morphed into a clear sectarian divide, with the Wahabi/Salafist VEO's in the forefront of a regime-change, and anti-West agenda, preaching extreme revivalism. As swathes of land got swallowed by these terror organisations, the only military opposition came from the rag-tag forces of Syria and Iraq, along with Iran supported Shia militias.

Surprisingly, the man then-heading the CENTCOM (US theatre command that handles Middle East, Af-Pak, North Africa, and Central Asia), General James Mattis, noted rather incredibly that the three gravest threats to the US then were, "Iran, Iran, Iran".

Amidst clear pointers to the contrary, General James Mattiss's Iran-fixation caused the Marine culture-hero to be removed from the hot-job in CENTCOM by Obama, before his tenure end. Today, James Mattis is back as the US Secretary of Defence, and is invoking the familiar American line of Iran to be the, "world's biggest sponsor of world terrorism".

As the only Marine to head CENTCOM, the Pattonesque James Mattis has an institutionalized and traumatized memory that afflicts all Marines--the 1983 Beirut suicide attack by the Iran-trained bomber, which accounted for 241 American deaths, including 220 Marines.

Despite the essential change in the terror landscape, nationalities, and established progenitors; such as, ISIS, Taliban, Lashkar-e-Taiba (all Saudi-Wahhabi offshoots of petro-dollar funded nurseries), this Iran-fixation has retained the American imagination, and defied ground realities for the last 15 years, as a deserved counter-narrative.

Former US President Barack Obama made the first tentative steps towards the much needed rapprochement with Iran by signing the "Joint Comprehensive Plan of Action" (JCPOA) or the "Iran Deal", along with the P+1.

The resultant thaw and the unfreezing of Iranian assets, expectedly riled the Gulf Arab nations led by the US-ally, Saudi Arabia, who were in the midst of a sectarian proxy war with the Iranians in Yemen, Bahrain, Syria, and even Southern Saudi Arabia (hosting a Shia enclave).

The consequences of the invaluable Iranian participation in the crucial anti-ISIS operations saw unprecedented reverses for the ISIS, from Aleppo in Syria, to Mosul in Iraq, though the mainstream media coverage, especially in Aleppo, was concertedly against the Syrian-Iranian operations.

Clearly, the Arab-Turkish lobby (Sunni nations) were not very comfortable to see the emergence of Iran and its proxies in the anti-ISIS success, and the brazen hold-out of the Saudi-forces by the Shia Houthis in Yemen, further angered the Arabs.

On the rebound, they formulated the Saudi-led, 39 nations (all Sunni ruled) force called the "Islamic Military Alliance to Fight Terrorism" (IMAFT), to fight "terror". Providentially for this alliance, the surprise election of Republican Donald Trump is poised to rearrange the Middle Eastern pieces, to their original positions of anti-Iran posture.

The latest US executive order on the immigration ban is a pointer to the reneging of track and policies. The seven "countries of concern" include all the three Shia-ruled nations (irrespective of their contribution and sacrifices in the anti-ISIS operations), of Iran, Iraq, and Syria.

The other four countries include the politically irrelevant and virtually lawless Somalia, Libya, Yemen, and Sudan. Not surprisingly, the countries which contributed to the principal 9/11 fiasco (i.e., Saudi Arabia, UAE, Lebanon, and Egypt), find an honourable omission. None of these seven countries have a trail to the recent terror attacks in the US; from the Boston Marathon, Charleston Church, Chattanooga shootings, San Bernardino, Orlando nightclub, to the most recent, Fort Lauderdale.

America's incomplete perspective on Iran started from the 1979 "Islamic Revolution", which toppled the pro-US monarchy in a popular uprising, and later resulted in a 444 day siege of the American embassy, in Tehran. The essential shortcoming in this American narrative, and oversimplification, is that it completely obliterates the prior context of the Iranian conviction of the CIA hand, in the 1953 coup, which overthrew the folk hero leader, Iranian Prime Minister Mohammad Mosaddeq (he was voted with 90% votes).

Mosaddeq had opposed the extremely unfair sovereign deal that gave Iran only 16% of oil profits (even these payments were pending), and had taken the issue to the International court in The Hague--expectedly he won the suit against the British, and went on to espouse many more progressive changes for Iran. Meanwhile, the West restively watched the vassal-status of Iran slipping away, and the CIA launched the infamous "Operation Ajax" to remove Mosaddeq in a coup.

Declassified documents from the US National Security Archives have since confirmed the dirty involvement, but in the US, the history of Iran revolves around the partial-truth of the US Embassy hostage drama, and the Beirut attack.

Expectedly, to magnify, protect, and perpetuate the theocracy in Tehran, the Ayatollah's swung sharply and ranted rabidly against the

West and Israel, in defiant posturing. Given that the US had allied with Saddam Hussein (a fact that is played down) in the bloody Iran-Iraq war, besides funding the Mujahedin in Afghanistan, in propagating their cold-war agenda, it was all kosher for the US. Later it would dump the Afghan Mujahedin, Saddam Hussein, overlook the dangerous Saudi funding of Wahhabism in *madrassas* across the globe, and continue playing the Iran bogey.

Israel too joined in the Iran-bashing, along with the Arabs, as in the 1980's and 1990's, when the Arab nations were no longer a threat; the Iran supported Hezbollah in Lebanon, and Hamas in Palestine were the only ones to offer resistance, while the Saudi's, Egyptians, and Jordanians had bought their peace.

Today, Arabs and Israeli's converge on Iran, and Donald Trump with his dual instincts of upsetting the previous regime's policy applecart, and owing to his ostensible mercantile investments in the Arab-Jewish world, has re-raised the ante against Iran.

The US, like Iran or any other country in the Middle East has blood on its hands--peace necessitates overcoming and overlooking the ghosts of the past, like Iran did in the case of the US.

However, the new US regime is bent upon invoking some truths, partial-truths, and complete untruths to short-change Iran, and the recent progress made in the anti-ISIS drive, as a whole.

Silence of the Sheikhs

(STATESMAN, 10 Feb 2017)

President Donald Trump's controversial executive order on the immigration ban, from seven Muslim-majority countries (Iran, Iraq, Sudan, Somalia, Syria, Yemen and Libya), for the next 90 days, and the suspension of refugee-entry for the next 120 days, has expectedly shocked and riled the world, and drawn accusations of a "Muslim ban". As global leaders from Canada, UK, and Germany weighed in, expressing their concern over the brazenness and the implied religio-specificity of the order, leaders from the influential Gulf Sheikdoms were conspicuous by their pusillanimous and vacuous stand on the US order. Even though, the world's largest body of Islamic nations, the 57-nation Organisation of Islamic Countries (OIC) spoke of "grave concern" and warned, "Such selective and discriminatory acts will only serve to embolden the radical narratives of extremists and will provide further fuel to the advocates of violence and terrorism", the muted acquiescence and understanding showed by Saudi Arabia, and the UAE, are reflective of the subservience of the Gulf monarchs, to the US.

Even though, Trump spoke to the Saudi King, Salman bin Aziz Al Saud, after the executive order was issued, accounts from neither side suggested that the immigration subject was even broached, whereas the UAE Foreign Minister Sheikh Abdullah bin Zayed al Nahyan defended the US order as a "sovereign decision" and added, "Some of these countries that were on this list are countries that face structural problems". The other influential voice in the region, Qatar, was equally considerate towards the US move, and hoped that it would "do the right thing" regarding immigration. Kuwait went one-up and enforced its own ban on five Muslim countries: Syria, Iraq, Pakistan, Afghanistan and Iran.

On the contrary, Iran, which surprisingly finds itself in the list of seven countries to be subjected to the US ban, was unequivocally forthright in slamming the move with its Foreign Minister,

Mohammad Javad Zarif, stating that the move, "will be recorded in history as a great gift to extremists and their supporters". The Saudi Arabian regime posits its moral supremacy, and the accompanying national narrative owing to the historical and geographical relevance of the Kingdom, as the birthplace of Islam. This has afforded the Saudi monarch the singular honour of attaching the symbolically revered title, "Custodian of the two holy mosques". This religious sanctification along with oil-generated affluence (Saudi Arabian reserves are about one-fifth of the world's total conventional oil reserves), has ensured that the Saudis are the leading voice in the Islamic world. Historically, it has been in the forefront of shaping the Arab multilateral forums: Arab League, Gulf Cooperation Council, Muslim World League, Organisation of Islamic Countries, and supporting the envisaged Arab Customs Union and Arab Common Market.

Often the "cheque-book" diplomacy of the Saudi Arabian regime ensured that the less affluent Islamic countries were given financial largesse--over $70 billion has been doled out by Saudi Arabia since the 1970's, under "overseas development aid". UAE, Qatar, and Kuwait who have similar bounties of nature, and stacked treasuries of affluence, have been "net donors" to various "Islamic" causes like Palestine, Bosnia, Chechnya, etc. However, politically and militarily, the Gulf Sheikhdoms are in a complex situation; wherein, they remain indebted and physically sustained by the invaluable security cover provided by the US. The contradictions within the region are exemplified by the US arming, protecting, and guaranteeing the sovereign integrity of the various Gulf nations, along with the parallel arming and supporting of the historical nemesis of the Arabs--Israel (both sides have F-15's, F-16's, AH-64 Apache Attack Helicopters, Stinger Missiles, etc.).

This eerie silence and tolerance by the Gulf Sheikhdoms is attributable to three principal threats to these regimes: firstly, the unleashed strains of ultra-religiosity that come in the form of organisations like ISIS, Al Qaida, Muslim Brotherhood, etc., who are intrinsically anti-monarchists, and active in the rebellion against the existing governance systems. The US and the Western powers aid the fight-back and suppression of such entities, as these militant organisations also have an inherently anti-West agenda, and routinely threaten Western interests and assets in the region. Secondly, the sectarian angularity of the emergence and assertion of Iran, and its proxies like the Houthis in Yemen, Hezbollah in Lebanon, etc. In the fight to contain the spectre of a rising "Shia-crescent" in the Gulf Peninsula, the US ,with its own anti-Iran agenda and posture, is aligned to the sensibilities of the Gulf Sheikhdoms (even more stridently under President Trump's watch). Thirdly, the implosive restlessness and internal tendencies that recently accompanied the "Arab Spring". These popular uprisings later petered out with the subsequent mayhem and lack of alternative solutions that they generated. Given these factors, the US and the Sheikhdoms converge, agree, and are aligned on the ostensible commonality of their respective threat perceptions; hence, the long rope of patience to each other.

With the US already over-committed across the globe (from containing China, Russia, North Korea, Afghanistan, etc.), and simultaneously tackling the economic pressures overall, it can ill afford to further escalate economic and military chaos with potential disruption to its energy supplies, from this oil-rich area. This had propelled the US to defend the Kuwaitis in "Operation Desert Shield", in the First Gulf War. The US has since stationed troops on Saudi soil, besides having the US Navy's Fifth Fleet based out of Bahrain, and maintaining large air installations in Qatar, UAE, and Oman. Even though, the presence and footprint of the US soldiers in the region has fuelled radical militancy, and has been essentially counterproductive, immediate withdrawal of US troops would severely jeopardise the ability of the Sheikhdoms to sustain themselves.

So, regime-survival instincts, a possible sectarian angle (as all the Shia-ruled nations like Iran, Iraq, and Syria are among the banned nations), along with the plausible theory of protecting commercial interests of the Trump corporate empire in the Gulf Sheikhdoms, has ensured a convenient *quid pro quo*, wherein maintaining ostensible "normalcy" and acceptance is in the mutual interest of both the US and the Gulf Sheikdoms. Thus, invaluable US support to these repressive, undemocratic, and authoritarian regimes of the Gulf Sheikhdoms, with the required leniency and legitimacy that is critical for their internal and external survival, buys reciprocal silence on matters like the immigration ban, which unquestionably irks the common man on the streets of the Gulf Sheikhdoms.

Diplomatic Coup that Overcomes the Past

(MILLENNIUM POST, 3 Feb 2017)

The UAE is arguably the second most important Arab country, after Saudi Arabia. Unlike most of the *ummah,* which is embroiled in internal fissures and strife that manifested in the failed "Arab Spring", the moderate and economically progressive Sheikhdom of the UAE has bucked the trend. Even as the debt-laden Dubai model (ruled by the Al Maktoum family) went belly up, and the palace intrigues settled in favour of Abu Dhabi (Al Nahyan family), the fundamental UAE narrative of an influential "soft power", remained unchanged. Jointly, the UAE has the largest sovereign funds in the world (estimated at over $1000 billion), and it is the rare beneficiary of US trust; with the signing of the US–UAE 123 Agreement for Peaceful Civilian Nuclear Energy Cooperation.

Pakistan, too, shares a fraternally powerful relationship with the UAE. Symbolically, Pakistan was the first country to recognise the state of UAE in 1971, and since then has benefitted from the relationship, with the UAE echoing the Pakistani line on Kashmir in the OIC forums, gaining invaluable petrodollars directly, or indirectly, through remittances made by over 1.2 million Pakistani expatriates in the UAE. The Shaikh Zayed International Airport at Rahim Yar Khan, Shaikh Zayed hospital in Lahore, and the "UAE Project to Assist Pakistan" (UAE PAP), are recent symbols of UAE's financial benevolence towards Pakistan. This declared "special relationship" extended beyond the commercial domain, with the Pakistani military training the UAE Defence Forces, UAE leasing the Shamsi Airfield in Pakistan's Balochistan province, besides partaking in sensitive moves like recruiting the former Pakistani spymaster, Lt. General Shuja Pasha (retired ISI chief), to head the UAE Secret Agency. However, the UAE is a practical oddity amongst the Arab nations. It hosts a large Iranian expatriate community in Dubai, and unlike Saudi Arabia, it exhibits no overtly demonstrated vitriol against Iran (passive dispute over three islands, notwithstanding). Even though, it does not recognise Israel, unlike other Arab countries, Jewish expatriates and Israelis with dual citizenship are allowed into the UAE. The UAE royalty is a frequent invitee to the US Presidential retreat, Camp David. All in all, mercantile prudence and geopolitical sensitivities have ensured that the UAE routinely shuns puritanical traits, and adopts more prudent policies that are in consonance with the times. This deft balancing of conventional Arab sensitivities and the extended global community, results in the dexterous management of both Pakistani and Indian sentiments, albeit earlier, they were diplomatically tilted in favour of Pakistan.

Today, the economically emerging India, the effects of the global war on terror, and its confirmed progenitors, along with the accompanying repercussions, have seen the UAE correct the bias in the Indo-Pak equation. The successful visit by the Prime Minister, Narendra Modi, in 2015, resulted in the barely concealed shift, with a joint statement which toed the Delhi line, by stating that they, "condemn efforts, including by states, to use religion to justify, support and sponsor terrorism against other countries", and called on nations to, "dismantle terrorism infrastructure where they exist and bring perpetrators of terrorism to justice". Ironically, just last month, members of the UAE royal family, including the Deputy Prime Minister Prince Sheikh Saif bin Zayed Al Nahyan, had a narrow escape with terror in Pakistan, when their cavalcade was brutally attacked in the Guchak area by Baloch rebels, whilst on a Houbara game hunt. The UAE has been swift and ruthless in keeping Islamic terror off its soil, and the recent bloodlust in the Middle East has only strengthened the regime's resolve towards a more pragmatic outlook, which no longer falls for the vacuous charm of Pakistan's persistent claim, as a "brother Muslim" country. Now, the strategic import and optics of the second-visit-within-a-year, of the Crown Prince and the Deputy Supreme Commander of the Armed Forces of UAE, Sheikh Mohammed bin Zayed bin Sultan Al-Nahyan, as the Chief Guest at the 68th Republic Day of India, is yet another unmistakable signal of the shifting sands towards India's relevance at the global stage.

The Republic Day proceedings were initiated with the poignant Ashok Chakra ceremony for the brave-heart, Havaldar Hangpan Dada, for, "killing four terrorists who had infiltrated

South Kashmir", with the UAE royalty in the Presidential box; a symbolic acquiescence of India's stand on Kashmir. The comfortable dichotomy was inherent in the joint presence of the UAE marching contingent, along with Indian military muscularity that is increasingly powered by Israeli wares-- Tejas (with AESA radar), Jaguars (with listening pods) etc. The reality of India as the largest buyer of Israeli military equipment, and Israel emerging as the second biggest arms supplier for India, mattered little, as the old hyphenated hang-ups of the past were given a royal miss. On the contrary, more real threats, like the recent terror attack in Kandahar which killed five UAE diplomats, with the inevitable shadow of the Haqqani network-ISI looming all over it, spurs the UAE away from the blind rationale of supporting a country, on the sole basis of religious affinity. The unequivocal phrasing of the latest UAE-India joint-statement nails the patented Pakistani bogey of "non-state actors", when it captures without mentioning Pakistan, "... deplored efforts by countries to give religious and sectarian colour to political issues and pointed out the responsibility of all states to control the activities of the so-called non-state-actors". With India, the talk revolves around increasing the existing $50 Billion mutual trade, to $100 Billion by 2020, a language of engagement that is strategically progressive, and not mired in the regressively narrow delusion of co-religiosity. The breaking of protocol to court UAE, with the Indian Prime Minister personally receiving the guests at the airport, extending the red carpet (unprecedentedly, to a Non-Head of State) is a laudable punt, and reflective of India's diplomatic march over its immediate neighbour, at many levels. This diplomatic coup follows previous year's dignitary in Barack Obama, who too, like the UAE, cannot candidly express his opinion on Pakistan, given the historical and existing stakes involved; yet, chose to symbolically assert their future course of strategic direction, by gracing moments that exemplify everything that India stands for!

The Andaman Angularity with China

(THE CITIZEN, 9 Jan 2017)

The neologism of the 21st Century as the "Chinese Century" (as opposed to the 20th Century as the "American Century", or the 19th Century as "Pax Britannica") has ensured a wary spotlight on China, through 2016. Historian AJP Taylor notes, "The test of a great power is the test of strength for war", and on this count, China has displayed unabashed propensity to take on the established world order, economically, militarily, and diplomatically. Having displaced the USA as the biggest economy in the world, by routinely flexing its military muscle in the neighbourhood, and by patronizing a certain roughish set of nations (North Korea, Pakistan, Philippines etc.), it is displaying the copybook behavioural pattern of an emerging, Great Power.

Militarily, the restive South China Sea has been the cynosure of strategic posturing between the Chinese bloc, and the rest. Two developments dominated the headlines last year: firstly, the continuing belligerence of the Chinese Military in the disputed and contested waters of the neighbouring countries (whilst, claiming sovereign rights on the small islands, lagoons, atolls and reefs, or even constructing artificial islands therein). Secondly, the formal rebuke from the International Tribunal in The Hague, in a case initiated by the Philippines, which rejected China's claim of historic rights on these disputed waters (ironically, the maverick new Filipino President, Rodrigo Duterte unexpectedly decided to steer away from Washington's security umbrella, and has moved towards the Chinese).

However, the South China Sea has remained dangerously choppy with the reciprocal hostility exhibited by the US Navy, to call off the Chinese bluff and bluster. The year ended with the dramatic capture of a US Unmanned Underwater Vehicle (UUV), or an "ocean glider", by a Chinese warship. Even though, the underwater drone was deployed by an oceanographic survey ship, USNS Bowditch (with an, "an all-civilian crew of civil service mariners and scientific support personnel"), the optics of the incident riled the President-elect of the USA, Donald Trump, to shoot back, "We should tell China that we don't want the drone they stole back – let them keep it!"

At the heart of the Chinese aggression in the region is the heightened-sense of vulnerability of its economic juggernaut, which survives on the free passage of its seafaring routes, via the South China Sea. As the largest oil importer of the world, fuelling its gargantuan industries and the furious stockpiling of its Strategic Petroleum Reserves (SPR), and as the largest exporter of goods in the world--both the fear of a debilitating blockade of energy resources, and the hopes of sustaining its hyper-production based economy are rooted in securing its seafaring abilities towards the Western axis, skirting India, for both essential sustenance and continuing the lucrative exports.

The recent South China Sea bullying tactics are a localised form of its extended and famed, "String-of-Pearl Ports" theory, which strategically envisages these Chinese ports along the seafaring routes to protect the Chinese access, to and fro. Unlike the US Navy which has true "Blue-Water" capabilities, the Chinese Navy needs support facilities in such "Pearl" ports and establishments *en route* to provide the requisite cover (hence, the coercive appropriation of disputed landmasses, and in an unprecedentedly brazen manner, the creation of artificial airstrips in the middle of the disputed seas).

However, the real sense of vulnerability, and a spectre for the worst nightmare of the dreaded Chinese seafaring blockade, is further westwards from the South China Sea, towards the Indian sovereign waters of the Andaman and Nicobar Islands. This shining-outpost of India, juts out strategically at the virtual "windpipe of fear", the Malacca Straits. Even though there is a relative lull, and the famed Chinese belligerence is concentrated upstream in the South China Sea, the ultra-narrow Malacca Straits (4-8 nautical miles, width), accounts for nearly 40 percent of the world trade.

With an estimated 90,000 cargo ships sailing across the Malacca Straits, the traffic is twice that of the Suez Canal, and thrice that of the Panama Canal. Geographically and providentially, positioned at the very mouth of the Malacca Straits, is the Campbell

Bay area, of the Indian Nicobar Islands. Unlike, the South China Sea, the Chinese have not opened any contentious claims or flexed military assets in these waters, yet the nervousness of the Chinese is palpable. Instead, the area was sought to be ring-fenced with "Pearl Ports" in Coco Islands of Myanmar (15 nautical miles away from the Northern tip of the Andaman and Nicobar Islands), Sittwe in Myanmar, Chittagong in Bangladesh, and Hambantota in Sri Lanka--encircling the Andaman and Nicobar "theatre" with a menacing and strategic, Chinese counter-presence.

However, the change of political guard with a decidedly pro-India dispensation in Myanmar, Bangladesh, and Sri Lanka has put to rest the Chinese "Pearl Port" plans, as of now; therefore, a possible explanation for the alternative strategic axis of the CPEC (China Pakistan Economic Corridor), which is underway at a furious pace of development, to connect the Chinese heartland with the Arabian Sea port of Gwadar, in Pakistan, with a series of road and railway networks.

For now, the Chinese angst and restlessness is concentrated on its immediate frontiers. Last week, in a show of strength, its first indigenously developed aircraft carrier, Liaoning, along with a flotilla of five other warships ratcheted up the heat by sailing past the Pratas Islands (or Dongsha Islands), a Taiwan controlled atoll, in the Northern part of the South China Sea, which saw a familiar mounting of tensions between China and its old nemesis, Taiwan. In yet another sign of the times to come, Donald Trump had earlier broken the long-standing hypocrisy by calling up the Taiwanese President, Tsai Ing-wen (Trump had noted, "Interesting how the U.S. sells Taiwan billions of dollars of military equipment but I should not accept a congratulatory call").

While, a lot of Chinese seafaring belligerence is historical (e.g., with Japan and Taiwan), the essential cause for the same is rooted in its obvious nervousness of protecting the passage of its survival-depending, seafaring routes. The weakest link from a Chinese vulnerability perspective is the Malacca Straits--which, for now, is beyond the immediate theatrics and capabilities of the Chinese military wherewithal, and hence the lull in the area. However, given the impending hostility of the incoming US presidency that has centered China as the principal foe, the emergence of the "pivotal lever" in the Malacca Straits will see the Andaman and Nicobar Islands emerge as a natural location of counter-poise. The Andaman angularity is inevitable to the Indo-US dimension of containing Chinese hegemonic instincts, though subdued for now, given the Chinese focus upstream in order to consolidate its presence in the immediate waters, before the strategic seismic zone shifts to its logical epicentre, the area in the proximity of the Malacca Straights, near the Indian sovereign land of the Andaman and Nicobar Islands.

More to Presidential Imperatives than Muscularity
(THE CITIZEN, 28 Nov 2016)

Donald Trump has regressed the sub-text of being "Presidential" to the narrow confines of misogynistic undertones, of appearance and gender, when he seemingly teased the men in the audience with an audacious, *"Does she look presidential, fellas"*?

The not-so-subtle implication in the words, and tone, suggesting that the men in the audience would automatically comprehend his concern. Aspects of gender, looks, and aesthetics were implied as the sole pre-requisite of Trump's definition of "Presidential". The social-contract mandated in the hallowed preamble to the US constitution, "to form a more perfect union" has held a certain characteristic of sobriety, inclusivity, and dignity that has been maintained for over two centuries, from the Presidency of George Washington (1789-1797) to that of the outgoing President, Barrack Obama (2009 onwards).

Politically, George W. Bush, and Barrack Obama, represented the exact opposite instincts and popular imaginations, yet the mandated transition from one Presidency to the other, was a textbook case of constitutional civility and grace afforded by one-to-the-other. Obama's trademark courtesy was extended to his then, vanquished Republican opponent, Senator John McCain in 2009--Obama made John McCain the guest of honour at a black tie dinner celebrating Obama's inauguration. More importantly, he valued and consulted John McCain's input about nominations to the sensitive security positions, and other issues. Obama even ensured that his running-mate in both his Presidential elections, was Joe Biden, a one-time fellow Presidential contender from the Democratic Party. Later, he made his principal Democratic-aspirant for the Democratic nomination in 2008, Hillary Clinton, his Secretary of State.

A certain pacifism, dignity, and accommodative spirit typified Obama as the generous victor in a graceful and consistent act of truly acting "Presidential". Even with the successful campaign of extreme polarization accompanying Donald Trump's recent victory, Obama has emerged as amongst the most popular Presidents ever (with the approval ratings at 56%, in the last leg of his term), owing to his trademark behavioural conduct--even as he overcame the initial sleights of his "Muslim ancestry", and the racist overtones of first "black" President. Clearly, the benchmark and imperatives of being "Presidential" in Barrack Obama's dictionary were bed rocked on wisdom, humility, and empathy; accompanied with a generosity of spirit, and hope.

India too, has been fortunate to have had leadership exemplifying behavioural "Statesmanship" across the political spectrum--from the erudition of Jawahar Lal Nehru, the simplicity of Lal Bahadur Shastri, the sobriety of Rajiv Gandhi, the intellect of IK Gujral, the eloquence of Atal Bihari Vajpayee, and the dignity of Manmohan Singh--the nation has essentially retained its unique sense of inclusivity, constitutional propriety, and liberality. The ingrained Gandhian DNA that values communal harmony, social integration, and progressive emancipation has been the leitmotif of most of the political leadership, irrespective of the political divide. The transition of the NDA government, to the UPA government in 2004, was marked by an inherent decency that came naturally to a truly Gandhian Statesman like Atal Bihari Vajpayee, as he passed the baton to another Gandhian (in thought, speech, mannerism, and conduct), Manmohan Singh. But, as the much quoted verse of the latest Nobel Laureate for Literature, Bob Dylan goes, "Times, they are a changing…"

Assuming the constitutional chair, whether "Presidential" or "Prime Ministerial", necessitates the transition from a "campaign" mode to a governance mode. Two aspects offer a sneak view of the potential flavour of the presidencies. Firstly, the choice of advisors and key aides is absolutely critical, as that cushions the initial continuum of the pre-election campaign vitriol towards a more nuanced, inclusive, and balanced policy making and executive decision making. Secondly, the approach towards the media, as liberal democracies warrant free space and breathing ground for impartial "connect", to act as an effective countercheck and voice, of both the constituents and the executive--any semblance of coercion or drowning of contrarian views is extremely frightening in the long run.

On both these counts, Donald Trump is clear about where he stands when he apparently told media honchos after his successful nomination to the White House, *"We're in a room of liars, the deceitful, dishonest media who got it all wrong"*. But in a more fundamental sense, the nation got a foreboding sense of the governance fabric with the appointments of Steve Bannon, Michael Flynn, and Jeff Sessions--these ostensible "best people" have a track record of proximity and empathy with white supremacists, are anti-minorities, and have extremely polarizing track records. The construct of the "Presidential" tenure is eerily poised to mirror the campaign populism, discrimination, and radicalization.

The acid test of the "Presidential" credentials in President Barrack Obama's tenor was exemplified by his inspiring and hoary intonation of "the audacity of hope", whereas the "Presidential" cues from Donald Trump are visible in his book, *"When people wrong you, go after those people, because it is a good feeling and because other people will see you doing it. I always get even"*. Seemingly, in the new reality across the globe, radical ideas, fear mongering, and belligerence are hot currency. The new-age leadership style is an ominous potion of unapologetic hubris, clumsy jingoism, and self-aggrandizement (Donald Trump had once stated that he would be, *"the greatest jobs president that God ever created"*, while calling his critics and rivals "losers" and "stupid").

The "Presidential" imperatives clearly go beyond sharp-suits, razzmatazz, and theatrics. The wistful sensitivity and inclusivity that was implied in Prime Minister Atal Bihari Vajpayee's *"insaaniyat ke dayere se"*, typified the constitutional values and the healing touch that went beyond party positions and electoral considerations, a parallel analogy of the unmistakable, "Prime Ministerial" imperatives, in a wounded country of diversities and opinions. Optics of derision, taunts, and threats do not behove the constitutional chair that ordains intellectual openness and tolerance towards contrarian views.

Perhaps, the subtler pre-requisite of the "Presidential" debate was nailed by President Barrack Obama, when he spoke at the Asia Pacific Economic Cooperation summit in Lima, about the supremacy of the "spirit" of law, over the letter of the law; he spoke about how he converted his assets into Treasury Bills, to avoid any potential conflict of interest, during his presidency. Clearly, in participative democracies, optics matter. The "Presidential" imperatives are a lot more profound than bravado and muscular posturing.

Mosul, and the Day After!

(MILLENNIUM POST, 22 Nov 2016)

Arguably, the three most violent conflict zones in the world are the ISIS-led Syrian-Iraqi swathes, the unforgiving terrain of the Taliban-led Af-Pak region, and the distant madness in the Libyan deserts with the bloodlust of the myriad Islamist/tribal militias. All three conflict zones have an eerie similarity--each of these zones was under some "benign dictator" (Saddam Hussein in Iraq, Muammar Gadhafi in Libya, and Muhammad Najibullah in Afghanistan) who was fundamentally opposed to the West. Each of these dictatorships were tolerated (sometimes even covertly supported e.g., Iraq in the 80's), as long as they did as per the West's bidding. All this would suddenly change when the dictatorship reneged on favourable politico-commercial interests of the West, who would then unleash a furious agenda of regime change, without any post-regime-change plans, and support for governance. To actualise their single-point agenda, the West instigated and supported bloody rebellions against the "no-longer benign" regimes, and would conveniently walk away leaving the natives high and dry in a cauldron of abject deprivation, and destruction.

The West's lack of strategic and long-term vision, the absence of compelling, credible, and empathetic justifications, and an arrogant display of military might (e.g., drones) has always left these zones with a pathologically, anti-West sentiment. That the phenomenon of ISIS is borne of the "secular" but abandoned Baathists, who later found bloody succour in radical Salafist ideology to avenge their humiliation, and sectarian grievances, is a well-known reality. Likewise, the ancestry of Taliban is directly traceable to the West supported-mujahedeen of the 1980's, who were hosted and *fêted* at the White House and 10 Downing Street, and even compared to the founding fathers of the nation! That these bearded ultra-outlaws would disprove the inert naivety in Brzezinski's theory of supporting a "few crazed Muslims" to be worth the price to pay, for the destruction of the Soviet Union, is a telling pathos. Lastly, the rare candidness of President Obama, in accepting Libya as the "worst mistake" of his Presidency, in failing to prepare for the aftermath of ousting Muammar Gaddafi, is a repetitive testimony to the subsequent chaos, bloodshed, and extreme violence initiated by the sudden vacuum created by the West's disappearance, after achieving its narrow and selfish aim of regime change. Obama's prescient insight on his Libyan failure was, "Probably failing to plan for the day after"!

This monumental failure is the bugbear of modern global unrest, as the Mujahedin of the Af-Pak regions mutated into the modern day Taliban, and have accounted for nearly 2400 US casualties. The cost of war on ISIS itself, is estimated in excess of $8 billion, and the ensuing air strikes are costing $11 million a day, besides triggering a genocidal loss of life. In Libya, known loyalists of Gaddafi are said to have extracted revenge for their slain leader by killing the US ambassador to Libya, J. Christopher Stevens. The war in all these "vacated" conflict zones only exacerbated and extracted a huge toll for the West, the local population, and the world as a whole. With this backdrop, talks of the "decisive battle" against ISIS, in Iraq's second largest city, Mosul, are foreboding. While it is undoubtedly a prized catch in Abu Bakr Al-Baghdadi's "caliphate", the impending retreat of ISIS hides the familiar fault-lines that beset the Middle East.

The assorted cobbling of unlikely allies in the form of Kurdish Peshmerga, Iraqi Armed Forces, Shia militias, Turkish soldiers, US "advisers" etc., is militarily, a formidable challenge for the ISIS to withstand. Consequently, the estimated 5000 ISIS fighters, in a city of 1 million, are expected to succumb after milking a bloody price through the indiscriminate use of suicide bombs, and civilian human shields. Arriving at a governance model in Mosul, post the ISIS defeat, will be the ultimate challenge. Deep rooted animosities, and wounds of the recent past, will posit the wary Sunni-majority populace into an uncomfortable huddle by the sectarian adversaries like the Iraqi Armed Forces, and the other Shia militias, or under the "alien" rule of Kurds, Turks, and the Americans. Flashback, to the-then rule of the regressively sectarian and brutal government of Nouri al-Maliki, is inevitable, as comparisons are odious with the new fellow-co-sect government of the current Prime Minister,

Haider al-Abadi. Further, the co-existence of Kurdish militias, and the Turkish Armed Forces in the joint fight against ISIS has an uncomfortable dynamic and augury for these two estranged forces, amongst themselves.

The ISIS is not simply an armed group; it is an ideological force that transcends borders, and attracts adherents from over 80 countries across the world. Militarily, Fallujah, Tikrit, Ramadi, and Baiji have been reclaimed from the ISIS in Iraq--but the general sense of Sunni marginalisation will haunt and fester, and the ongoing Iranian-Saudi proxy wars will create their pressures as well. The old and unresolved tussle for redemption and tribal honour will create violent dissonance. The fact that there is no agreement, or even eye-to-eye discussions amongst the myriad forces, who are simply concentrating on evicting the formal presence of ISIS from Iraq, has a familiar ring to it. The tinderbox of the Middle East is a veritable playground for geopolitical shadowboxing and grandstanding. The Russians have their axe to grind in supporting the West-loathed, Bashar al-Assad in Syria, whereas the Turks are fancying their irredentist claims in the region (the Turks have never fully digested the incorporation of the former Ottoman province of Mosul, to Iraq, in the 1920's). With no concrete alignment, or understanding amongst the key stakeholders in and around Mosul, the post-ISIS picture will severely test the permanency of the "divisive battle". Even though the Gulf monarchies and sheikhdoms are nervous about the ISIS presence in their backyards, the spectre of Shia forces controlling a predominantly Sunni township of Mosul, will not go down well in the cash-rich capitals of Riyadh, Abu Dhabi, or Doha. If the uneasy tentativeness of the "humanitarian truce" in the neighbouring Syria's besieged town of Aleppo is anything to go by, in terms of operational alignment amongst the major partakers of the fight against the ISIS, Mosul could see an unfortunate, familiar, and utterly premature declaration of "mission accomplished", as was signalled by President George Bush in 2003, atop the USS Abraham Lincoln.

U-turn by Philippines

(STATESMAN, 17 Oct 2016)

When Rodrigo Duterte took over as the President of Philippines, on June 30, this year, attention was focused on China's belligerence in the South China Sea, and the ensuing judicial case between Philippines and China before the Permanent Court of Arbitration at The Hague. On 12 July, the court ruled strongly in favour of the Philippines. It observed that China had no historical rights over the disputed Scarborough Shoal. The wary neighbourhood sighed a collective relief at the verdict, calling the Chinese bluff of the brazen "nine-dash-line" approach, which even threatened the sovereignty of other countries like Malaysia, Vietnam, Taiwan, and Indonesia. It seemed the famed Pivot approach--as propounded by Hillary Clinton in the seminal "America's Pacific Century", with undertones of recognizing the emergence of a hegemonic China, and therefore the need to contain the same--was finally playing out and taking shape with the strategic alignments in the region. Except for the fact that Rodrigo Duterte was a maverick, which no one had anticipated.

His background betrays traits of his extreme unpredictability. A self-confessed socialist in a very pious Catholic majority country, he had even cursed Pope Francis during the Pontiff's visit last year. He is a selectively outspoken populist and crass in language. For a country that is statistically the most pro-American country in the world, with 89 per cent having confidence in Barack Obama, in 2014, he has brazenly reneged the special US-Philippines equation, which afforded a political-diplomatic-military shield as the most strategic Non-NATO ally of the US. What is baffling is the preferred trajectory towards the traditional foe, China, in an unexpected drift that threatens to tilt the balance of power in the restive South China Sea.

The unexpected U-turn by the Philippines was crafted by President Rodrigo Duterte immediately after the International court's verdict, when he avoided his trademark triumphalist bluster and offered a conciliatory approach, "War is not an option. So what is the other side?", peaceful talk to calm the angry shock-waves in Beijing. However, this understated sobriety was unusual for a man who had earlier promised to jet-ski in the disputed waters, and plant the Filipino flag on the Spratly Islands.

On the contrary, his bluster was wholeheartedly reserved towards the Western powers. For a man who has claimed to have shot a fellow student in his youth, made despicable comments about a gang-rape victim saying that he should have been the "first to rape", bragged about his licentious and adulterous life, and willy-nilly encouraged vigilante justice in his anti-drug drive--said to have claimed 1400 alleged criminals, drug users, and street children in his recent sobriquets of "The Punisher" by Time magazine, or "Duterte Harry", in an ode to his language--he has made international capitals sit up, and take notice of the latest strongman who is scripting an uncharted course for the Philippines. And it is a course that has strategic import for the rest of the world.

His angst is inexplicably targeted against the US, where he is packaging himself in Cold War theatrics, and positing the accompanying "imperialism" of the US interests, and military forces, along with stakes in his country. From his infamous description of Barack Obama as "a son of a whore" to his cavalier comparison of his anti-drug drive, to likening the same to Hitler, "Hitler massacred three million Jews. Now there are three million drug addicts. I'd be happy to slaughter them".

A shocked world watches the new realities in Manila. Beyond the crassness of his words is the implied strategic drift towards China. In order to please the Chinese before his impending visit to Beijing, he has asked the US to withdraw its troops fighting the Islamist militants in the Philippines, and has also accused the CIA of trying to kill him. He declared that the ongoing US-Philippines military exercises on the Island of Luzon would be the last, and further threatened to withdraw from the United Nations, and instead form an alternative multilateral equivalent with China and its vassal African nations.

Clearly he is playing one international power against the other, and thus far his approach is holding well on the domestic streets, as he is seen as an assertive nationalist who does not shy away from calling a spade a spade. While the international bodies and human right groups are aghast at his anti-drug methods, and the accompanying killings, he remains unmoved, "Do the lives of 10 of these criminals really matter? If I am the one facing all this grief would 100 lives of these idiots mean anything to me?"

Despite the international shockwaves, his domestic popularity chart remains robust as ever. With the open pandering to the sub-conscious and latent "anti-imperialist" sentiments, the strongman bravado and tactics resonates with the populace. Even his shift from the Western group to the Chinese fold is attributed to practical pragmatism. The contours of his new-fangled "independent foreign policy", envisage an active reach-out to both China and Russia. As Washington refused to sell arms to Manila, he is supposed to have reacted furiously and said, "Instead of helping us, the first to hit was the State Department. So you can go to hell, Mr. Obama, you can go to hell".

The Chinese are gleefully lapping up the providential turn of the tide, and a red carpet awaits President Duterte, in Beijing. An unprecedented *quid pro quo* is said to be in the offing. The Philippines will play down the territorial claims on the disputed waters, in exchange for mega-bucks from the Chinese, for the decrepit and desperate Filipino infrastructure, soft-term loans, and military aid, as well as assistance for his anti-drug drive. The traditional suspicion between the Chinese and the Filipinos is giving way to a new realm, which threatens the traditional equation between the US and the Philippines.

Clearly it is a U-turn, and a gamble of unprecedented international ramifications, with the Philippines falling for China's "cheque-book" diplomacy. Earlier, Maldives had gone the same way. Further, the reassuring and gratifying silence of the Chinese towards the strong-arm tactics on domestic issues such as human rights, endears Duterte towards China. However, the military in the Philippines has historical and strong ties with the US, in terms of training equipment and outlook. Therefore, a sudden political U-turn, with the enemies of yesterday suddenly becoming best of friends today, will not go down very smoothly. The cultural integration of the US-Filipino connect, and the accompanying sovereign-compromise *vis-à-vis* the Chinese, will put on test the gamble of President Duterte. For now, the strategic balance in the South China Sea and the Asian waters at large will be monitored very carefully, and the process of re-calibration is guaranteed as the situation unfolds.

Enter the Dragon

(DECCAN HERALD, 13 Aug 2016)

CHINA IN AFGHANISTAN: Along with Pakistan, China continuously seeks to limit the ever-increasing Indian stakes in Kabul by keeping it out of Afghanistan.There are two contradictory strains that tug at the Sino-Afghan dynamics. The first is the need to control, and avoid the spill-over of radical Islamic groups into the restive Chinese province of Xinjiang (which has the Chinese Uighur Muslim population). The second is to counterbalance the growing geostrategic imbalance, of China's "all weather" friendship with Pakistan. Islamabad is seen as the principal supporter of the Afghan Taliban.

However, staying out of the Afghan theatre is not an option for the Chinese, given the solidification of the alternative Western-Indian-Iranian axis, interest within the Afghan government in Kabul, and the ultra-radicalisation of militancy in Afghanistan, which includes the China-centric East Turkestan Islamic Movement (ETIM). The ETIM has been designated as a terror organisation by the United States and the United Nations.

The 76-km Sino-Afghan border harbours the famous "Wakhan Corridor", which was a creation of the "Great Game" in the 19th century, between the imperial powers in Russia, Britain, and Afghanistan. Earlier requests by the Afghan authorities to the Chinese to open the corridor, and facilitate an alternative supply route for the Afghan-NATO forces expectedly fell on deaf ears, given the Chinese animosity to Western interests, and concerns about its own sovereignty.

A violent flare-up, in the near proximity of the China Pakistan Economic Corridor (CPEC) on the Pakistan-Afghan border, is reflective of the Chinese concern to safeguard the multidimensional Corridor, with stable relationships in the region. This, given the backdrop of the mammoth Chinese investments in the $49 billion CPEC initiative. The CPEC dangerously skirts the Afghan territories.

As it is, Pakistan is seen as an unnecessarily meddling, and irascible neighbour that cannot be trusted in Kabul. Hence, the urgency for the Chinese, to cool tempers, and arrest the geostrategic and geopolitical slide against the Pakistanis, and by its strategic default extension, against Chinese irrelevance, too. The recent signing of the tripartite agreement between Tehran, New Delhi, and Kabul on using the Chabahar port in Iran as a transit hub is seen as a strategic counter to the Sino-Pakistani interests in the Gwadar port, which links the CPEC up to the Chinese hinterland.

Last year, Chinese Foreign Minister Wang Yi, US Secretary of State John Kerry, and CEO of Afghanistan Abdullah Abdullah met on the side-lines of the United Nations General Assembly. This paved the way for the quadrilateral format, and talks on the Afghan Peace Plans, with Pakistan in tow. However, Pakistan's subsequent inability, or deliberate undoing of not getting the Afghan Taliban to the negotiation table upset the Chinese applecart, leaving Beijing to undo the damage done by the Pakistani intransigence, and the effects of its perennial hostility towards the government in Kabul.

In parallel, China, too, had been courting the Taliban covertly, by hosting their representatives for many years. Even last month, the Chinese were supposed to have met Abbas Stanakzai, head of Taliban's Qatar-based office, who discussed their "occupation", by the US-backed Afghan government forces. This is to enable them to maintain a toehold of Chinese influence, relevance, and equation within the Afghan Taliban, and to have a say in the regional confabulations.

Duplicity of action

The Chinese have been understandably discreet about their parleys with the Taliban, while in parallel suggesting to the Afghan government, its willingness to "deepen counter-terrorism intelligence, joint drills, personnel training and other areas of practical cooperation." This was in tandem with its famed "cheque-book" diplomacy in the region, where the Chinese offered substantial commercial investments to aid the rebuilding of Afghanistan.

The duplicity of the Chinese action is typical realpolitik, where the need to assert Chinese relevance in the region drives it to engage, and entertain the Taliban. This is to the consternation of the government in Kabul, while simultaneously offering the economic-military carrots to a cash-strapped Afghan government.

This is in return for strategic influence and understanding, to protect its own infrastructural investments and interests, like the CPEC, and to ensure the reigning-in of the ETIM elements within Afghan soil itself. Domestic issues like containing the Uighur militancy posits its own actions against itself, while pandering to the Afghan Taliban simultaneously.

Along with Pakistan, China continuously seeks to limit the ever-increasing Indian interests and stakes in Kabul, by successfully keeping India out of the Afghan discussions, whenever it can, like it did during the quadrilateral talks. Now, given the recent flare up and military muscle-flexing in the South China Sea, and with the unfavourable decision by the International Court of Arbitration against Chinese interests, the criticality of an alternative trade, commerce, and energy corridor for the Chinese survival, becomes even more so. The stakes for CPEC rise significantly, and will draw in the Chinese even more prominently into the Afghan theatre.

Recently, the Chinese Defence Minister Chang Wanquan met the head of the Afghan Army, Chief Qadam Shah Shaheem, and alluded to the delicate duality of the Chinese concerns, by acknowledging the Afghan government's "valuable support in combating the East Turkestan Islamic Movement terrorist forces, on issues related to China's core interests."

He then expanded the scope to encompass a more holistic security dimension by stating, "I hope the two militaries can continually enrich the shape and content of cooperation, and make greater contributions to safeguarding both countries' security, and creating a favourable environment for joint development."

The Chinese are past masters in strategic realpolitik, and balancing their hegemonic instincts and aspirations, which necessitates their willy-nilly entry into the Afghan scene, to protect their own interests and ambitions. In doing so, their moves would typically run inimical to the Indian interests, as the ground situation is playing out currently. The Chinese are aware of the vulnerabilities, sensitivities, limitations, and the new strategic equations in the region; therefore, the Chinese footprint and interests will surely see an escalation in the days to come.

Fault-Lines in Pakistan and Turkey are different

(THE PIONEER, 7 Aug 2016)

Similarities between Pakistan and Turkey are eerie--both were borne of Islamic lands that portended an aspired identity of modernism and secularism, afforded genealogically by Muhammad Ali Jinnah in Pakistan, and Mustafa Kemal Atatürk in Turkey. Both nations have seen the sparring oscillation of rule between the Armed Forces, and civilian leadership. Both are continuously trying to rationalise, and nuance their inherent religious tendencies, along with the post-modern necessities of integrating in the global order. Both have had bloody histories of managing the minorities, one with the Kurds; and the other with its myriad sectarian trysts.

They are the only two Islamic countries with nuclear weapons on their soil (Pakistan has its own arsenal, while the Incirlik airbase in South-East Turkey is the North Atlantic Treaty Organisation's largest nuclear weapons storage facility). One has a "Bangladesh" to its behavioural infamy, and the other, an "Armenia" to its blotted history. Between themselves, they are undoubtedly the two most powerful militaries in the Islamic world, with standing Armed Forces that are professional, and revered in popular perception and culture.

The commonality of the multiple strains, instincts, institutions, and compulsions have afforded them a unique relationship and partnership between themselves, which has held its own, in the most trying times--for instance, the India-Pakistan war of 1971, which saw rare and active Turkish support for Pakistan that was both diplomatic and military.

It was not just the Pakistani *Quaid-e-Azam* Jinnah, who looked up to the Turkish revolutionary Atatürk as a role model. It is said, Gen. Pervez Musharraf, who spent close to 10 years of his childhood in Turkey, and speaks fluent Turkish, modelled himself to be the modern *avatar* of Kemal-ism. Fittingly, in 2009, the Turkish President Recep Tayyip Erdogan, was honoured with the highest civilian award in Pakistan, in recognition of "the highest degree of service to the country and nation of Pakistan", the *Nishan-e-Pakistan.*

On the face of it, Pakistan is like Turkey. Even today, although civilian rule is in place, the brooding shadow of the Generals, looms in the background; an uneasy truce, and unsaid looking over the *epaulettes* on the shoulders, continues. However, the recent failed attempt of the Turkish *coup d'état* attempt, has thrown some stark questions about popular perceptions of the Turkish Armed Forces.

While it is true that the military putsch was not a unified attempt, and it lacked uniformed fraternity. Yet, unprecedented scenes of civilians hauling out uniformed soldiers from their armoured vehicles, and publically flogging them on the streets was an unimaginable spectre for a country that is known to cherish, revere, and hero-worship their soldiers.

Adding to the insult was the veritable joining-of-hands by people of all political affiliations--from Erdogan's Justice and Development Party (AKP), to the Opposition Republican People's Party (CHP), and the Nationalist Action Party (MHP). Irrespective of the bitter politics, and bad blood amongst the various political entities, the combined angst and disgust at the prospect of a military take-over, was overwhelming.

Clearly, the popular democratic impulses, and frameworks that have been nurtured assiduously by President Erdogan's efforts since 2003, have taken deep root. Simultaneously, the neutering and defanging of the military top brass, with the gradual chipping away of powers, and purging the barracks of the "non-compliant" cadres, has literally saved the long night for Erdogan, and participative democracy in Turkey.

The current landscape in Pakistan is markedly different, as the ruling politicos are losing the reigns of state control, and popular perceptions *vis-à-vis* the Pakistani Army. The dominant role in Pakistan has shifted from the National Assembly in Islamabad, to the General Head Quarters (GHQ), in Rawalpindi. It is General Raheel Sharif, and not his less imposing namesake, Prime Minister Nawaz Sharif, who is perceived as the saviour, given the prospects of self-implosion--not just from military threats or the security imperatives, but also from sure-shot economic degradation.

In the ongoing turf-war for control of the "game-changing" hype-infrastructure project of the China-Pakistan Economic Corridor, or managing international affairs and diplomacy, the "Army house" has emerged as the must-stop-port-of-call for any foreign dignitary, and the frequent dashes of the Army Chief to discuss strategic affairs in Riyadh, Kabul, or Washington, D.C., is reflective of the real boss in Pakistan, ensconced in the GHQ Rawalpindi.

The chairman of Pakistan Tehreek-e-Insaf, Imran Khan, stirred the hornet's nest by stating that, "People will celebrate a military takeover in Pakistan. The democracy here is threatened by Nawaz Sharif's monarchy, not military". He went on to say that the Pakistanis would, "celebrate and distribute sweets!"Undoubtedly, General Raheel Sharif is the alpha-male in Pakistan, and in a foreboding move, an obscure political party called "Move on Pakistan" put up posters on the main streets of the big cities, with a commanding photo of General Raheel Sharif, and a singular message, "For God's sake, take over".

The popular perceptions of the Army as the only institution that is selfless, patriotic, and can get things done, is at an all-time high. Aiding the image is the visible "fight-back" by the Pakistani Army, in the form of Operation *Zarb-e-Azb* in North-West Pakistan, operations in Baluchistan, and even on the trigger-happy streets of Karachi. Even from the perspective of a sub-continental proclivity towards sentiments of "anti-incumbency", the timing augurs well for the military (the last military government was of General Musharraf's in 2008).

Like in Turkey, all political parties slammed the Turkish coup attempt, in Pakistan. Understandably, the nervous Prime Minister, Nawaz Sharif, demonstrated his finest democratic beliefs with, "We deeply admire the resolve of the brave and resilient Turkish people, who stood up against the forces of darkness and anarchy to express their support and commitment to democracy".

Further, the Pakistan People's Party (PPP) chief, Bilawal Bhutto Zardari, added for good measure, "The people of Turkey deserve to be complimented for coming out into the streets and face military tanks and artillery with bare hands to force the coup makers run". The truth is, even with the combined numbers of all the political party members in unison, the average Pakistani's perception about a potential takeover by the military, cannot be safely imagined or likened to the ground reality in Turkey.

The fundamental difference is that while the popular disillusionment in Turkey is with one party's ideological mooring (and agenda), versus the alternative's, the popular disenchantment in Pakistan is with the composite perceptions of ineptitude, corruption, and inabilities of the political classes, versus the solidity and decisiveness, of the soldiering fraternity. Pakistan is not Turkey, and all eyes are on General Raheel Sharif, with his supposed retirement in September.

Awkward Truths of the Middle Eastern Crisis

(THE CITIZEN, 22 Jul 2016)

From Walter Benjamin, Napoleon Bonaparte, Winston Churchill, to Dan Brown, all have alluded to the "victor", defining the essential and definitive narrative, and perceptions, surrounding an event or history--except, in the burning cauldron of the Middle East, there are no "victors", only "victims" who have to suffer the partial-truths, convenient versions, and the ultimate ignominy of the established narrative, written by the "mightier".

Ignorance of history, context, and oversimplification has been the bane of the "truth-crusade" in the Middle East, which belies various facts that have led to the current inferno. Pronto, the popular narrative established in the Western capitals becomes deliciously appealing, and palatable, to the uninitiated, restless and impatient masses, who seek a "quick-end" to the Middle Eastern crisis (read, military solution only).

The part-declassification of the remaining "28 pages", of the official US Congressional Report, in the lead-up to the September 11, 2001, terrorist attacks, and on the alleged ties of the US "ally", the Saudi Arabian establishment with the perpetrators of the terror act, along with the parallel tabling of the "Iraq enquiry", or the "Chilcot Inquiry" (the timing is coincidental), across the Atlantic in the UK, paints a very dim view of the West's track record leading up to the horrors of 9/11, and the subsequent actions in the Middle East, which germinated the foundation for regressive strains like the ISIL etc.

Expectedly, the embarrassment of the formalised facts, as established by the Western experts themselves, will be played down and contained--in his last days as the Prime Minister of Britain, David Cameron, refused to accept a "mistake" on part of the Conservative Government, and observed conveniently that he did not see "a huge amount of point" in "replaying all the arguments of the day", and added rather sagely that the focus should instead be on learning, "the lessons of what happened, and what needs to be put in place to make sure that mistakes cannot be made in future".

The West's historic tolerance and support for the various Sheikhdoms, and dictators, as long as they abided by Western interests is well documented. The sudden waving of human rights manuals, literature on democracy, and civic freedoms gets flashed only on the selective non-compliance of the energy and geopolitical agreements of the said Middle Eastern establishment, and the West (Saddam Hussein was the preferred business partner in the Iran-Iraq wars, irrespective of his known indulgences of chemical weaponry).

The toxicity and malignancy of the Western disinterest, in the reckless excesses and largesse of the Sheikhdoms, who fuelled the *madrassa* inspired angst, ignorance, and anger as far as the Indian-sub continent, and the Sub-Saharan deserts, was ignored and *pooh-poohed* with a "look away", as then the shores of the US, and continental Europe, were still thought to be very far away from any danger; something that haunts the doorsteps of Paris, Nice, Brussels, New York and London, today. These deliberate oversights are indefensible and unforgivable, pointing to the complicity domain, well beyond the commonly known contours of the currently apportioned, "blame-framework".

For 13 years, these 28 pages of the US Congressional report were kept away from public gaze, fuelling rightful suspicions on the content, intent and implication of the same. Even now, certain sections and portions containing specific details have been "blacked-out", or withheld. The official spin put on the declassification of the "28 pages" is that it actually exonerates the Saudi's, although the 9/11 report did mention Saudi support to certain "charities", which ultimately bankrolled the likes of Al Qaida, earlier. Clearly, even now, the strategic compulsions are still getting the better of the entire truth, related to the conception of the events, leading up to the 9/11 act.

Institutional complicity is getting differentiated from direct individual complicity, hence, offering a dangerously convenient and perilous escape route--raw truth without any qualifications, is still the casualty.

On the other hand, the "Chilcot Inquiry", which was led by Sir John Chilcot, a career diplomat, along with other committee members--including a military historian, a former ambassador to the UN, a civil historian, and the chairwoman of the Judicial Appointments Commission has formally inked the worst kept secrets of Britain's war in Iraq. The Guardian described it a "crushing verdict", while the BBC described it as "damning".

At a fundamental level, it found the very case for going to war in Iraq as insufficient, with an inadequate legal base, tantamount to "undermining the Security Council's authority", given that it had proceeded without a Security Council resolution. Further, the report alluded to the limited say Britain had on the war in Iraq, vis-à-vis the US, and the planning for the war as, "wholly inadequate". To compound matters, it clearly stated that the military objectives were not met, and the situation on ground had deteriorated after the invasion.

The well-known bogey of Iraqi WMD's was supposedly made on the basis of flawed intelligence, and worse, while it should have been challenged, it never was. Now, prickly questions of "lying", or the extent of "lying", or even just plain mistakes by the British leadership are getting debated--though there is, like in the US, a brave front put up to mitigate the implications.

The West's instinct to protect their own track record, intelligence sources, and strategic relationships (e.g., avoid upsetting Saudi Arabia) is realpolitik. It is also very powerful in defining the construct of the "story" of Middle East, which is both damaging in the long run, immoral, and counter-productive.

Unless, the whole truth prevails in its entirety, and not in selective leaks and releases, the understanding of the context and the application of the remedial steps required, will always haunt the region, as indeed the entire world. Europe and the US are no longer unreachable from the elements of the regressive forces that they have willy-nilly created, and about whose origins they choose to still remain naïve.

That the emergence of the Taliban has something to do with leaving the Afghan turf in a lurch, in the supposedly safe hands of another reliable "ally", Pakistan, or that the progenitor of the phenomenon of ISIL are the disgraced remnants of the erstwhile Baathists, left to fend for themselves by the US forces, is something that needs to be discussed, addressed, and internalised in the mainstream, a lot more; this truth, and reconciliation, is the only way to mend the increasing polarisation with the masses, and the ultimate isolation of the fundamentalists.

However, historical facts about the Middle East, and the games played within, is a can of worms that the West prefers to avoid opening, or accepting.

Rough Waters Ahead

(*INDIAN EXRESS, 21 Jul 2016*)

The verdict of the international tribunal over the South China Sea dispute has collaterally vindicated the maritime concerns of Japan, Taiwan, Malaysia, Vietnam, Brunei and obviously, the principal litigant Philippines. Enforcement of the verdict aside, the legitimacy of China as a responsible power is formally tainted--a dangerous import for China's strategic aspirations. Incompatibility and belligerence with prevailing international laws, and verdicts, can impact crucial transactions in a globally aligned world, especially for China, which is the world's largest export economy.

While the verdict nailed the Chinese falsity of historic claims on the rocky outcrops at sea, sovereign rights, construction of artificial islands, commercial aspects like fishing and petroleum exploration etc., it did not mention the overarching sweep of geo-strategic intent that subsumes the intentions and actions of the Chinese behaviour.

China's bizarre claims to 90 per cent (using the "nine-dash line" methodology) of the South China Sea, owe its brazenness to insecurities of ensuring control on the $5 trillion seaways. In 2015, Chinese exports and imports were $2.2 trillion, and $1.6 trillion respectively, leaving a very positive balance of payment status. This bankrolling hinges on the uninterrupted free flow of goods out of, and into, the Chinese mainland. The oft quoted "overheated" economic infrastructure, and model, is essentially energy-guzzling and vulnerably thirsty. This economic susceptibility, coupled with historic disputes with wary neighbours, and the US, posits the real issue of regime survival and the seaway to a bi-polar world, with China fancying itself as the fundamental "other". Pursuant of this hegemonic dream are tectonic initiatives like the "One Belt, One Road", which connects the energy-flush Central Asian nations, and Europe, with China's hinterland, and the China-Pakistan Economic Corridor. However, the more immediate and semi-working geopolitical approach of safeguarding and promoting the

Chinese interests and assets is the fabled "String-of-Pearls". This envisages a dual, commercial-military Chinese footprint along the Sea Lines of Communication (SLOC's) dotted with both natural and artificial ports (like the recently contested Spratly archipelago, which saw over 3,400 acres of land reclamation) in the contentious South China Sea, right up to the ports along the African coastline. Besides, the South China Sea based "Pearl Ports", the foreign ports envisaged to be stringed are: Sittwe and Coco Islands (Myanmar), Chittagong (Bangladesh), Hambantota (Sri Lanka), Marao Atoll (Maldives), Gwadar (Pakistan), Port Sudan (Sudan) etc. These "Pearl Ports" conceptually ensure clear passage for Chinese traffic, and especially protect and dominate veritable choke points like the Strait of Mandeb, Lombok Strait, and Strait of Hormuz. However, the proverbial "Chicken's Neck", and the uber-vulnerable passage, is the narrow and unavoidable, Straits of Malacca, in the dangerous proximity of the Andaman and Nicobar Islands.

Given that 80 per cent of Chinese fuel passes through this narrow strait (only 1.5 nautical miles wide at the Philips Chanel), connecting the Indian Ocean and the Pacific Ocean, coupled with the reality of two to three weeks of known strategic fuel reserves available on the Chinese mainland, the nightmare of even a temporary blockage would be debilitating; and irreversibly damaging to the Chinese juggernaut. It is unarguably the world's worst maritime choke point, with over 1,00,000 vessels crossing annually, and accounting for a fourth of the world's trade. Choking herein, is the ultimate (and the most plausible) doomsday situation for China, from a traffic perspective. Militarily and legitimately, only India has the real estate to dominate the mouth or the entry of the narrow passage, given the providential geography, and the clean status of the property papers (unlike the ports involved in recent *fracas* of the South China Sea, the Andaman and Nicobar is a shining outpost, and indisputably Indian from a "claim" perspective). India, like China, is a signatory to the UNCLOS (United Nations Convention on the Law of the Seas) that mandates a certain maritime behaviour, and norms. In 2014, India had accepted an unfavourable ruling versus Bangladesh, in the Permanent Court of Arbitration. For now, the International Court of Arbitration's verdict is restricted to the China-Philippines context. However, the narrative, template, and ground rules for future engagement with China, and any of the other sparring countries, has been irrevocably altered. India is not a direct party to the issue, but given that the China-Philippines *impasse* is a sub-component of a wider ecosystem, the national capitals along the South China Sea, Bay of Bengal, and the Indian Ocean will be keeping a close watch on the developments as they evolve.

For now, the International Court of Arbitration's verdict is restricted to the China-Philippines context.

Turkish Army Losses Sheen

(TRIBUNE, 20 Jul 2016)

Turkey's long night of the failed *coup d'état* owes its genesis to the simmering political turmoil, and President Erdogan's authoritarian counter-instincts. The disunited and restricted participation of the Turkish Armed Forces ensured adequate providence and timing to the masses, to pour onto the streets and upstage the lightening putsch. Images of civilian protestors shouting down soldiers in armoured vehicles and tanks, in defiance of the armed personnel, and with the subsequent arrest of over 3,000 military personnel, and the supposed killing of over 100 "coup plotters" (read, soldiers)--the scenes were an unprecedented comedown for an institution that is the second largest standing military force in NATO (after the US).

Completing the humiliation of the military coup plotters was the defiant language of President Erdogan who stated that the coup supporters, "will pay a heavy price for their treason to Turkey", with Prime Minister Binali Yildirim suggesting that the Constitution Council could even consider the reintroduction of the death penalty, after the coup din settles down. The immediate "mop-up" action included the dismissal and arrest of five generals, and 29 colonels. Many more senior officers were taken to "unknown locations". While the status of who exactly was controlling Turkey during the dark night kept yo-yoing by the minute, with multiple and contradictory claims, It finally culminated in the rare sight of the coup-plotting TAF component (Turkish Armed Forces) abandoning their tanks and vehicles on the streets, and surrendering *en masse* to their own comrades and countrymen, as they were marched with "hands-up", into custody by the pro-government forces.

The Turks have a glorious martial history, with official records tracing the lineage of the Turkish Armed Forces to 209 BC, as the foundational year of the first Turkic Army. The later-day legacy of the Ottoman conquests, and the more recent beneficence of the legendary soldier, and first President, Mustafa Kemal (later the exclusive honorific "Atatürk", The Father of Turks, was added), is the continuing linkages of the Turkish Armed Forces on the national psyche. The very early moves of abolishing the Caliphate, promoting secularism, insisting on education and modernisation, committed Mustafa Kemal "Atatürk" (and by that extension, the Turkish Armed Forces) to a certain legacy, role, and position that often posits them against the more avowedly civilian, political, and religious elements of the Turkish society.

Recep Tayyip Erdogan, the twelfth President of Turkey, personifies the exact combination that is anathema to the principles of Kemalism and therefore, the Armed Forces--he is civilian, decidedly political, and the most religious man to adorn the position of leadership in Turkey, since Mustafa Kemal Atatürk. The recent political undercurrents had more to do with Erdogan's party of "conservative democracy", or the Justice and Development Party (AKP), versus, the principal opposition Republican People's Party (CHP) which is based on the principles of "social democracy", and Kemalism. The fact that all opposition parties, and the bulk of the Armed Forces, came out in support of the democratically elected government alludes to a less politically conspiratorial rationale, and to a more unbearable angst amongst a certain section of the Turkish Armed Forces.

This didn't stop President Erdogan from prematurely pointing fingers at his earlier ally, and now political rival, the US-based cleric Fethullah Gulen. The increasing presence of Gulenists in the judiciary, police, and the Armed Forces had earlier prompted President Erdogan to go in for a very public and massive purge of these government institutions. However, Fethullah Gulen's Hizmet movement was quick to disassociate itself from any support to the disgruntled elements in the Armed Forces by stating, "We have consistently denounced military interventions in domestic politics. These are core values of Hizmet participants. We condemn any military intervention in domestic politics of Turkey", reiterating the probability of an exclusive military-led coup composed of minority elements, within. Even the ostensible logic proffered by the coup leaders in their brief *communiqué* during the long night was a nebulous and apolitical statement stating that they had taken control, "to reinstall the constitutional order, democracy, human rights and freedoms, to ensure that the rule of law once again reigns in the country."

Whatever the trigger for the coup plotters--the Turkish Armed Forces have had an uncomfortable history with Erdogan's politics, and have been subjected to various "clean-up" drives to neuter their political efficacy and role. They have always fancied themselves as the flag-bearers of Mustafa Kemal Atatürk's legacy of mandated secularism, and nationalism; leading to formal interventions in 1960, 1971, 1980, 1993, and 1997. So much so, that in 1998, Erdogan was sentenced to 10 months in prison for inciting religious intolerance--an unforgettable hurt and forbearance, of latter day run-ins, which would see Erdogan clipping the wings of the Army leadership with brazen changes and legal actions. Aiding Erdogan's belligerence in the last 15 years is the growing wave of Pan-Islamism in the region that has seen a resurgence and celebration of the Islamist instincts, which Mustafa Kemal and the Turkish Armed Forces had managed to suppress. While the last shot has not been fired as yet, Erdogan would have a dual and contradictory task of demonstrating public control by further emasculation of certain elements of the Turkish Armed Forces.

Beyond a point, pushing the Turkish Armed Forces to the brim will be counter-productive. With a known nuclear defence system in place, NATO military bases, multiple operational commitments against Kurds, Syria's Assad, and the ISIS in the Middle East, as also in the forefront of an angry relationship with Russia--the Turkish Armed Forces cannot allow themselves to be run over. For a professional and nationalistic army, aspersions of "treason" are unmanageable. The Bosporus sails silently in the aftermath of the failed coup--the progeny of the legendary military commanders like Fevzi Cakmak (who commanded the "Great Offensive" in 1922), General Kazim Karabekir, and Cavalry General Fahrettin Altay, this coup attempt and the accompanying taint slapped on the uniformed elements of the Turkish Armed Forces, is a nightmare that will haunt the Turkish soldiers for long.

China sitting on a Tinderbox in Xinjiang

(TRIBUNE, 22 April 2016

China has been a cradle of religio-cultural diversities, which were historically tolerated by the various ruling dynasties. These dynasties claimed the "mandate of heavens" to shape overarching traditions, philosophies and cultures, as opposed to the rigidity of a formal and definitive religion. However, since the Communist Party of China's reign in 1949, Mao Zedong initially suppressed all expressions of societal religiosity, only to see a certain liberal acceptance of religious autonomy in recent times, as long as it didn't conflict with regime survival.

Amidst a total population base of 1.4 billion, an estimated 1.7 to 2 per cent are of the Islamic faith (approximately 25 million). In addition to the majority Han population (91.6%), the Chinese government officially recognises 55 ethnic minorities (8.4% of population), of whom 10 are predominantly Sunni Muslims. Old manuscripts claim the advent of Islam in the seventh century (about 620 AD), when Sa'd ibn Abi Waqqas, an uncle of the Islamic Prophet, supposedly came to China on a mission, and established the Huaisheng Mosque, over 1,300 year ago.

Broadly speaking, there are two distinct groups of Islamic adherents in China--the majority Hui people (who are similar to the majority Han Chinese in terms of ethno-lingual profiles, spread across China), and the more restive Turkic ethnicity based Uyghurs, who are concentrated around the Xinjiang Autonomous Region.

Interestingly, official Chinese cartography encompasses the Indian territory of *Aksai Chin*, within the Xinjiang Autonomous region, affording it borders with India, Pakistan, Afghanistan, Kazakhstan, Kyrgyzstan, Tajikistan, Mongolia, and Russia. Within the cauldron of Xinjiang, the majority Uyghurs (46.4% of population) aggressively jostle with the Han (39% of population) to practise, preserve, and perpetuate the Uyghur identity, and relevance.

It is the forbidden lands of Xinjiang that test the Chinese regime's stranglehold, over the global Pan-Islamic wave of puritanical militancy and secessionist tendencies--often, resulting in violence, popular unrests, and hidden fissures that are kept away from the glares of the world. Chinese absolutism is practised to ensure the lid is kept on the region's simmering dissent by the Uyghurs. However, the Chinese government's Uyghur-specific discrimination has resulted in further alienation, and hardening of the Uyghur Muslim identity, and their causes for separatism.

The famed Chinese "strike hard" approach against the "three evils of separatism, extremism, and terrorism", has clearly divided the Islamic adherents into two groups: one, of the "patriotic Chinese Muslims", that is, the Hui people (they have no secessionist groups or tendencies), who are allowed to practise their faith and beliefs, and the other of the discriminated Uyghur, who pray in different mosques from the Hui, and who formed the East Turkestan Islamic Movement (ETIM) as the main secessionist group, to form an independent "East Turkestan".

The divide-and-rule of the Chinese government is clinically effective with the Hui Muslims, who have been seamlessly integrated into the Chinese mainstream. The taint of Islamic terror and fundamentalism is restricted to the Uyghurs. The usual tactics of repressive security cover to blank out news, and demographic resettlements of Hans, have been employed. Economic discriminations have increasingly marginalised the Uyghurs, and turned Xinjiang into a veritable tinderbox.

The footprint of the ETIM is visible from the cadres operating in Afghanistan (where they were trained by Al Qaida, with 22 of them arrested, and detained in Guantanamo Bay), Pakistan (where they attacked Chinese engineers in the port city of Gwadar), and even in the ongoing conflict in Syria-Iraq, where the Uyghur cadres are seen fighting along the Al-Qaida affiliate, Nusra Front.

However, the ETIM (or Turkistan Islamic Party, as they call themselves) have been designated as a terrorist group by the US, under Executive Order 13224 (blocking financial transactions), and the US Terrorist Exclusion List (which debars members from entering US). This terror designation is further confirmed by the

UN, UAE, Afghanistan, Pakistan, Russia, Kazakhstan, Kyrgyzstan, and obviously China, thereby squeezing and limiting international support, and funding. However, they have competing baiters amongst the ISIS, Al-Qaida, and even the Taliban, who empathise with the Uyghur cause, and recruit their foot soldiers, arming and training the frustrated Uyghurs to the ultimate consternation of the Chinese.

Strategically for China, the import of Xinjiang unrest goes beyond the fears of Uyghur Islamic fundamentalism and militancy. It also tests the Chinese ability to cover its intrinsic fault-lines in Tibet, Inner Mongolia, and Taiwan, each of which has its own secessionist rationales against the mainland-Han Chinese rule. It forces doubts in the minds of the Chinese strategists and policy planners to invest in a restive area, which is the principal highway of the strategic China-Pakistan Economic Corridor (CPEC), as indeed the gateway to the energy-flush Central Asian Republics, which are key to keep the Chinese engines of economic growth running.

So far, heavy boots on ground and providential international environment of most countries clamping down on terror groups, has spared Xinjiang from going completely out of control, though over 200 terrorist strikes have been attributed to the ETIM. There is no visible or credible Chinese governmental effort to economically, or socially, try and integrate the restive Uyghurs. On the contrary, it is the sole "strike hard" approach, bereft of any inclusive imperatives, which is getting deployed, and the same has diminishing returns in the modern era, especially for a religious movement and insurrection that knows no official border or emotional appeal amongst its adherents across the globe. Its appeal is theoretically more readily available than say for a Tibet or Taiwan that is restricted to its constituents, beyond a point.

Xinjiang is the underbelly of a glaring Chinese reality that potentially posits the duplicitous Chinese stand of vetoing against India, in the UN forum, towards Indian efforts to designate Maulana Masood Azhar as a terrorist, as the Chinese still feel comfortable to egg on the Indo-Pak game of cloak and dagger, as a willing accomplice of Pakistan. Although, much like Pakistan, which self-admittedly is atoning the sins of supporting fundamentalism, this is Chinese augury for chickens to come home to roost in Xinjiang. The dynamics and intrigues of international diplomacy may force the wary Western powers, and the other stakeholders, to recognise the tactical utility of the Xinjiang unrest as a counter-check to Sino aggression, duplicity, and hegemony in the region.

Venezuela in Crisis

(STATESMAN, 11 Jul 2016)

The year, 1989, witnessed Caracazo (or Los Saqueos) mass lootings and riots in Venezuela, against the IMF-prescribed austerity measures. The security clampdown led to the death of hundreds of protestors. Unlike, in 1989, when the government in Caracas was apparently caught unawares, the current situation is escalating towards absolute mayhem. There have been food riots with mobs raiding supermarkets and vehicles, protests and road blockades; uncontrollable chaos on the streets. Starvation, violence, and desperation is driving the country-- once hailed as "Venezuela Saudita" (Saudi Venezuela) because of its oil-driven boom--into a catastrophic economic and social freefall. A 700 per cent-plus inflation is still steadily heading south (estimated to go to 1600 per cent by 2017), symbolizing the proverbial riches to rags story of modern times.

The reality in Venezuela belies the fact that it is still home to the world's largest oil reserves. However, global oil prices and extreme mismanagement of both the overall national economics, and specifically the oil infrastructure and industry, has brought the nation to its knees; almost a failed nation. Oil constitutes 95 per cent of its export revenues, this "liquid gold" had been financing populist subsidies, specifically schemes such as free housing, and other unrealistic and unsustainable ultra-leftist utopias. This "Chavist Shangri-La" came to a grinding halt as oil revenue plummeted from $ 80 billion in 2013, to just about $20 billion in 2016 (with foreign debt standing at a crippling $130 billion). The economy is actually contracting.

The Venezuelan economic model of "Socialism of the 20th Century", was developed by the maverick Hugo Chavez (2002-2013, in office as the President). Aided by the record-high global oil prices, he fuelled the popular imagination with electorally populist doles, which made him invincible at home, and strident against the Western world.

He expropriated industries, discouraged private enterprise, filled the state oil company, PDVSA, with his own loyalists instead of professionals, and milked the oil inflows for unsustainable welfare benefits. His untimely death due to a prolonged fight against cancer, saw his deputy Vice-President Nicolas Maduro assume the mantle, but Maduro also inherited a stuttering economy, and a very unfavourable global oil scenario followed. In two years (2014 to 2016), the Venezuelan Bolivar has collapsed from 64 to a US dollar, to nearly 1000 per dollar! Clearly, unfettered spending, domestic price controls, and printing more currency arbitrarily made for very bad economics.

Today, defaulting on debt is not an option as that would completely cripple the only inflow-trickle that comes through the state-owned oil company, PDVSA. Most imports are curbed, a 60-day state of emergency has been declared, and everything is rationed; from food and water, to electricity. However, the politics is still getting the better of economics, and President Maduro is playing the age-old card of Latin machismo in waving off humanitarian aid as, "a guise for foreign intervention". However, this is no longer cutting ice, either with the desperate Venezuelans or other Latin American countries who are watching the empty bravado with horror, as Venezuela slides into inexplicable regress and contraction--even though it is blessed with gargantuan levels of oil resources. The head of the Organization of American States, Luis Almagro noted, "These challenges cannot be blamed on external forces. The situation facing Venezuela today is the direct result of the actions of those currently in power. Venezuela should be one of the most prosperous and influential countries in the region. Instead, it is a state mired in corruption, poverty and violence".

Almost daily, either a particular food staple, medicine, or industrial part goes missing. The public queues are becoming longer and longer, and it can take several hours to get the subsistence stocks. Frustration and tempers are rising beyond control, and the policing apparatus is jittery, and crumbling in the face of public fury. Amidst all this, the parallel economy of the black market, and crime, has received a virulent fillip. This has made the society still more restive. In such times, unnecessary intransigence, and hope, make for a very feeble reconstruction. Waiting for the oil prices to go up, waiting for rainfall to kick-start the hydroelectric plants, waiting for bailout loans or extended credit terms, and cutting the working week of state employees from five days to two in order to soothe the nerves, is like hoping against hope. No sane creditor, institution, or country (not even China) is willing to depend on oil prices moving north (at least, to the extent desired), in order to extend a breathing space to the cash starved Venezuelan government. In such a situation, closing doors on humanitarian aid is irrational.

Economic implosion threatens Venezuela. Devaluation of the Venezuelan Bolivar is one option; such a move would sharply raise the prices of all essentials, currently provided in the state-run stores, which are the only source of survival for the majority of people. Devaluation will further aggravate the already-unserviceable debt levels of $130 billion. The country lacks the funds to pump more oil, as the oil industry infrastructure is crumbling, and there have been no investments to correct the decline. Oil production is falling substantially by the day.

Venezuela is a case study of economic mismanagement, matched with unrealistic populism, unnecessary bluster, and ideological intransigence in an increasingly inter-dependent world, and a dire wake-up call to diversify and expand the repertoire of national output, exports, and capabilities. Temporary autonomy, and a voice on the world stage, facilitated by milking a finite resource (oil in the case of Venezuela) is inadequate preparedness for hedging against future headwinds. Ideally, harnessing of other vital sectors, political systems, timely infrastructure investments, and enforcing fiscal discipline should have been undertaken. Venezuelan *chavismo* was the foundation of the leftist revival in Latin America (Bolivia, Ecuador, Nicaragua etc.).

However, the more inclusive, and pragmatic, left-of-centre model and approach adopted by the post-Augusto Pinochet-Chile, has managed the delicate transition more peacefully, sustainably, and in a relatively harmonious manner. The impact of Venezuela on India will be minimal, given the distance and the relatively limited interactions, both economically and socially. However, the lessons of swerving either to the extremes of the left, or the right, while pandering to populist demands, are invaluably relevant and pertinent for Indian politicians. Venezuela is the country with the largest oil reserves currently, and it is self-combusting for want of adequate infrastructure.

China's Veto Wars

(ASIAN AGE & DECCAN CHRONICLE, Apr 13 2016)

Historically, China has been the least obstructive member of the United Nations' Permanent Security Council (comprising the United States, Russia, United Kingdom, France and China). The exclusive membership of the P5, which is rightfully sought by India, grants the power to veto, and therefore enables any member to prevent the adoption of any "substantive" draft resolutions--the criticality of which is in the formal declaration (on behalf of the UN) of an individual, group, or country to an act of commission or omission, directly or indirectly, within the context of the proposed draft, and its implicit perceptions.

Since 1945, the Chinese have exercised the veto power just 11 times. Although, for such a reluctant participant, it has habitually snubbed India on Pakistan-related terror issues. In June, 2015, China blocked an Indian resolution to question Pakistan on releasing Zaki-ur-Rehman Lakhvi, key commander of the terror group Lashkar-e-Taiba, who was accused of the 2008 terror attacks in Mumbai that had led to the loss of over 160 lives. This, in the face of overwhelming evidence, as corroborated by various international intelligence agencies.

So, to that extent, China has been blocking India's bid to ban the terror outfit Jaish-e-Mohammad's chief, and mastermind of the Pathankot terror attack, Masood Azhar, which follows an established Chinese diplomacy and policy pattern. If, in the earlier case of Lakhvi, the Chinese line was that India had "failed to provide enough information", this time the Chinese foreign ministry spokesperson, Hong Lei, stated that China acted on such issues on facts and rules in an, "objective and just manner".

He probably gave away the real reason when he said, "The Chinese side has always been in communication with relevant parties on the listing issue," alluding to the real arrangement of the famed, "irreplaceable, all-weather friendship" of Pakistan and

China that invariably converges on such platforms and issues, masked in vague diplomatic semantics.

This consistency of selective interventions at the cost of standing out as the lone opposing voice, and vetoing Indian proposals amongst the P5 members played out three times, when India sought to get Jamaat-ud-Dawa (political arm of Lashkar-e-Taiba in Pakistan) added to the UNSC's terror list (finally added to the sanctions list in December 2008). Even the leaked 2010 US state department cables revealed how the Chinese placed "technical holds", at Pakistan's request, to block UNSC sanctions against Lashkar-e-Taiba, the Al-Akhtar Trust (charity front for Jaish-e-Mohammad, designated as a terrorist support organisation by the US), or even list the dreaded terrorist Syed Salahuddin, of the Hizbul Mujahideen.

Unsurprisingly, such unstinted support to Pakistani positions on untenable logic, led the Pew Research Center to report in 2014 that the Pakistanis have the most favourable opinion of the Chinese, outside of China. Therefore, the strategic development of the "Pearl Port" in Gwadar, the $46 billion mega-infrastructural China-Pakistan Economic Corridor, the joint development of the JF-17 Thunder fighter aircraft, and Chinese help in building the Khushab nuclear reactor, are all symptomatic of the Pakistani-Chinese equation of geopolitical *quid-pro-quo*.

The single-party regime in China has allowed for a consistent and overtly strategic roadmap of China's vision, diplomacy, and an unflinching quest to challenge the hegemonic run of the US. The world at large, and the West in particular, has been successfully lulled into believing that the opening of the Chinese economy would automatically lead to the emergence of a liberal, democratic, and pacifist instinct--towards that end, unprecedented acts of technology transfer, business opportunities, and most-favoured nation (MFN) status have been extended by the Western powers, whilst the odd behavioural streaks, like China's recent veto, have been tolerated as it was India-centric.

If anything, the Chinese have dug in their heels with aggressive military build-ups, asserting their military footprint in the restive South China Sea with surreal brazenness, and maintained a duplicitous stand on global terror, as exposed by its support to

Pakistan and North Korea, even at the cost of international outrage. The reality is, unlike its ready condemnation and support for proposals against the Taliban and ISIS, which have a global impact (especially for the Western nations), it realises that it can get away by selectively cocking a snook at India.

The essential reality, post Chinese President Xi Jinping's visit to India in 2014, and the reciprocal visit by Prime Minister Narendra Modi in May 2015, has exposed the hollowness of the initial claims of "personal chemistry", and the "highest level receptions". The fact remains that even prior to the UN veto snub, the promised investments between India and China only stuttered in. Flare-ups on the India-China border continue with a certain regularity.

There's dangerous meddling in the fragile Indo-Nepal area, where sentiments are stoked with condescending concern for Nepal's plight, by China. Even economically, India still has a massive trade deficit with China, which increased by about 34 per cent in 2014-15. Suggested semblance of thaw between the two suspicious nations has changed little on ground. There is still no respite on the issue of Chinese restrictions on import of value-added Indian goods and services, such as pharmaceuticals and IT expertise.

Embarrassing reneging on the principal of reciprocity by Pakistan's joint investigation team (JIT) on Pathankot, and the flanking Chinese intransigence *vis-à-vis* India, has been a vital lesson on India's focus on managing optics versus the Pakistani-Chinese realpolitik. India has to go beyond the theatrics of frenzied NRIs, ultra-nationalistic chest-thumping, and charm offensives. It has to grind itself for the long haul of professional diplomatic engagements and hardnosed realpolitik. Initial enthusiasm for managing international headlines, and appropriating the most "internationally-savvy" credentials, needs to be sobered down and handled with less fanfare, and more dexterity.

The Pakistanis have reiterated their stand of duplicitous absurdities, the Nepalis are increasingly cosying up to the Chinese, and China continues with its strategic chicanery. The US, amidst all this, ends up giving F-16s and attack helicopters to Pakistan (ostensibly to take on terrorists!). In the end, India ends up looking silly, sulky (pointing to the imminent Islamist threat within China, and its dangerous import to them in the days to come), and amateurishly over-enthusiastic about country-hopping, but really ending up with a disgruntled neighbourhood like never before.

The Sectarian Wedge

(DECCAN HERALD, 25 Apr 2017)

Shias are essentially the minority within the Islamic world, with only about 15%-20% of the total Islamic adherents.

For an estimated 10% (about 20 million) of the total Pakistani population today, the Pakistani Shias have punched above their weight in terms of historical relevance, and consciousness of the nation. From the founding father of Pakistan and *Quaid-e-Azam* ("Great Leader") Muhammad Ali Jinnah, first president Iskander Mirza, president Yahya Khan, Commander-in-Chief of the Pakistani Army in the Indo-Pak war of 1965, Muhammad Musa Khan Hazara, to the politically-omnipresent dynasty of the Bhuttos; the Shias were an integral part of the Pakistani narrative, at least initially.

Globally, the theological divide of the Sunni-Shia denomination dates back over 1,400 years of Islamic schism, with each side questioning the legitimacy of the other sect. However, the sectarian wedge amongst the *ummah* acquired a violent inter-sovereign dimension after the Iranian Revolution (or the "Islamic Revolution"), in 1979. This milestone event lit the spirit of Shia revivalism, as Ayatollah Khomeini was perceived to be following the footsteps of the revered Shia Imam, Hussein Ibn Ali.

As Shias are essentially the minority within the Islamic world, with only about 15%-20% (about 300 million out of 1.6 billion) of the total Islamic adherents, they were traditionally oppressed till the re-emergence and assertion of a theocratic Iran, in whom they found a spiritual and material benefactor of their suppressed rights.

Since then, a competitive spirit accelerated within the region, with the Arab Gulf States (led by Saudi Arabia) generously funding the propagation of its puritanical form of Sunni Islam (or Wahhabism), while the Iranians stepped up support for Shia-movements in the other West Asian countries; such as, Hezbollah in Lebanon, Sipah-e-Muhammad in Pakistan, and more recently the Houthis in Yemen.

Today, beyond the ostensible and the more visible "fight against terror", and its prominent manifestations like the Islamic State (IS), or Al Qaida, lurks an equally dangerous undercurrent of a sectarian divide that is tearing apart the countries in the region. This irreconcilable divide has ensured the shift in the principal focus from the traditional ire of anti-West, and anti-Zionist agendas, towards angularities of bitter sectarianism, with Iran championing the Shiite sensibilities.

Besides Iran, there are a few other countries that are Shia-ruled: Iraq (where the majority Shias were earlier brutally ruled by the minority Sunni leader, Saddam Hussein), Syria (ruled by the minority Shia-offshoot, Alawite ruler, Bashar al Assad), Azerbaijan, and Bahrain. A prominent Shia-minority also exists in Lebanon, Yemen, Saudi Arabia, Pakistan, and India.

The bloodlust in the ongoing "fight against terror" in the IS-held Iraqi-Syrian swathes also has a clear sectarian divide, with the composite Shiite forces, in the form of the modern day Iraqi Army, elements of Iranian Revolutionary Guards, Lebanese Hezbollah, Assad's Syrian Army, and the private Shia militias fighting together as one principal bloc, as opposed to the other Sunni bloc of the combined forces of Saudi Arabia, Turkey, Qatar, and the UAE composing the broad alternative grouping.

The Western powers have dragged themselves into the conflict for their own geopolitical reasons. This sectarian mayhem has spilled over to Yemen (where the Saudi Arabians have been bombing the Iranian-supported Houthis), Lebanon (where the armed Hezbollah retain a parallel armed force, besides the official Lebanese Army), and Saudi Arabia (where the restive Shias in the Qatif region were exacerbated with the hanging of the Saudi Shia cleric Nimr al-Nimr in 2016).

Worsening the sense of mutual suspicions has been the geopolitical success of the Shia-led forces, from Assad's inevitable continuation in Syria, the Houthis, holding ground in Yemen despite concerted efforts by Saudi-led forces, and the most game-changing acceptance and integration of Iran in the global arena, after the signing of its nuclear deal.

These parallel tensions morphed into the Iranian ban on the mandatory pilgrimage for all Muslims, the Haj, in Saudi Arabia.

Amidst this backdrop, the Saudi-led initiative of launching a 39 country "Islamic military alliance to fight terrorism" (IMAFT), ostensibly as a counter-terrorist force, is laced with sectarian implications as all 39 countries are Sunni-ruled. Ironically, most of the current Islamic terrorist groups like the IS, Al Qaida, or Taliban were overtly or covertly supported by countries of this grouping who are now taking on their own Frankenstein-creation.

Sleepless nights

However, the ground gains for the "Shia Crescent" (as the wary King Abdullah of Jordan alludes to a spectre of Shia-dominated landmass, from the shores of the Persian Gulf to Levant Countries, and Yemen) is giving sleepless nights to the Arab-Sunni nations who face the dual task of regime-protection against the IS, and their ilk, along with parallel dangers from Iran and its Shia-supported proxies breathing down their neck in a competitive tug-of-war.

Pakistan, with its own fragile history of extreme sectarian-related violence, did well to avoid joining the Saudi-led alliance initially, given the obvious ramifications of further emboldening the Sunni supremacists within, and upsetting the powerful neighbour, Iran. However, its recent move of approving the services of the former chief of Pakistani Army General Raheel Sharif, to lead the Riyadh-based alliance, has put the nation in a quandary.

Having found itself in the crosshairs of expected sectarian intrigues, the Pakistani NSA defended Gen. Sharif's move with incredulous logic, "He will become a reason for the unity of Muslim *Ummah*"! Given the prevailing Saudi sentiments and intentions, the inherent messaging in Gen. Sharif's move is one of forsaking the supposed neutrality that Pakistan maintained on the Saudi-Iranian rift, and will willy-nilly rile the Iranians dangerously.

The economic-military-strategic calculus within the Pakistani establishment would have accounted for the invaluable financial and strategic support expected from the Arab countries, as its own relationship with its principal ally, the US, is on very thin ice. This, given Pakistan's undeniable dalliances with terror groups, besides the ever-growing proximity to its "all weather friend", China. The internal considerations for Pakistan aside, Raheel Sharif leading a Saudi-funded military force is bound to redraw the strategic equations and implications in the dynamic global order, internally in Pakistan, and in the sub-continent.

Marshal to Mattiss

(STATESMAN, 5 Jan 2017)

Donald Trump will inherit at least eight active combat theatres with direct US involvement (Iraq/swathes of Syria, Yemen, Pakistan, Afghanistan, Nigeria, Cameroon, Somalia and Uganda), up from the three that Barack Obama inherited in 2009 (Iraq, Afghanistan, and Pakistan). The "war-related" commitments have increased from $ 811 billion under the Presidency of George W. Bush, to $ 866 billion during the Obama tenure, while the overall annual Defence spending for 2016 would be approximately $ 600 billion. However, given the aggressive posturing, and unpredictable nature of Donald Trump's position on dealing with terror and managing foreign policy, these Defence figures could spiral stratospherically.

In the US context, the Secretary of Defence is the key executive whose powers over the US military are in the chain of command, second only to those of the US President. The US Secretary of Defence is also sixth in the Presidential line of succession. So, given the existing operational commitments and the foreboding portents owing to the growing belligerence of Chinese threats, the selection of the new Secretary of Defence in the Trump cabinet is keenly awaited, as the incumbent would have the definitive "authority, direction, and control over the Department of Defence". Historically, the US Secretary of Defence has always been a civilian, except in the case of General George Marshall who was the Secretary of Defence in 1950-51. He was brought in to resurrect the morale and confidence of the US forces in the aftermath of the recent demobilisation, and to get them combat ready for Korea, and the ensuing Cold War theatrics. Therefore, the choice of the Secretary of Defence is a sure-shot indicator of the tenor and approach that is sought to be adopted by the new Trump regime.

Herein, the choice of the retired Marine, General James "Mad Dog" Mattis, is a veritable statement of intent. While it is still subject to a Congressional waiver, as the federal law requires the Secretary of Defence to be off active duty for at least seven years, and General

Mattis retired as the 11th Commander of the United States Central Command (USCENTCOM) at Tampa, Florida, in 2013. This 4-star General is part of the popular folklore with monikers like "Mad Dog", "Warrior Monk", and the ubiquitous imagery of a stoic and expressionless General with the call-sign "Chaos" staring out of posters, with statements like, "Be polite, be professional, but have a plan to kill everybody you meet", or, "Actually it's quite fun to fight them, you know. It's a hell of a hoot. It's fun to shoot some people. I'll be right up front with you, I like brawling"!

Now, a certain amount of *brouhaha* and swagger comes naturally to the Marine Corps fraternity, and it needs to be discounted. However, this life-long bachelor with a penchant for voracious reading is a cold-blooded intellectual, who became a legend much earlier as a Major-General commanding the 1st Marine Division, during the 2003 Iraq war, when he immortalised the 1st Marine Division motto, "no better friend, no worse enemy".

However, he is unlike the only other former veteran as Secretary of Defence, the Democrat appointee, General George Marshall, who was an inherent pacifist (recipient of the Nobel Prize for Peace, in 1953, for his seminal "Marshall Plan", for the European Recovery Programme), and was also avowedly opposed to the idea of recognising the State of Israel. On the other hand, General Mattis, is--as the rightist Donald Trump introduced him, a "true General's General"--an old-school American who still believes that Iran is the principal threat to US interests in the Middle East, and not the ISIS. He is still cast in the anti-Russian mind-set of the Cold-War era, and is believed to be intrinsically confrontationist in his operational deployments.

Already, the conciliatory tones of "inclusiveness" that were alluded to, and invoked by, Donald Trump, after his electoral victory, are falling apart with the prospective appointments of Jeff Sessions as the next Attorney General, Mike Pompeo as the CIA Chief, and Michael Flynn as the National Security Adviser--all of them come with taints of racism or xenophobia, and a track record of regressive and incendiary statements. The proverbial "walls" Donald Trump promised are inevitable, at least in the crucial policy-making framework of the next Presidential governance.

The quintessential Marine Corp General Mattis will have to make an unknown, and uncomfortable transition from the familiar "Semper Fi" intonations and muscular "Oorah's" to the statelier sobriety of continuous engagement and disengagement of the American military footprint. This will have to be done in such a way that the diminishing might and respect of the US military is both restored, and protected, from the heavy price it is paying in terms of personnel lives, material, and sustenance investments. The recent thawing, from a decidedly hostile to a cautious status of "frenemies", in both Cuba, and Iran, stands risked with Trump's advent as he threatens to reverse "better deals" for the US.

Increased military spending, blunt speak, and concern for the last US man standing would be logically expected from General Mattis, but at question is his ability to bring the requisite "political" astuteness to manage often contradictory strains and realities, such as the Pakistan theatre with its duplicitous and "selective" stance on the "war on terror". With a track record of undeterred and apolitical soldiering, the military commitments will have a more military rationalisation as opposed to the often obfuscated rationales professed by part-time civilian bureaucrats in the Defence set-up, or by semi-informed politicos who have hidden angularities to their statements. While the US Secretary is akin to our Defence Minister, the formula of an ex-military man at the helm of military affairs will be put to test. The only parallel example of a veteran as the Defence Minister, in India, was Jaswant Singh, arguably among the finest; albeit, for a short period. If the appointment of General Mattis was aimed at sending an unmistakable message of deterrence to interests inimical to the US, and to prop up the flagging morale of the over-stretched US Forces, then on both counts, the result will be unambiguously achieved. However, the acid test for the Secretary of Defence goes beyond conventional combat "General-ship", and requires statecraft and protracted engagements with enemies, which will require General Mattis to go beyond his practised instincts and inclinations. Herein lies the doubt about someone who famously said, "I come in peace. I didn't bring artillery. But I'm pleading with you, with tears in my eyes: If you (expletive) with me, I'll kill you all".

Indian Security Framework and the Indian Defence Forces

Who does the Indian Army belong to? Answer: To all Indian Citizens, not to Political Parties

(TIMES OF INDIA, 8 Apr 2017)

In Independent India, as survival instincts ebbed, socialistic dreams drowned, and the opening of the economy ushered in an "emerging India", its fractured and deeply polarised society sought a unifying rallying cause, which embellished quasi-majoritarianism under the garb of hyper-nationalism. Alongside, the political appeal of appropriating the army became an irresistible device to enhance nationalistic credentials.

The general elections, in 2014, saw the soldier-rabbit pulled out of the hat, to conjure a seductive image of muscularity, decisiveness, and patriotism. Still, while its suitors are many, and the Army has taken failed promises on its chins; it has remained steadfast, ramrod straight, and absolutely silent on the question as to who exactly owns it. It rightfully swears to the Constitution of India, and not to any political party, person, or religion.

Does the Indian Army belong to Raj Thackeray who offers Rs 5 crore to it, or to the Kargil martyr's daughter, Gurmehar Kaur, to Mohan Bhagwat, Kanhaiya Kumar, *gau rakshaks* or Umar Khalid? The simple answer is, it belongs to "all of the above", and to the 1,300 million other Indians, irrespective of their opinions about the Armed Forces.

Recent times have seen the Armed Forces being inserted into so many political contexts--from AFSPA to surgical strikes, Pakistani artistes, even demonetisation. The "soldier" is the leitmotif of the nationalist, rationalist, and even anti-nationalist, getting redefined by usage and context. All the while, the Armed Forces officially choose to keep mum, as they have for the past 70 years.

The vicarious voice in the form of the veterans, which emerged powerfully in the OROP agitation, has sadly but successfully been divided with the old fogeys echoing party lines with typical military bluster, on social networks. Many among them have morphed into "newsroom warriors", in tilted regimental hats, adding incontestable patriotism to party flags. Yet, despite multiple provocations, interferences and allusions, the Armed Forces have not chosen one Indian over the other!

The recent State elections saw the tragic misuse of the Indian soldier in watermark, with reference to "surgical strikes". Similarly, the woes of demonetisation were brushed aside by rote invocations of, "if our soldiers can stand for hours every day guarding our borders". The inherent danger of such a casual invocation, of the Indian soldier, is the willy-nilly invitation to force a political flavour on an institution that is proudly apolitical. The last and only successful bastion of inclusivity, secularism, and region-agnosticism runs the risk of prefixing "pseudo" to most of these adjectives, which define and exemplify their current conduct.

Political parties weigh every action from the tactical and dynamic prism of electoral relevance, but the Indian Armed Forces have historically been spared the blatant misuse of context. We must continue with this tradition, and the Indian soldier needs to be spared the condescending words, and worse, the *"jumlas"*. Instinctively, the Army believes in actions not words, and therefore needs to be given space and time to do what it does best; that is, protect the nation at any cost, as it is India's army.

Veteran Soldier caught off Guard!

(DAILY EXCELSIOR, 6 Feb 2017)

Primetime news-hours on the TV are peppered with repeated allusions to the Indian Defence Forces, from invoking the "soldier" on legitimate issues like the Indo-Pakistan *impasse*, to the utterly disconnected issues like demonetisation, and standing during the national anthem in cinemas. Convenient propping of the symbolic Indian "soldier" to inject hyper-nationalism is underway with military precision, by the accompanying retinue of the latest "newsroom warriors", who employ the veterans, in resplendent military regalia, to creating political "no-fly-zones", and guarantee a nationalistic high ground for political parties. This is a new medium and phenomenon for the essentially "barrackised" soldiers, who are more attuned to relative isolation from the political mainstream, ensconced in either the "forward areas", or the picket-fenced cantonments.

Part-historical and part-deliberate, the institution of the Armed Forces has evolved its own governance, ethos, and values that have withstood the parallel degradation of most other governmental agencies. It has its own laws, and redressal and operational systems, which have ensured that the efficacy of the "Sword-Arm" is maintained, from the frozen, minus 50 degrees (-50 °C)of the Siachen glacier, to the infernos of plus 50 degrees(50 °C) of the Thar Desert. The systems are not perfect, and are susceptible to aberrations and derelictions like the Adarsh scam, Tehelka sting, Tatra Trucks amongst many others; however, the proverbial bad apples are still a minority that is incomparable to any other Governmental body. Unfortunately, it does have a brewing angst and ire that is dangerously glossed over (e.g., OROP, successive Pay Commissions etc.), a testimony to the price that befalls any disciplined institution that delivers more than the mandated, and yet remains "voiceless", by design, choice, and good reason.

The frustration of "voiceless-ness" first burst forth during the OROP saga, which sadly continues with the emotional and financial humiliation of the fraternity playing out on the footpaths of Janpath.

The OROP struggle was political in its inception, as it presupposed that all political parties had contributed to the regression of the Indian Armed Forces, notwithstanding the condescending invocation of the "Indian Soldier". Sadly, the TV's lost interest in the technicalities of OROP and the civil bureaucracy managed to kick one more in, when the Seventh Pay Commission perpetuated the "secondment", and disallowed the promised parity.

The OROP movement is symptomatic of the institutional discipline, which is oddly enough, abused and ignored, as the dual reality of tanks parading down Rajpath on Republic Day is juxtaposed with the spectre of aging warhorses, with rusting medals, sitting silently across the road on Janpath, unable to comprehend the indignity of "*jumlas*".

Apathy breeds division, and the governmental procrastination almost succeeded in creating a hitherto unprecedented and explosive divide--a few meters away from the principal OROP movement tent was an alternative OROP protest, which was ostensibly protecting the rights of "other ranks"; the principal movement was unfairly projected as propagating the issues of officers, only. The first fissures of internal divide surfaced. This owes its genesis to the governmental twiddling-of-thumb, and risking the sacred covenant between the officer and the soldier. Like all divided protests, OROP totality was essentially lost. Despite the institution exemplifying the motto of living by the sword in Pathankot, Pampore, and during various other natural disasters, these elicited a jingoistic fervour for a few days, before settling down to concerted apathy.

OROP was primetime TV baptism for veterans, and soon, many joined the varied debates, and propounded the blunt military angularities--unquestionable in import, and with the running risk of sounding "anti-national", should a less kinetic option be suggested. The political appropriation and showcasing of these veterans was irresistible, as they offered the plausible justifications and "cover-fire" for muscular posturing of the executive. Except, this pawned overreach led to veterans joining the "shouting brigades", and navigating debates to convenient political positions. This tactic was fraught with inherent risk, as initially the conversations were essentially outwardly, and therefore even extreme solutions like, "let us raise our own *fidayeens*", were given a long rope. The cookie crumbled when the dispassionate TV channels picked up a story of disgruntled soldiers on social media, to milk, for primetime TRP's--for once, the veterans were forced to stare at their own navels, and get caught in the line of fire of TV sensationalism. The no-holds barred platform of the TV newsroom pitted officers, versus the "other ranks", and watched them squirm with glee, TRP's were guaranteed, and institutional sensitivities and implications be damned!

The construct, history, and conditions of the Armed Forces are so contextually complex that to make immediate sense of the situational status is impossible, and to twist the same, extremely possible. The "viral" of the BSF *jawan*, to the CRPF *jawan*, to finally the Army *jawan*, was almost expected, given the immediacy of chain-reactions of the medium. Again, this is not to suggest that there are no lapses or issues warranting redressal and review; however, this act and means are tantamount to portents of unimaginable disciplinary consequences, and it belies the reality of the multiple redressal systems that exist within the Armed Forces. General Rawat was spot on to call the bluff of sensationalism, and insist on raising the valid concerns in the appropriate form and forum. Frankly, given the overall governmental apathy, the institution would not be able to deliver a Kargil, a surgical strike, or continue winning in the most hostile and inhuman combat conditions, but for the exceptional internal leadership and redressal systems that exist, and keep the chin up, across board. The systems in the Forces work better than anywhere else.

The veterans have paid a price for their own naivety--from politicians to the TV studios, the fraternity reposed its faith, and found itself stuck in the quagmire of selective usage. Recently, the apolitical voice of the Armed Forces acquired a deeply political overtone with the wilful allowing of the "soldier", in almost all sundry political posturing. The continuing slide of the Armed Forces is a legacy reality that needs a voice in unison, stripped of all political colours and loyalties, when it is about the institution itself. Veterans must engage carefully, avoiding the political usurpation of the "soldier", and steer clear of minefields of the divide that come from an ignorance of the institutional functioning--as the politicians and TV studios are only driven by ratings, political or viewership, fickle either ways.

Dispelling the Flawed *Fauji* Narrative

(TRIBUNE, 21 Sep 2016)

Narratives about *fauji* laziness often dominate conversations about the Indian Armed Forces. Firstly, the typical separatist talk about the ostensible "policies" of the Indian Army in conflict zones. Secondly, the frequent lament of the Indian masses venting their frustration with the politico-bureaucracy combine to see the Armed Forces "take over" the reins of the country, to "sort out" the problems and lastly, the suspiciously-mystified-awe with which other governmental functionaries abuse the operational efficacy of the Indian Armed Forces.

Indian constitutional mandate has ensured the supremacy of the democratic-civilian rule, even though the state has entrusted the Armed Forces with a wide and powerful latitude of manpower and weaponry (including nuclear). The sheer physicality and muscularity of the Armed Forces aside, the delicate national equilibrium of governance, is nested and respected, with predefined "jurisdictions" afforded to various government agencies. The police and the para-military are entrusted with maintaining internal peace, and law and order, while the Indian Armed Forces are responsible for meeting external threats to the sovereignty of the nation--the increasing overlap (only in one direction) is reflective of the invariable necessity of calling in the "last resort", that is, the Indian Armed Forces, to do additional tasks for which they are not fundamentally designed, trained, and equipped (ranging from armed insurgencies, to civic disturbances like the Haryana riots). This frequent requisitioning of the Army owing to the sub-optimal performance of the other arms of the executive, coupled with the intrinsic "kinetic" approach (operationally), and "silence" (behaviourally, owing to a sworn institutional code of conduct) is fodder for imagination and creative aspersions.

Firstly, the operational deployment of the Indian Army in the hinterland (e.g., Jammu and Kashmir Valley) is not out of any military doctrine or desire. The process of determining the deployment pattern of the Armed Forces is exclusively with the elected civilian government of the day, after the other local governmental authorities (who are the real custodians of the constitutional responsibility of controlling internal situations, for example, the police, bureaucracy, state politicians etc.), have thrown in the towel, citing inability to control the ground situation, therefore requisitioning the Army.

Ascribing a motive in wanting to remain deployed in "internal" matters, is factually wrong. Unlike the Pakistani Army, the Indian Army does not control policy matters, or voice independent opinions (which might be contrary to civilian governmental positions). The Indian Armed Forces would rather concentrate on their real professional task of soldiering at the borders, or training at bases, rather than be pulled into a cauldron of politico-bureaucracy mess, like Kashmir.

In short, the military has no political "opinions", ambitions, or aspirations on say, a political unrest like Kashmir, other than executing the only "opinion" that it respects; that of the state. It restricts its thinking to operational tactics, accompanying requirements, and subscribes to unprecedented self-policing (the tenets and remedial measures of which are infinitely more stringent, rigorous, and permanent than any other judicial system).

Specific and isolated incidents of individual culpability are not tantamount to an organisational "opinion", as the predominant instinct and track record of the Army's operational conduct is contrary to the one constantly propagated by the separatists. Herein, operational necessities like the AFSPA are not privileges, recreation benefits, or any form of tangible or intangible benefits that accrue to any soldier. Importantly, the Army is not trained for mob control or curfew enforcement. They are intrinsically trained to "engage and destroy", by using military wherewithal in terms of weaponry and instinct (standard infantry training ordains the soldier to charge and stab the dummy enemy with their bayonets). Obviously, certain restraint and circumstantial conduct is implemented to tone down trained instincts, whilst managing domestic strife, but individual accidents do happen and are not condoned or rewarded, neither are they borne of any organisational intent or opinion.

Secondly, the no-nonsense and time-tested record of "nation before self", differentiates the soldier from all the rest, hence, the view that the Armed Forces "take over" the country, and correct all the prevailing administrative, societal and infrastructural failings is overly-simplistic. This belies the universal truth of similar experiments across the globe, wherein, the reality is, all progressive nations and societies emerge only with the sustained practice of a participative democracy, as opposed to military rule. The Armed Forces are simply not meant to make or implement polices pertaining to things like tribal affairs, agrarian economy, or corporate law. The perception of clinical efficiency about the Armed Forces should not be extended to suggest martial law (the euphoria accompanying the Musharraf coup was soon consumed by yearning for democratic rule in Pakistan, and vice versa now!).

Thirdly, insularity from societal morass, incomparably rigorous training, and most importantly, the self-mandated behavioural standards, have honed the Indian Armed Forces into an extraordinary band of military individuals who can execute the impossible (e.g., Kargil), unfailingly, consistently, and silently. No specialised "natural disaster force" or "police commando force" can hold a candle to an Army detachment in handling either a natural disaster, or a man-made disaster. This professionalism owes its efficacy to the disallowance of any political, religious, casteist, regional leanings, or any other expression of divineness, to infect the day-to-day working tenets of the Indian Army. Indeed, there are "caste"-based regiments but the unique (and often inexplicable) formulas of secularity (one room can be a common temple, *gurudwara*, mosque, and church, to all soldiers in the unit!), and camaraderie of the Indian Armed Forces, personify the idea of "India", in all its glory. The Armed Forces are brutally effective because they have been kept away from the politics, bureaucracy, and civilian society (iron-clad gates of cantonments host an idyllic of discipline and respect).

This very reason for operational efficacy, is sadly also the bane of the current dismay that is seeping in the Defence Forces, as they see their faltering cousins in other governmental institutions (who have the eye and ear of the political classes) climb the ladders of hierarchy, status and financials, whilst, dumping the flotsam and jetsam of their professional shoddiness in the firm hands of the Armed Forces to manage.

Contrary to Mr. Geelani's view, the Indian Armed Forces have no ulterior motive or "opinion" in Kashmir. To the millions of the Armed Forces loving Indians--the *izzat* afforded needn't extend to "take over", the Armed Forces are already carrying the can of multiple failures of the other arms of governance. Lastly, to other governmental institutions who wish to "maintain primacy" (ironically and shockingly, suggested in the Seventh Pay Commission as opposed to the mandated "parity"), it ought to be remembered that the Armed Forces are the last bastion of governmental recourse and hope. All ongoing dilutions, and empty condescending voices, as in the aftermath of Uri, and delays in arming and equipping the forces, are not just risking the spirit of the soldier, but also the last hope (that is, the "last resort") of the nation.

Veteran Affairs – A Glaring Contrast

(MILLENNIUM POST, 26 Aug 2016)

There is an interesting parallel in the electoral culture of the two largest democracies of the world, the rival political parties in both India, and the US, try to appropriate more nationalistic credentials by appearing more "martial" (therefore more decisive, assertive, and security concerned than the other). Appearing so, necessitates championing the security framework in terms of policies, preparedness, and most importantly, the people. Therefore, inclusion and showcasing of the veterans in the party ranks, and their issues in the manifestoes, becomes imperative and highly competitive. In violent times like today, with bloody military deployments both internally and externally (for the US), posturing a military veteran friendly face is a positive electoral cause that cuts across other societal divides, and arguments. Given that Hillary Clinton's own father Hugh Rodham was a Chief Petty Officer in the Navy, during the Second World War, she invokes the inseparability of veteran affairs from that of strengthening the military, and protecting the nation, "I believe in making sure that people who sacrifice for us are given all the care and the benefits and support that they need. And I believe strongly that taking care of our veterans is part of our solemn duty as Americans".

Whereas, Donald Trump, of the Republican Party, who benefits from the statistically proven traction of the veterans towards the Republicans party, makes "Veterans Administrations Reforms" as one of the only seven declared positions on his campaign site. The hullabaloo and *fracas* of the veterans expressing indignation, at the insults heaped on "one of them", in support of Captain Humayun Khan's legacy notwithstanding--veteran affairs is a strikingly powerful and effective symbol of the uber-muscular Trump-ism of "Make America Great". The electoral formula works true in India too. The run-up to the 2014 General Elections saw a similar traction amongst the 5 million odd ex-servicemen voters, who voted almost *en bloc* for the currently ruling dispensation as part of its overarching theme of "India First", an instinctively ingrained concept that resonates automatically amongst the veteran fraternity.

The essential codes of conduct for the ex-servicemen, and the BJP's promises, mirrored the overall intent, approach, and plans. The BJP manifesto explicitly had three points specific to the veterans; Implement One Rank One Pension, build a war memorial to recognise and honour the gallantry of our soldiers, and appoint a Veterans Commission to address the grievances of veterans (including reforming ECHS, and re-employment of ex-servicemen). Whereas the Congress manifesto stated that it had fulfilled the long-standing demand of the One Rank One Pension, and it would instead establish a "National commission for ex-servicemen" to provide an impetus for welfare and opportunities. Presumably, the active wooing and hyper-nationalistic posture adopted by the BJP was more successful in swaying the veteran votes in its favour. That the veterans would get a subsequent rude shock with the apathetic and condescending treatment which followed, was something that the essentially apolitical veteran had not considered. The explicit nature of the promises was soon relegated to disgraceful common homilies like "*jumlas*", and a very mercantile approach of bargaining ensued, which insisted on "lowering the expectation", this after an unprecedented protest by veterans and war heroes on the footpaths of Janpath; the war memorial, and the fabled Veterans Commission is also, almost forgotten.

The Seventh Pay Commission was the proverbial last nail in the coffin, and the veterans are left ruing the trust they reposed in a political formation that projected, appropriated, and successfully "banked" the veteran vote. However, like any other composite formation, the veterans are not just an emotive showpiece but have emerged as a unique constituency of like-minded people, of a sizeable scale and presence. Uniquely, the veteran fraternity is region agnostic, caste agnostic, and religion agnostic group, and is spread across the country in varied socio-economic classes.

This emerging veteran bloc has some peculiar trends that emerge from the American experience--for instance, they vote more than other groups, as 70 percent of the 14 Million veterans voted in the 2012 presidential elections (civilian voting rate was

61 percent). This made the "American Service Members" account for 17 percent of American votes. The veterans typically vote for a party that puts the nation before any regional, racial, religious, or societal cause; therefore, the logical empathy towards, "India First", in the 2014 General Elections. Also, the swing or preference of the veteran votes is typically seen as a huge endorsement of patriotism, honesty, and efficiency that can swing and sway the civilian votes in favour of any particular political party. Hence, the reverse implication of a damaging indictment by the veteran community will have far reaching consequences, for any political party in the future. Equally, efforts to divide and fragment this veteran community bloc is fraught with risks and damage to the Armed Forces, and the nation, as a whole. Unfortunately, successful efforts of dividing the OROP agitation, as indeed ignoring the Seventh Pay Commission inequities, has sadly initiated a sort of a very public wedge of grave political colour and flavour.

President Barack Obama once said that too many people who adorned the nation's uniform with much aplomb are now struggling on the streets--sentiments that reflect the Indian story too, albeit, by and large, the Obama administration has a successful record of fulfilling most of the campaign promises to the US Veterans. One of the most profound statements made in the bitterly contested American primaries, by the Democrat Bernie Sanders who said, "If you can't afford to take care of your veterans, then don't go to war". This is deeply reflective of the growing sentiment amongst the Indian Veteran community who are increasingly despaired at the callow and frivolous way the Armed Forces get deployed in harm's way, for meeting any internal disturbance, natural disaster, or societal flare-up (which ought to be the reserve, and preserve of the political classes, the police forces, and the civilian administration--who invariably melt away at the first sight of trouble, to let the Armed Forces take charge, while they get busy increasing their own respective emoluments, pay, and statuses in the system).

Mealy-mouthed platitudes and empty promises have a short shelf life, especially with the soldiering fraternity which is not trained to forgive and forget very easily. As JF Kennedy famously said, "As we express our gratitude, we must never forget that the highest appreciation is not to utter words but to live by them". This, more than anything else, separates the soldier/veteran community from their civilian counterparts, as it is the only profession where one knowingly dies for his/her country, as they value the nation more than their own lives, and by that extension expect the same from their civilian leadership.

Respecting a Soldier's Code of Honour

(MILLENNIUM POST, 20 Aug 2016)

When Prime Minister Narendra Modi visited the United States of America, his first pit stop of symbolic diplomacy was to invoke the American conscience, by paying homage at the Arlington National Cemetery. This military cemetery houses the national heroes and brave hearts of America, including the Indian-American astronaut, Kalpana Chawla. One among the 400,000 odd graves is of Captain Humayun Saqib Muazzam Khan (September 9, 1976 – June 8, 2004), a US Army Captain of Pakistani descent who had died in a suicide car bomb attack in Iraq, while trying to save the lives of his fellow soldiers. This gallant action had earned the 27-year-old Ordnance officer, the decoration of the "Bronze Star" and the "Purple Heart" that is given for those, "wounded or killed in any action against an enemy of the United States or as a result of an act of any such enemy or opposing armed forces".

Now, the fractious and deeply polarised debate leading up to the presidential elections in the United States has inadvertently brought back focus on Captain Humayun Khan's legacy, and its peripheral import on the buzzy electoral discourse. His name was first invoked late last year by the Democratic nominee, Hillary Clinton, to posit her anti-divisive credentials against the Republican, Donald Trump, when she eloquently stated, "If you want to see the best of America, you need to look no further than Army Captain Humayun Khan. He was born in the United Arab Emirates. He moved to Maryland as a small child. He later graduated from the University of Virginia, before enlisting in the United States Army." The political ante was further raised when Captain Humayun Khan's parents were brought to the Democratic National Convention, to punch holes in the no-holds-barred and anti-immigrant (also anti-Islamic) campaign of Donald Trump. Not one to take it lying down, Donald Trump retorted back by escalating the feud, and alluding to the silence of Humayun Khan's mother while on the convention podium, and attributing the same to their Islamic faith. The politicisation of the electoral narrative has willy-nilly given a soldier, a political (in this case, religious) "prefix" to his/her identity as a soldier, beyond the flag that he/she serves under, and runs the real risk of returning from the battlefront, wrapped in only one flag; the national flag.

The debate has expanded the identity of Captain Humayun Khan from a simple US Soldier to a "Muslim", and therefore its political interpretations--a trustworthy identity for one political candidate, and a pejorative identity for the other. It is a statistical fact that the military veterans in the United States tend to be more Republican than Democrat. But, this latest war of words has left many Republicans and veterans red faced. They have criticised Donald Trump's insensitivity towards the grieving "Gold Star family". This sleight of the soldier moved the "Veterans of Foreign Wars" to state, "Election year or not, the VFW will not tolerate anyone berating a Gold Star family member for exercising his or her right of speech or expression". The inherent soldier in the senior senator from Arizona, John McCain (also the 2008 Republican nominee in the Presidential elections), came to the forefront when he said about his fellow Republican, "I cannot emphasise enough how deeply I disagree with Mr. Trump's statement. I hope Americans understand that the remarks do not represent the views of our Republican Party, its officers, or candidates". Himself a decorated Vietnam veteran, the Naval aviator, and a prisoner of war (his plane was shot down and he was captured and tortured by North Vietnamese, which has left him with lifelong physical limitations), John McCain alluded to the sacred and deeply personal sense of the faith-agnostic spirit that binds a soldier by adding, "Scripture tells us that 'Greater love hath no man than this, that a man lay down his life for his friends'."

Captain Humayun Khan of the United States Army showed in his final moments that he was filled and motivated by this love. His name will live forever in American memory, as an example of true American greatness, "In the end, I am morally bound to speak only to the things that command my allegiance, and to which I have dedicated my life's work: the Republican Party, and more importantly, the United States of America". Increasingly, political parties across the countries try to appropriate electorally rewarding nationalistic credentials by posturing a pro-soldier stance. However, in mature democracies like the Western nations, and India, the

Armed Forces play a decidedly apolitical role and remain confined to strict professional conduct.

This deliberate insulation from the political humdrum ensures the perpetuation of unique codes of conduct, camaraderie, and an inert sense of the age-old ethos that is bereft of the prevailing societal morass, and degradations. Honour, nobility, and devotion find an invariable expression across all Armies, Regimental mottos, and war cries--if it is *"Semper Fidelis"* (Latin for "always faithful") for the US Marine Corps, it is "Service before Self" for the Indian Army, and *"Iman, Taqwa, Jihad fi Sabilillah"* (English for "A follower of none but Allah, the fear of Allah, Jihad for Allah"), for the Pakistani Army.

A similar and uncompromising code exists to defend the flag of the nation. Military history is replete with tales of reciprocal honour and dignity amongst the soldiering fraternity, afforded on both sides of the border--Captain Karnal Sher Khan, of the Pakistan Army, was posthumously awarded the *Nishan-e-Haider* (highest gallantry award of the Pakistan military) for his bravery in the Kargil war, on the recommendation of the Indian Army, who viewed Captain Sher Khan's gallantry as soldier-to-soldier respect; and not out of any political, religious, or personal prism of animosity or bigotry.

The most touching story of the sub-continental vivisection, and bloody wars between the two countries, is when Brigadier ML Khetarpal (father of India's pride and Param Vir Chakra awardee in the 1971 Indo-Pak war, Second Lieutenant Arun Khetarpal) decided to visit his birthplace in Sargodha, Pakistan, after 30 years of his son's martyrdom. Unknown to Brigadier Khetarpal, was the past of his host in Pakistan, Brigadier Khawaja Mohammad Naser, of the Pakistan Army, who went out of his way to personally supervise Brigadier Khetarpal's visit--a last day confession by Brigadier Khawaja Mohammad Naser, about being the man who thirty years earlier in a battlefield had fired the last and fatal tank shot on Arun Khetarpal's tank, was met with a bittersweet recognition of the hard realities of a soldier's life that still salutes, respects, and recognises the opponent's courage and dignity in battle. Later, Brigadier Khawaja Mohammad Naser sent a poignant note, along with the photos of Brigadier ML Khetarpal's visit, which read, "To: Brigadier M.L.

Khetarpal, father of Shaheed Second Lieutenant Arun Khetarpal, PVC, who stood like an insurmountable rock, between the victory and failure, of the counterattack by the 'SPEARHEADS' 13 LANCERS on December 16, 1971 in the battle of "Bara Pind" as we call it, and battle of "Basantar" as 17 Poona Horse remembers. --Khawaja Mohammad Naser, 13 Lancers, 2 March 2001, Lahore, Pakistan".

The strings that bind one professional soldier to another, despite serving different flags is often inexplicable to the political classes, who are not very clear on the difference between a professional soldier and a mercenary. A soldier is a complex entity that is woven with values of nobility, and codes that transcend armies, continents, and allegiance to various political dispensations; therefore, the disgust of a die-hard Republican like John McCain on the sullying of a fallen American soldier, or the respect afforded to a gallant warrior by professional armies on both sides of the Indo-Pak LoC. Unfortunately, the more recent instances of mutilating bodies, and tell-tale signs of torture, are reflective of the advent of political, religious, and other regressive strains that are not becoming of a professional soldier. Politicians across the spectrum pay lip service and would happily encroach, impact, and erode a soldier's code of conduct and sense of professional fidelity to their regiment, and to the flag of the nation, to suit their ulterior aims of igniting negative passions for electoral gratification.

Counter-Questioning "Flab" in Defence Forces

(DAILY EXCELSIOR, 29 June 2016)

The ongoing debate of a "leaner and meaner" Defence Forces reveals as much as it hides--the imbalanced "tooth-to-tail ratio" (or T3R) propounded as the ostensible reason is a valid concern; albeit, masking a convenient military solution to what is essentially, a non-military problem. The real devil lies in the spiralling national budget that calls for immediate pruning of certain "non-essential" spends, and herein lies the difficult government task of "cutting spends" on sectors that could have severe electoral repercussions; like, MNREGA (hence, electorally "less relevant" sectors attracted cuts, e.g., allocation for University Grants Commission (UGC), was reduced by a staggering 55%, from Rs 9315 crore to Rs 4286 crore, or even cuts to the Child Health Interventions). Similarly, and unfortunately, beyond the optics and shenanigans of hyper-nationalism, the Defence Forces are not electorally unified or relevant, and therefore perennially suspect to enduring governmental decisions in their strides.

The reality is, the size and scale of the Defence Forces are in direct correlation to the threat perceptions--it is no one's case that the neighbourhood is more peaceful now, than before. China and Pakistan are jointly belligerent with unprecedented military investments and brazenness (e.g., South China Sea build up, CPEC investments, joint JF-17 Fighter Aircraft Program, and the growing Pakistani nuclear arsenal estimated currently at 120, are few of the obvious joint strategic moves), and now, even Nepal and the Maldives are openly sulking with India; and dangerously flirting with China. Internally, Jammu and Kashmir, and the North East remain tense and active. Unanimously, the strategic fraternity is of the opinion that India needs to be prepared for a "two-front" eventuality. Such a collusive scenario is to be contextualized according to current levels of preparedness/unavailability (e.g., Air Force has 35 fighter squadrons against a requirement of 45). The contradiction of real military requirements versus external (non-military) exigencies is personified with the urgency of raising a Strike Mountain Corps, facing China (envisaging additional 90,000 soldiers approx.).

The strategic imperatives that are integral to improving the "tooth-to-tail" ratio has inherent prerequisites of redefining military concepts, and doctrines, like unified command and control structures, rapid mobility, weaponry, and process modernisation etc., none of which is accompanying the current "flab" debate or committee mandate. An isolationist and simplistic "headcount" is a typical bureaucratic approach of "*salami-tactics*", without appreciating the military construct of either the head, or what constitutes the tail. Any review of the "tooth-to-tail" discussion without rewriting the National Defence Strategic outlook is puerile and disastrous, as there is no parallel urgency in either "integrating" services, or appointing CDS etc., which are key to constituting a "leaner and meaner" organization, in its true operational spirit.

It is true that there are structural inefficiencies and opportunities to optimize roles and responsibilities within the Defence Forces. However, an institutional track record would bail out the Indian Defence Forces from taints of functional sloppiness or inertia *vis-à-vis* other governmental institutions like the Police Forces, Railways, PSU's, or even civilian set-ups in the Defence sector like DRDO, BHEL, or HAL. Seemingly, there appears to be no committee or urgency constituted on cutting the ostensible "flab" in any of these set-ups (These have delivered sub-optimal solutions like the Arjun Tank, Tejas LCA, and worse, could not even produce a standard rifle for the Infantry). In any case, there is an ongoing process of reviewing structural issues and preparedness of the Armed Forces (e.g., Perspective Planning at the Army Headquarters), which could be nudged to either accelerate or sharply review the existing structures in a less public manner, to ensure optimisation of resources; however, to allude to simplistic examples, like when the Defence Minister stated, "Every military station has telephone operators. What is the need for operators in today's time when everything is automated?" might be factually true, though politically expedient, convenient, and not really germane to the real issue of modernising the Army into a "leaner and meaner" force. This, besides offering a misleading logic, which could lead to irreversible disservice to the totality of the Indian Defence Forces, and ultimately to the nation.

Increasingly, there are extraneous non-core-functional commitments and requisitions enforced on the Defence Forces, owing to the institutional failings and shortcomings of other governmental institutions. Neither is there a similar call to cut "flabs" in other such institutions, nor is any committee instituted to curb the easy requisitioning or deployment of the Defence Forces, from bailing out the other faltering governmental structures; for example, from policing jobs on the border, and in the hinterland (for which a host of State and National Para-Military forces exists), natural disaster relief works(for which Disaster Relief Forces exist), civic responsibilities like ensuring water supplies by opening canals when a domestic stir takes place, to more recently laying yoga mats or building pontoon bridges for Godmen! The fact is, there is a certain pent up frustration that haunts the Defence Forces with the background of OROP, and the subsequent Seventh Pay Commission that confirmed the "secondment" of the Defence Forces when it came to any issue of parity and equality, even though the track record of the institution would suggest otherwise.

There is an urgent need for a comprehensive and holistic review, of both modernising the Defence Forces (with robust threat perceptions built-in), and also defining the role of the Defence Forces in non-core commitments. This should finally define the processes and organisation reviews and structures, capital investments, and optimisations in Toto, given the reality of finite budgetary constraints and environmental assessment. However, a convenient, lazy, and piece-meal approach that keeps both eyes on the balance sheet, without adequate attention to the capability levers, is short-changing the institution, once again. Unfortunately, the other inefficient sectors of the government do not endure such fine-combing, and arbitrary review of staffing--a systemic curse where the ultimate reins are in the hands of time-serving bureaucrats in the Defence Ministry, with limited appreciation of military matters and doctrines. Even, staffing "flab" review committees with ex-servicemen without the complete and holistic "modernisation" mandate, allows the government the plausible line of deniability of interference or vested interest, whilst, ensuring the institutional tinkering with impunity.

Genealogically, the term "flab" is an anathema for the Defence Forces--it is not reflective of their physical, mental, or psychological character. The disciplined comity of the Defence Forces has seen a gradual deterioration of internal health with continuing chipping-away of its tangible and intangible constituents. The fact that the Army is deficient by 12,000 officers is a telling testimony of the "unattractiveness" of the profession, and the operational risks it entails. Amidst all this, the silent soldier endures the barbs of "flab", till the next requisitioning of a task. It is not that the issue of a "leaner and meaner" Defence Force is wrong. It is the spirit, real intent, and half-baked rigour behind the *brouhaha* of a "leaner and meaner" force, which warrants a questioning concern.

Indian Soldiers' Unique "Unlimited Liability"

(TRIBUNE, 18 Dec 2015)

Last month, when the nation was waking up to the news of the raw gallantry of Colonel Santosh Mahadik, Commanding Officer of 41 Rashtriya Rifles, who was killed while leading his men in a fierce counter-infiltration operation, in the Manigah forest, of Kupwara--a poignant and pertinent point made by the Northern Army Commander was lost in the din. The General said, "The ethos of the Indian Army, the culture of the Indian Army —these are things that are sometimes not very well understood. We have a concept of unlimited liability. A man goes into battle, a man faces terrorists, and he faces them sometimes with certainty that he could lose his life". The fundamental import of the concept of unlimited liability is unmistakably military, and Indian in nature--an underlying sentiment that sub-consciously informs the beliefs, customs, and practices of an Indian soldier.

International military historians and observers often marvel at the operational daredevilry and leadership of the Indian Army, with Kargil counting amongst the finest displays of operational unit-level and company-level command, by relatively young officers and bloodied subedars--a lesser known fact being the Indian combat casualty ratio of "officer to men", which is arguably amongst the highest of all militaries in the world. Not surprisingly, earlier in the year, Colonel MN Rai, another commanding officer of a Rashtriya Rifles unit, went down leading from the front; an intrinsic tenet of unlimited liability.

The etymological origin of the better understood concept of "limited liability" is essentially mercantile, and corporate in nature. It is a concept which is defensive, and self-protectionist in spirit, and which seeks to absolve the protagonist of any liability beyond the officially stated definition. This is in complete contrast to the more cavalier, and noble concept of unlimited liability that offers no such comfort or escapist approval in operational responsibility. This concept necessitates a soldier's behaviour to be contrary to human instincts, and morally (yes, only morally) binds him to walk in the line of fire, irrespective of personal danger. Importantly, no formally signed covenant at the time of joining service spells out any such specific need to face losing life, or limb, as part of the job--it comes unwritten, unsaid, and largely remains unknown outside of the soldiering fraternity.

Across the canvass of public life, in the political space, corporate turf, and other civilian administrative domains, there are myriad instances of leadership exhibiting limited liability in all its sophistry; for instance, the case of a well-known corporate liquor baron, who until recently was seen personally endorsing a swanky new dream in the form of a brand-extended airline. This, only to see its disintegration, and devastating financial impact on the hapless employees, and vendors. Even today, there has been no change in his flamboyant lifestyle which continues unabated, secure in the legal comfort of a limited liability with no moral bindings, or call to honour. Most political virtuosos of legally convicted status tom-tom the oft-repeated, and convenient "political conspiracy" line, and prop surrogate candidates in the form of wives, sons, or relatives to retain their fiefdoms--morality be damned.

A visit to a government set-up for any paperwork or clearance is usually met with cold and sharp explanations of the scope of the actions, and inactions, which define the limits of the said desk or individual on the movement of a file (if at all). But, the nature of military service is different. It comes with its own inexplicable and extended codes of conduct, sense of history, and Regimental *"izzat"*, uncompromising quirks of culture and ethos, nail-biting training, and the seclusion of its barracks, operational theatres, and deployment--creating a distinct and unique set of battle-hardened separateness from the mainstream civilian society. Military service is clearly not a job but a calling in life; it subconsciously drives a moral burden on the soldier, who is expected to answer the call to arms at the state's directive, even at the sure cost of losing a life or limb.

Unlimited liability is all-encompassing in the soldiering eco system, and straddles up the chain of command. It is also equally relevant for the men directly under command. It extends to the veterans, as well, who are afforded higher respect, and honour than those still in uniform. An interesting corollary to the same principal is seen in the struggle of the veterans for the OROP cause, wherein literally the struggle is a composite agitation for all three services: soldiers, officers, early retirees, widows, etc. The underlying principle being the motto, "Leave no man behind".

Structurally, for a soldier there can be no selectivity, individuality, or limitability of thought and action. However, given the increasingly commercial and transactional leadership dominating the national narrative, it is often commented (rather ignorantly and lazily) that the soldiers ought to be aware of the risks that "come with the turf"--thereby, invoking a certain justification on the unnecessary hardships, and dangers that would be unacceptable for bureaucrats, civilians, and political administrators.

The premium in the military uniform is always on "going beyond". Last year, when the lion-hearted Major Mukund Vardarajan, of the Rajput Regiment, was conferred the Ashok Chakra (highest gallantry award in peacetime action) for counter-insurgency action in Shopian district of J&K, his gallantry citation alluded to the unsaid but sworn commitment of an Indian soldier, "...for display of valour beyond the call of duty...". Yet another Indian Army officer had answered his clarion call, towards fulfilling his unlimited liability towards his nation, his regiment, his unit, and his men.

For the military, anything short of such conviction, and belief systems would be devastating for itself and the nation. The nature of the service affords no second chances, bargaining, or discussions in pursuit of the state's order, making it the most lethal and effective organisation in trying times (a fact that is selectively remembered only in such trying times, like the recent flood aid in waterlogged Chennai, when all other governmental functionaries came to a grinding halt). There is a crucial lesson in such selfless leadership concepts for all countrymen to imbibe, wherein the country sleeps safe at night, with the solid assurance that the military still swears by their unflinching commitment to unlimited liability towards the nation, not because of the prevailing political or civilian leadership in the country, but in spite of the same.

End Politics over OROP

(ASIAN AGE/DECCAN CHRONICLE 26 Nov, 2015)

Even in the most avowed democracies, wars, terrorism, insurgencies, and natural calamities ensure the relevance and respect of the Defence Forces, and their veterans. Matters pertaining to the military and its veterans are also hot currency, politically. Not surprisingly, the run up to the US presidential elections are witnessing similar emotional pitches with Democrat Hillary Clinton stating, "Today we are failing to keep faith with our veterans," and pledging "zero tolerance for the kinds of abuses and delays we have seen", to Republican Jeb Bush stating emphatically on his campaign website that, "We don't have the money, is not an acceptable answer when it comes to providing choice and care to veterans. This is a problem of priorities, not funding."

In India, too, the ruling dispensation was able to punt and cash the electoral cheque, of appropriating ultra-nationalistic credentials, by passionately espousing veteran causes and promising to implement "One Rank, One Pension" in a time-bound manner with the exact specificities as passed by Parliament. The subsequent reneging via the concept of electoral *jumlas* is "friendly fire" that the Indian soldier was unaware of. Instinctively, the Indian soldier does not have the requisite skills or inclination to negotiate, bargain, or doublespeak with his own government, and seeks reciprocal dignity and the time honoured tradition of a "word" given.

Now, the OROP's avoidable narrative is getting dangerously political. Unlike our neighbours, the Indian Defence Forces have been fiercely apolitical, restrained, and bereft of any internal divisions in the rank and file. Today, the continued *impasse,* insensitive handling of the issue, and procrastination are leading to implosive fault-lines. Initially, the campaign was studiously apolitical (despite trophy visits by certain Opposition party leaders), absolutely non-mutinous in tonality and phraseology (given the intractable link between the serving and the retired), and presented in the most "officer-like" manner, despite multiple provocations and temptations to be otherwise.

Now, it is showing strains of quasi-unionisation (a definite no-no in military operations), with multiple bodies championing alternative formulas and approaches, each accusing the other of a "political benefactor"--an avoidable outcome of the delay. Similarly, symbolic medal-returning by soldiers gets wrapped up as part of the larger debate on the "politics of returning awards", by artists and writers, with all its political allusions and import. Now, the Indian soldier is even asked to "prove" that he/she is apolitical, and is getting ticked-off by the first-time Union Minister for Defence, on the "un-soldier-like" conduct of the campaigning veterans (some of whom are war heroes and have given up to 40 years of their lives in the uniform)!

The curse of the delay is causing divisions within the fraternity, with a set of pro-government and anti-government OROP campaigning bodies--the classic "divide and rule" gets the better of the innocence, and desperation of the veterans, and the politics set inside and outside the movement.

The divide then gets even more dangerous and innovative within--it potentially posits the officers *vis-à-vis* the other ranks, it divides those retiring after completing 20 years in service versus those who serve the full term; it even divides the Defence Forces with their cousins in the para-military and so on.

For an ecosystem that has survived the curse of the combined apathy of the political classes and civilian bureaucracy, by minding their own, in their respective barracks, this unprecedented infusion of politics within the comity of the Defence Forces is cancerous, and sure to impact the efficacy and fine record of the Indian Defence Forces.

The tragic martyrdom of Col. Santosh Mahadik, who died in an encounter, leading his men from the front and placing himself in the line of fire, is a shining example of the institution's ethos and classless nature. It is suchlike spirit that is at risk of getting squandered with overt politicisation, and polarisation of a so far watertight outfit.

The key deterrent to rapprochement is one of trust deficit between the stakeholders--the seeds of which were laid by the governments post-Independence, which saw the Defence Forces as a legacy of the colonisers, and a potential challenge to the acceptance of the political classes; thereafter, the task was conveniently accomplished by the willing *babudom*.

Now, the ghosts of suspicion need to be addressed with a transparent and inclusive approach by the government. Cherry-picking of pro-governmental OROP campaigners is tactically tempting, though strategically disastrous--it politicises the institution, and impacts efficacy. An immediate joint committee (with time-bound mandate for resolution) needs to be formulated. This committee can hear out the grievances, facts, and clarify the pain points of the OROP movement, directly. The earliest, and still the largest body of the OROP campaigners, led by Maj. Gen. Satbir Singh (fighting for the original scope of OROP without any dilution, as passed by Parliament) needs to be represented. Given the sensitivity of the case, the Prime Minister himself should hear out the final outcome of the committee report, in person. Given the fractious history, an inclusion of any civil servant in the committee would only vitiate the discussions (more so, given heightened emotions within the Defence Forces, after the tabling of the Seventh Pay Commission, and its implications for the Forces). Post the agreement, surely the bureaucracy can step in to execute the modalities, and conduct business as usual.

The OROP campaigners claim to have diligently done the financial calculations and considered all implications related to the implementation of the same (core issue in government's dishonouring the OROP in toto).

However, addressing the veterans through spokespersons of political parties, condescendingly debating on TV, or surrogates, has only led to the current stalemate. Let the nation know the hard facts, and it is possible that the OROP campaigners may have erred in calculations, let that also be clarified factually. However, in an era of multi-thousand "packages" being doled out to politically relevant states, it would be interesting for the government to quote the exact amount of differential monies, which it feels it cannot pay for the cause of veterans, and the Defence Forces of India.

Gentleman Officer Unaware of Political Googlies

(TRIBUNE 14 November 2015)

The unfortunate (though not surprising) comment, by the ostensible voice of the Defence Forces in the Union Cabinet, Manohar Parrikar, about the behaviour of the protesting OROP veterans, which was "unlike that of a soldier" and, "These acts are not in line with the Army discipline. It is hurting the basic ethos of the Army", is the sad unfolding of a telling reality, beyond slick political observation.

To understand the sophistry of this comment, it is imperative to understand the genesis of the 40-year-old OROP *impasse*, which was conveniently propped up, and repackaged in the run-up to the 2014 parliamentary elections. Amongst many other political and electoral deceptions, a stridently "military" campaign which allowed the ruling dispensation to appropriate a martial, nationalistic, and soldier-friendly posture, and perception, was successfully undertaken. An innocently apolitical comity of the Defence Services (a familial setup of brothers-in-arm from all services, irrespective of race, religion, region or rank), fell for it hook, line, and sinker, and took the political promises (of a very exact and detailed nature) in the innocent spirit of a true soldier; OROP, a specific and key component of the political spiel.

Subsequently, reneging on a word given, bargaining, and procrastination of the electoral promises by the political classes, were a new and unfamiliar battleground for the Defence Forces. Pyrotechnics of jingoistic bravado, inside and outside the country, barely concealed the horrific sight of decorated and gallant soldiers, sitting by the roadside, and asking the government to honour the word given; "honour", being the operative word for themselves, and for the government to keep. These dark times for the veterans also saw the birth of a slew of new military "experts", like a much-celebrated fiction writer, who condescendingly suggested, "It's time to analyse OROP with our head, not our heart", or another famous political spin master and journalist, who alluded to the financial burden and administrative issues as principal reasons against the OROP. Remember, this is not like decoding results of the Bihar election, where the famed political gravitas can come into play by deftly using sharp convincing logic, for and against a result, depending on how the results pan out during the day.

This subject is about the men, women, and their families who give up their lives knowingly, often using the heart and not the head--it is such raw sacrifice that keeps India, as it is. That said, we are a proudly democratic, and free society, where everyone is entitled to their views, however unpalatable or "half-baked" they might be.

So, what constitutes "soldier-like behaviour", as referred to by the Defence Minister? Actually, the proximate concept of a "Gentleman Soldier or Officer" is instilled in the new inducts, on the very first day of the initiation, or baptism, as a soldier in a training institution. It is unique, sacred, and beyond compromise, as a prerequisite for an officer, to be called so (note very carefully, applicable to all serving, or retired veterans, also).

It is a quality that stands out from the other citizenry, which is best reflected in the way they talk, walk, or conduct matters professional or personal--nothing that can besmirch the name of the nation, forces, or at a more granular level, the *paltan*.

You need to belong to the fraternity to understand and appreciate the nuances, and subtleties. Therefore, a rare journeyman, and a proud former cavalry officer, Jaswant Singh, as the former Defence Minister from the very same political party, stood head over heels in terms of military correctness, and restraint in all matters, including passing judgement on qualifications of soldier-like behaviour.

Therefore, before being commissioned as an officer in the Armed Forces, one is proudly prefixed with the nomenclature, as a "Gentleman Cadet", and not just as cadets: a tell-tale and irreversible augury of behavioural expectation and standards for life, which are expected to be carried along to one's graves. Which other institution, political, civil, or professional lays similar emphasis on behavioural uprightness, and correctness?

Perhaps, little known outside the services domain, are the prompt and strict codes of Army laws that potentially court-martial any serviceman, for any matter that is considered improper, or unbecoming of an officer or a soldier. Sometimes, the financial quantum of misconduct or misdoing is of an amount that would seem ridiculously low to warrant a dishonourable exit from the service, without any benefits; however, this is how the organisational construct is. The serviceman usually walks with his chin up.

It is this spirit of wrongdoing, or corruption, and not the quantum of the same, which is germane to the ethos of the institution. The codes of conduct and terms of engagement are above board, and there have been issues and concerns. However, the process of internal cleansing kicks in, and the institution is thankfully spared of any outside interference.

The current standards of the services, and public adoration is not without a reason. The conduct of the OROP struggle by the veterans is an unparalleled case study in terms of dignity and maturity. Nothing political, mutinous, or anti-national should be affixed to it. It should be spared of the political shenanigans, and condescending banalities. This institution is incomplete without its veterans--the bond is inexplicably strong. Therefore, distasteful and insensitive observations, such as those by the Defence Minister, reek of political chicanery, compulsions, backtracking, and inability to honour a given word. Thankfully, the majority of the fraternity do not comprehend the concept of electoral "*jumlaas*". Imagine, a situation of reciprocal logic from the military, to the extent that, "all demands cannot be fulfilled", filed back to the civilian masters when tasked to clear a breach on the border, or addressing a natural calamity. The Defence Services are justifiably proud of confining themselves to the call of the nation, either on the borders or internally, otherwise remaining content within their own barracks. There is nothing un-soldier-like about returning medals. It is an act of renunciation for something won by putting one's own life in danger, and is an act of immense heart, and love for the nation. The soldier does not indulge in doublespeak--he is loyal to the nation, and not to a particular political dispensation.

It is shameful enough for the nation to see veterans treated like common criminals, as had happened in Jantar Mantar, where the policemen forcibly tore up the shirt of a geriatric brave-heart. In a democratic nation, our conscience keeper with the civilian authority cannot be passing loose comments on "soldier-like behaviour", with political googlies, and subterfuge of facts and commitments, after reaping the political harvest.

Give the Sword Arm Honour & Dignity

(TRIBUNE 21 July 2015)

The proposed symbolism of celebrating the 50th anniversary of the 1965 war, in August, will look extremely distasteful against the backdrop of the very same partakers of the unparalleled gallantry of 1965, sitting on a hunger strike. Unfortunately, today, the One Rank One Pension (or OROP) conversations often digress into the emotionally charged, yet unnecessary territory of comparative political commitments, intra-functional benchmarking, financial and administrative implications, and such like bureaucratic meanderings. While all these are factual challenges, they end up obfuscating the real, and irreversible cost of OROP indecisiveness--the strongly perceived national apathy, and loss of conscience towards the Defence Forces, and their over 40-year-old cause. The debilitating and scarring consequences of such a "wait", haven't been understood by the polity.

In the composite concept of nationhood, the Defence Forces are the "Sword-Arm" of the body--a necessity that was born of the womb of Partition itself, and with the immediate role it played in the aftermath of Independence; and the protection of Kashmir in 1948. It formally reiterated itself in 1962, 1965, 1971, Kargil, and the umpteen counter-insurgencies, and undeclared wars across the length and breadth of India, and sometimes beyond. Its relevance temporarily rearing its head during the countless natural calamities, social disorders, and all other ills and challenges facing the country; none borne of its volition.

A silent, disciplined, and tireless epitome of the lofty idea of "India", the Defence Forces stood steadfast with the finest and rarest traditions, of plurality and secularity, in action. However, there is a fundamental difference of narrative *vis-à-vis* the Defence Forces of our neighbouring countries. Our Defence Forces stayed the course (at the borders or the cantonments, never straying), never eyeing "Delhi"--the same has not been true of Pakistan, Bangladesh, or Myanmar. Interestingly, the proclivity for the corridors of power, or the "stickiness" of Defence interference is best borne out of the fact that while the Indian Army is working under its 28th Head of Army (including the posts of "Commander-in-Chief", and later "Chief of Army Staff"), the Pakistani Army is effectively under its 14th head of the Pakistani Army. Some like Field Marshal Ayub Khan, General Zia-ul-Haq and, more recently, General Pervez Musharraf preferring to overstay their welcome, and democratic requirement. Meanwhile, the Indian Defence Forces have been fiercely and proudly, apolitical. Unfortunately, this very quality has seen the steady and consistent decline of its standing in the Warrant of Precedence, from second, in 1947, for the Commander-in-Chief, to twelfth today for its Chief of Army Staff--symbolic, yet, a telling tale of its consistent fate, ordained by the powers that be.

Perversely and ironically, the jubilation of its famed victory in 1971 was acknowledged with the seeds of the present OROP issue, with the first tinkering with its pension system, and a downward revision from 70 per cent of the basic pay, to 50 per cent in 1973.

The "secondment" of the Forces was in full-swing, and to compound matters, there was a societal, psychological, and financial new world emerging that was making the soldier think beyond the enemy, the border, or the cantonment--as the economy opened up in the 1990's, the unleashing of the private sector was being celebrated, and somewhere along the way, "pension" became a dirty word. Typically, the catchment of the soldiering stock was from "generational" families, and regions who started wondering about the fate of their parents, now being forced to sit on the footpaths near Jantar Mantar; an unprecedented act for those from the Defence Services. What was the option, and who cared in the new world order? Confusion and angst started setting amongst the forgotten uniformed fraternity, in or out of service.

I threw my weight behind the ageing soldiers, war widows, and families of this immensely patriotic lot of Indians at Jantar Mantar, last week. Unlike the typical protesters from any specific region, religious, social or cultural denomination, this was a set of diverse people who had earlier in their lives, stood ramrod straight during the *"Kasam Parade"*, swearing on their respective religious books to protect the country as soldiers of India; no region, or religion but simply put, protect India. Now, to find them sitting and fighting for their *izzat,* was indeed a sad reflection for the nation as a whole.

Today, many children of the OROP protestors are still staring down the "enemy", in the most inhospitable environs under bone-chilling state of danger, with their backs to the country--perhaps wondering why this issue still hasn't been resolved, and why their parents and loved ones are being told to be "patient". This, after an ostensible agreement across boards, as a justifiable right and deserved correction (not "privilege") to a governmental anomaly towards the Defence Forces. All subsequent comparisons with other government functions and departments are a deliberate bogey, unnecessary, and not germane to the issue. The fact is, any organisation that has service conditions similar to that of the soldiers of the Defence Forces has a case of "One Rank, One Pension" (read, retire at 35, risk both limb and life as part of standard duty. Not to mention the type of service locations, and implications on a soldier's family and financial life, post early retirement)--hand on heart, the answer needn't be debated, *ad nauseam.*

Thankfully, "patience" is not a standard soldiering *lingua franca.* Imagine, if the soldier were to profess the virtues of "patience" in handling a few of their own duty challenges? Let us not preach what can be immensely counterproductive.

Where then is the issue? My trysts with the civilian bureaucracy at the highest offices like that of the Supreme Commander of the Defence Forces, the President of India (as the Military Secretary to the Presidents, KR Narayanan and APJ Abdul Kalam), and even at the local panchayat level (as the Lieutenant-Governor of a territory without a state assembly) points that in the sad case of OROP, the issue is of *prathamikta* (priorities) and more dangerously of *neeyat* (intent), of a few disinterested stakeholders.

This is not a commentary of any political setup. The 1971 war was fought under the Congress rule, and Kargil under the BJP. Both major parties are alive to the sacrifices, justness, and specificities of OROP. My own experience suggests that administrative implementation challenges aside (to be expected), such like decisions, once taken by the highest authority to be undertaken in toto, breaks all roadblocks. I have no doubts that the OROP decision is irreversible and inevitable; it is a question of time.

The "Sword-Arm" does not get strengthened only by arms purchases, or replacing ageing equipment (which is also important). First and foremost, it is important to retain the *izzat* (and therefore the fighting spirit) of the combatant soldier--this *izzat* is now contextualised around OROP, and is being challenged with suggestions for "patience". After 40 years of collective indifference, the Defence Forces are not oblivious of the situation; July 26, *Kirgiz Vijay Diwas*, is a fitting date for OROP redemption and implementation. A visit by the Defence Minister to these OROP protestors would not be seen as an act of succumbing, but a large-hearted step towards acknowledging the sacrifices of these soldiers, and ensuring the dignity and *izzat* of those who put their lives before the nation, and ensure, India remains India.

Expectations from Soldiers in Politics

(THE CITIZEN, 20 Jan 2017)

Ill-informed orthodoxy of the past suggested that the "apolitical" mandate of the Indian Armed Forces should sub-consciously extend to the veterans, in the post-retirement phase of their existence. This ingrained shunning and contempt for the electoral process, and it's *"dhotiwallahs"*, was the bugbear of the eventual apathy for the Indian Armed Forces.

Without exception, political parties have been inherently disinterested in the institution, as it offered neither the valuable "notes", nor the invaluable "votes". Over time, an uninterrupted slide for the institution ensued in the official warrant of precedence, budgets were hair-combed towards crippling combat inadequacies; and creating insults like OROP. The successive Pay Commissions unambiguously pointed to the misaligned priorities between the national executive (politico-civil bureaucracy combine), and the extended family of the Indian Armed Forces, both serving and retired personnel of the three Defence Forces.

Today, opinions are divided on the participation of veterans in the political process of the country--unfortunately, history shows that no amount of impressive conduct, élan, or sacrifice for the nation is enough to warrant addressing the institutional concerns, in the corridors of power.

The veterans must partake the constitutionally provided opportunity to raise their voice in the State and National assemblies, which ultimately approves or disapproves the various imperatives. Given the track record of all political parties, and their governments, it would be puerile to attribute blind faith in any one political party for having championed their causes, as each has had blood on their hands, as far as commitments to the Armed Forces are concerned.

Therefore, any national party that ostensibly stands for the "nation" is kosher, as long as the outlook is to chisel, devise, and drive the subsequent agenda for the good of the Armed Forces. The more the participation in various parties, the better for the Armed Forces, as the dangers of a singular political party appropriating the supposed claims of pro-military support, invariably come home to roost. It is not to challenge the fundamental principle of civilian supremacy in the hallowed framework of our constitution, but to correct the dangerous perceptions of "use and abuse", within the institution, which is no longer based on emotions, but on hard facts.

However, given the construct of the Indian Armed Forces, as the single largest volunteer, and proudly "apolitical" Defence Force in the world, there are inescapable codes of conduct that are enshrined to be honoured, both inside and outside of the uniform. Veterans carry the rare dignity of carrying the prefix of "rank" to their graves, hence the duality of honour and responsibility to behave in a manner befitting the exacting standards of the institution. Arguably, the only governmental institution personifying the lofty "Unity in Diversity", the Armed Forces walk the spirit of national integration beyond the realms of religious, ethnic, linguistic, or casteist denominations in their unique ways (the supposedly "caste" based regiments never express themselves in any regressive or pejorative connotation, and are inexplicably integrative in the operative sense).

Unknown to most outside the "barracks", the institution hosts a supremely patriotic and dedicated array of Nagas, Manipuris, Kashmiri youths, and other supposedly irate sections of the national narrative. This DNA of inclusivity is unparalleled, celebrated, and expected out of all, irrespective of rank or service. Often this posits the sensibilities of a veteran in contrast to that of a provincial party, which clearly propagates a regional, religious, or specific agenda that is not becoming of the institutional ethos; hence, the appropriateness and conduciveness of National parties.

Political encomiums like the "first Dalit", "first Muslim" etc., which are personally attributable (as opposed to professionally attributable, like belonging to a regiment, or service-arm to associate relevance), is deeply frowned and looked down upon, as it violates the only approved hierarchy of loyalty that ought to come from a serviceman, serving or retired (i.e., unit, regiment, service-arm, and above all, the nation).

It is true, that fighting under any political flag automatically risks subsuming the absolute concurrence of the individual, to that of the party's antecedents. However, outstanding exceptions like Jaswant Singh, who wore his military pride, conduct, and deference expected out of a "Gentleman officer", made him stand out from the more political insinuations, and aspersions that were reserved for his party-members. Therefore, it is not necessarily the manifesto, or the history of the party that veterans join that is germane, but his or her subsequent conduct, whilst, in the political party.

If, it is the service-record (and seniority of rank) that is the principal leitmotif of invoking votes, it becomes even more onerous that the individual engages in the conversations, within the ingrained values and probity of expressions. Already, the Armed Forces, for reasons beyond their control are witnessing levels of divisiveness that are unparalleled--in terms of various service-arms, ranks, serving versus non-serving, and now, with the vicious angularity of blind political affiliations.

Unfortunately, some veterans have been propped up as the latest "newsroom warriors", who under the plumes of their hard-earned *fauji-hats* inject the unquestionable muscularity, and knowingly or unknowingly, defend the new-fangled interpretations of uber-nationalism (bordering on jingoism) that disallows any contrarian views under the garb of "nationalism". The wily politicos merrily deflect uncomfortable questions on unrelated issues like demonetization, playing the national anthem in cinemas, to other socio-economic crisis, by conveniently alluding to the "soldier".

To reiterate, no government since Independence, has covered itself with glory on matters pertaining to the Defence Forces, and all have been complicit in the downgrading with utter immunity-- the challenge is for veterans to join the political mainstream, and voice the hitherto, muzzled concerns of the institution (the serving forces must remain fiercely apolitical).

For sure, they can and must propound on matters beyond causes of the Armed Forces, like any other political person. However, given their existential, and principal electoral rationale for having invoked the votes, they owe their *alma mater* the dignity of conduct--else, an individual is free to "drop" the rank from his or her name, and seek votes in pursuant of either individual merits (non-military), or on behalf of the chosen party positions, but never invoking the military service-record as the plausible *raison d'etre*.

Be a Force to Reckon with, Shun Politicking

(TRIBUNE, 26 Oct 2016)

Jawaharlal Nehru was a utopian idealist, with a dim view about the role and relevance of the Armed Forces, "We don't need a defence plan. Our policy is non-violence. We foresee no military threats. You can scrap the Army. The police are good enough to meet our security needs". Seen institutionally, as a legacy of the Empire, Nehru suffered the looming suspicion of a potential *coup d'état, a la* Pakistan, in 1958. The debilitating "secondment" of the Armed Forces started immediately, with the banishment of the post of Commander-in-Chief of the Armed Forces--an earlier avatar of the much-bandied CDS (Chief of Defence Staff) today, who was second in the warrant of precedence.

Today, the Army Chief has been steadily relegated to 12th in the warrant of precedence, an inexplicable slide, which ironically followed every major engagement. For example, the 1962 war saw the COAS go below the Cabinet Secretary. In the 1965 war, it went further below, after the Attorney General, and the 1971 war saw the COAS go below the CAG, besides initiating the OROP disparities, *vis-à-vis* other governmental functionaries.

The damage was systemically infused, with the leftist-internationalist Nehru disregarding the "security imperatives", whilst propounding his strategic framework of policies. For instance, the disastrous "Forward Policy", which forced a loyalist, VK Menon, as the Defence Minister, to keep the Armed Forces in "check", and the *fracas* with General Thimayya. The military was consistently squeezed for critical equipment and wares, susceptible to political interference, and there was the emergence of the "pull" factor, in major appointments. The inevitable ensued in 1962. Even the subsequent turn-around with the military glories of 1965 and 1971, did little to change the narrative of a wary political class, milking the Armed Forces with disdain. All political dispensations, without exception, are guilty of appropriating military success for harvesting electoral yield. The "Indira Wave" of 1972, owes its energy to the 1971 victory. Since then, multiple deployments in counter-insurgency, Siachen, Sri Lanka, Maldives, Kargil etc., have only led to condescending motherhood statements, attributed to the Armed Forces. The political-civil-administrative nexus of all the political parties has perpetuated the rot, be it George Fernandes insisting that the then Army Chief, SF Rodrigues, apologise for calling some countries "bandicoot", to the sacking of the Naval Chief in 1999 by the NDA government, or the debilitating lack of investment by the UPA government. Of course, there is the now-successful espousal of the concerns of the Armed Forces, in the run-up to the 2014 General Election. However, what followed was the subsequent short-changing and reneging of OROP promises, and the inelegant political usurpation of the "surgical strikes", as a demonstration of political brilliance! The agenda of all politicians, irrespective of the theatrics and shenanigans during the hyper-nationalistic debates, in television rooms, has been guilty of politicising the Armed Forces. This is done while ensuring a parallel run of "secondment", by going back on OROP commitments, and worse, knowingly accepting the deviousness of the Seventh Pay Commission which retains the sliding trend.

Our national policies are bereft of adequate security dimensions, and appreciation. Therefore, we need more participation of the military, or the veterans, in the public domain. Unlike China, or the USA, the composition of the national security framework is devoid of military expertise (the NSA of Pakistan is a military veteran). It does not matter which political party is joined by a veteran. The more widespread the representation, the better would be the espousal of the institutional cause, perspective, and dimension towards political policies. However, the clear usurpation of the military to be an exclusive domain of any one party is a regrettable position, and a clear spin in political marketing. The concerns in the official status, emoluments, equipment, and investments in the Armed Forces remains unequivocally unfair. The increased pressure put on the military, to pick up the gauntlet for other failed governmental institutions, has only increased.

The much-required presence of military men in television newsrooms has unfortunately transgressed from propagating institutional concerns and domain expertise on security matters, towards political colouring, and a fixation towards certain political parties. For a proudly apolitical profession, which has maintained its operational efficacy--despite the disastrous political interventions and appropriations of the past--care must be taken to ensure the correctness, objectivity, and sobriety that is symbolised by the classical image of an "officer and a gentleman". Recently, the optics of shrill mud-slinging, bombastic bravado, and thunderous derision are reminiscent of political crassness and one-upmanship. The Armed Forces are the only institution that affords the unique dignity of pre-fixing "rank" to name. This warrants certain behavioural conduct and restraint, as the words of the veteran are willy-nilly tantamount to the institutional position and image.

Dangers of overt politicisation of the Armed Forces is manifested in the political baiting of the Armed Forces, for electoral gratification. Recently, a new low has been touched, with the provincial MNS chief using the Armed Forces as a convenient appendage. The "Rs 5 crore threat", to the pusillanimous and equally condescending Bollywood, is an affront of unbelievable proportions to the Armed Forces, and to the nation, as a whole. A politician, whose recent love for the Armed Forces was preceded by wont illiberalism, and hatred for non-state natives, would never understand how a proud "Maratha" officer, who went up to become the Chief of Army Staff, General JJ Singh, was actually Sikh, or how, arguably the finest brain to adorn the Indian military uniform was a "Mahar" officer, General K Sundarji, a Tamilian (if the demographic-geographical-historical connect of Maharashtra were to be linked to the Armed Forces).

The country needs more military men in the public and political space, and not less. However, it is the likes of the rare Jaswant Singh, who embellished his political journey with military aplomb, sensibilities, and care, which brought the much-needed security perspective, élan and institutional concern. Importantly, military men in political fatigues are free to postulate political positions in debates, on matters that are non-military, given their experience and tenure in far-flung areas. On military matters, they owe it to their *alma mater*, and the nation, to strip the same of any political colour and denomination. The influx of political flags, and appropriation, runs the real risk of the ensuing "secondment" getting accelerated with further fragmentation, and division in the ranks--all political classes have used and abused the military, for posturing muscular and nationalistic credentials.

Politicians do not send their children to the Armed Forces, they are content to soak in the blood-soaked glory of the Armed Forces. Never before, have the veterans been humiliated or had to sit on the footpath of Janpath, and face the parallel ignominy of ostensible support to the institution. Ex-military men must join political parties to influence the governance, policies, and politics of the politicians. They must not end up joining the "shouting-brigade" of the wily politicians, who would merrily lap up the spectre of the veterans joining their rank, and conduct. Politicising of the Armed Forces is in full swing. The onus of seeing through the same, and remaining committed to the institution and the nation, lies on the ex-servicemen only.

Magical Algorithm of our Defense Forces
(MILLENNIUM POST, 19 Sep, 2017)

Since the age of the Vedas and epics, the cultural instincts of the Indian soldier and his behavioural conduct has been subjected to and honed by certain martial traditions, values, and codes that thrive in the long-term muscle memory of the modern-day Indian Armed Forces. A unique framework of religio-social sensitivity without the accompanying bigotry or puritanical insistence, a regional-ethnic celebration without the exclusivist or supremacist dogma, and a carefully incubated and guarded interpretation of its own liberal moorings have evolved within its "barrack-ised" confines. Thus, unlike other security forces like the Police Forces or the Central Armed Police Forces, the relative isolation from the societal morass (politics, external interferences, or administrative *red-tapism*) has ensured that the glint in the bayonet is effectively deployed for any kinetic operation, without any fuss or favour.

One key differentiator from any other executive arm of the government is the quantum of investment that the Indian Defence Forces affords on history (both, good or otherwise) and "living up to it". This results in an elephantine memory for the institution that disdains forgetting and "moving on", without settling scores, albeit, in a heroic, noble, and soldierly (opposite of mercenary) manner. As the Indian Generals stoically underscore, following any terrorist attack, "We are unable to disclose how we will retaliate but we will do it at a time and place of our choosing", and settle the score they do, for they are wired not to fail a fallen fellow-soldier. It is specific revenge, not generalised vendetta against a populace or even a nation.

This unsaid camaraderie manifests in the silent pride that the institution feels on the commissioning of Swati Mahadik within its ranks. She is the wife of the Braveheart, Colonel Santosh Mahadik, who in an exclusively Indian phenomenon of military leadership, led from the front in the Kupwara sector, before succumbing to bullets in an anti-terror operation. The institutional pride gets doubled with the co-commissioning of Nidhi Dubey, whose deceased husband was a *Naik* in the Army. These women won their own individual battles in life, and retained their faith and trust in the institution to which they had lost an irreplaceable part of their own lives, for this calling. Like the "Surgical Strikes", the commissioning of these women is a cherished ode to "why we never leave behind our own".

As with glory, shame is deeply and profoundly personal, yet collectively felt, reposed, and shared. In order to comprehend the intensity of the passion and retaliatory urge, the composition party of the Indian Armed Forces that undertook the two recent "Surgical Strikes", one in Pakistan and earlier still in Myanmar, is a giveaway of the institutional ethos. Certain manpower from the affected units (which had earlier drawn blood owing to a terror-attack on it) were deliberately drawn and drafted into the final raid party that subsequently crossed the border to inflict the "Surgical Strike", as part of the deadly, limited, and calibrated response. The sacred *"izzat"* of a *paltan* is restored as it partakes the avenging of its fallen own. This unwritten code of "I have your back" presupposes the inviolable trust, commitment, and action within the fraternity. It is the impact of such cohesiveness and blind trust amongst each other that ensures that irrespective of the dangers, the Indian soldiers simply don't disintegrate. From Kargil, the classic infantry attack that reinfused the necessity of raw courage even in modern battles, to a civic disorder like the Dera Sacha Sauda *mêlée* in Panchkula, wherein the immediate impact of introducing just six columns of Army detachments, *vis-à-vis* the parallel spectre of hundreds of fleeing policemen, tells a story of the two parallel institutions. From time immemorial, supremacy has been accorded to the warrior codes of chivalry and the spirit of never-say-die, as opposed to "victory" at any cost--Maharana Pratap is revered more for his unbreakable pledge to protect and serve his land, his audacious courage, and commitment to the principle of fight-to-the-end, as opposed to military victories. Similarly, his progeny in the Armed Forces today hero-worship Captain Mahendra Nath Mulla, from the Navy, who went down with his ship in the 1971 war, or Major Shaitan Singh whose unparalleled heroics involved refusal to retreat in the face of certain death, in the 1962 Indo-China war.

Invoking such spirit, even from the ill-fated 1962 war led to a complete reversal of fortunes in 1967, when the Indian Armed Forces bloodied the nose of the Chinese in the Nathu La and Cho La clashes. It is this DNA, which held its own amongst the hardy soldiers in the recent Doklam impasse. No loss remains unavenged, no call remains unhonoured. The institution has inexplicably complex systems that often befuddle the mainstream understanding--from priding over "Battle Honours" won under the British Army, swearing on maintaining sartorial appropriateness whilst inspecting the "Guard of Honour", insisting on the term "Veteran" over "civilians" for those who have hung their boots, to being the only "profession" that is allowed to retain their "Rank" after retirement. The well-oiled system runs smooth and efficiently, without any interference or political beneficence. While emotions are all-prevalent, there is a very short-fuse against theatrics and everyone follows and respects the "order" that is handed down. The fact that the Indian Armed Forces has the highest "officer-to-men" casualty ratio amongst any armed forces in the world, is a blunt testimony to the preferred winds of leadership that blow in the cantonments. While the politicians and news anchors debates make condescending pronouncements and appropriations, the steely institution remains proudly silent and apolitical. It even handled the Lt. Col. Purohit issue based on the "orders" that flow, and not out of any sense of opinions as the contours of the case go beyond professional necessity.

This kinetic force, lethal but dignifiedly silent, is now the last bastion of inclusivity, secularity, and patriotism that differs from the majoritarian, illiberal, and jingoistic impulses that mark the current political climate in India. Gender is immaterial and the inclusion of women is based on their merit and not on any publically ordained sense of gender-balance, Swati Mahadik has earned her justifiable spurs to wear the uniform that was once worn by her husband with much aplomb and respect. As society wonders at the magical formula, the simple algorithm of unchanged history, balance of respect and discipline, spirit of nation-above-all, and tireless training are surprisingly missed on most occasions.

Governance, Administration
and Political Essays

Looking for a new President

(TRIBUNE, 8 May 2017)

THE 13th and incumbent President of India, Pranab Mukherjee, completes his term on July 25, and the grand estate on the Raisina Hill, Rashtrapati Bhavan, will subsequently witness the swearing in of the 14th President of India (not including the terms of acting President of India, VV Giri, Mohammad Hidayatullah, and Basappa Danappa Jatti). While the terms of the President are renewable for another five years, the only President to have been re-elected for a second term was Dr. Rajendra Prasad or *"Desh Ratna"*. It is to his credit that the office of the President has institutionalised a certain culture of non-partisanship, statesmanship, and apolitical conduct (the exceptional cases of presidential pusillanimity have thankfully been rare). Even though Dr. Prasad had a political colossus in Jawaharlal Nehru, as the Prime Minister, the first President set the precedent for independent opinions that could be expressed, even if they varied from those of the "parent" political party, or its leadership, to whom the President owed his appointment through indirect election. The articulation and style of presidential expression, dissent, or intervention since then has varied with various incumbents--from the openly expressive form during the tenure of Dr. Prasad, confrontationist tenor during Dr. Zail Singh, or even the more intellectually sober form during Dr. KR Narayanan's tenure.

The "First Citizen" of India is more than a constitutional necessity, or even more than the profound role of a "conscience keeper" of the nation. In today's politically fragmented India, it is a functional position of practicality, to protect and valorise India's commitments to its foundational values. The evolving narrative of Indian politics has ensured that the principal role of the President, as the defender of the hallowed Constitution, has acquired more interventionist and activist conventions. The principal of "equality of rights" is shaped by the Indian Constitution, which is intrinsically non-discriminatory, (and) irrespective of any socio-religious-economic divides. Hence, for the President who takes the unique oath to "preserve, protect, and defend the Constitution" (unlike the Prime Minister, and others, who "swear allegiance to the Constitution"), the answerability of the presidential position is only to the holy book of the Constitution, and its citizens; thus, the former President APJ Abdul Kalam modelled himself as the "People's President".

The process of selection--entailing the combined votes of the electoral college consisting of the members from both houses of Parliament, legislative assemblies of all states, including Puducherry and Delhi--renders the final process and outcome to be a political choice or decision. To think otherwise would be naïve, as all previous selections have been reflective of the strength of the ruling dispensations of the times. With the recent state elections delivering a strong verdict in favour of the ruling BJP party at the Centre, the choice for the 14th President would essentially be the predominant choice of the ruling dispensation. To go for a political person, an apolitical appointee, or even a party ideologue is the legitimate prerogative of political parties, as long as the subsequent conduct of the presidential appointee reflects constitutional correctness and probity, without any subsequent political biases or subjectivity.

Often the selection process of the candidates is subjected to topical posturing, which is rooted in attempts to symbolically integrate the myriad diversities of India. The affixations of "the first Dalit President", "the first Sikh President", "the first woman President" are societal nomenclatures in a show of societal assimilation and posturing, to garner moral acquiescence for the candidates, initially. However, to confine individuals to these nomenclatures often does injustice to their subsequent contributions. For instance, KR Narayanan was not just the first Dalit President of India, he was arguably the most erudite, upright, and dignified crusader in the Rashtrapati Bhavan. His compelling conduct, and heightened sense of constitutional propriety reintroduced the concept of "working President", albeit in a characteristically sensitive way, without threatening the democratic instincts of the system. The phenomenon of a "rubber stamp" President was given a quiet burial, with him constantly innovating, improvising, and pushing the envelope of presidential concerns. To remember his tenure as only that of the first

Dalit President would be grossly inadequate. That said, presidential selections afford a powerful signal of "composite India", and offers the opportunity to showcase India's aspirations, and commitments towards equality of opportunities, to the highest office of the land.

The Presidents can enforce a huge moral weight on any government, through the judicious exercise of "intervention", even if technically and ultimately the President is bound by "the advice of the government". Similarly, the President seeking expert "consultation", on a contentious point, is as powerful a message of reconsideration for the government of the day as, say, implied in the "return of the unsigned file". It loads the public imagination with a gentle, yet contrarian query. Even presidential speeches carry messages, and sentiments that convey far deeper meaning than the literal sense. KR Narayanan's famous banquet speech in honour of US President Bill Clinton was a subtle rebuke to the US's hegemonistic instincts when he stated, "The fact that the world is a global village does not mean that it will be run by one village headman", in a classic ode to his diplomatic finesse and gravitas.

Rumour mills have already started with the names ranging from those of certain prominent people, from the ideological fount of the BJP, corporate czars with a certain line of thinking, members from the geriatric *Margdarshak Mandal*, to even other senior governmental functionaries who represent the social diversities of India. The reality is, beyond a point, the previous political antecedents of the nominees are less important, than the subsequent will to behove and distinguish oneself, with the requisite constitutional propriety and sobriety, whilst in chair. While opinions on the performance of the previous presidential tenures vary, rarely can any of the Presidents in the last 40-odd years be accused of any overt political bias during their tenure. Today, India is a deeply polarised society with extreme positions acquiring prominence, preference, and political beneficence. Equally, the politics are mirroring the said churn, and it is imperative that the next "conscience keeper" be able to reign in regressive tendencies, with the constitutional and moral powers bestowed on the chair. There is no dearth of talent or suitability to choose from, yet the choice of the 14th President of India will prove the government's commitment to plurality, inclusivity, and independence of "institutions".

The Dignity of her Office

(INDIAN EXPRESS, 14 Jan 2017)

The larger point in the LG-CM tussle in Puducherry is not about the use of social media platforms, possible security issues therein, or even the impact of technology on governance--everyone agrees that speed is the leitmotif of modern governance. The issue is one of persevering with the constitutional spirit which necessitates that gubernatorial actions reflect contextual sobriety. This does not debar action-oriented measures, but mandates a certain tone and demands that the governor be the "benevolent elder", who could legitimately rein in the government of the day, even though it represents the larger will of the electorate, when a constitutional crisis looms. What constitutes a crisis to warrant public dissent is subjective, but the phraseology and text of the gubernatorial reprimand, is not.

The Indian Constitution has chiselled an active and executive role for the Prime Minister and Chief Ministers, and more "conservative" and "overlooking" responsibilities for the President and those holding gubernatorial positions. The means, methods, and implied perceptions emanating from such gubernatorial interventions, hold the key to this delicate system. The morality and dignity of the chair cannot be lowered to meet the mainstream temptations of "action-oriented-ness".It is true that the LG's office is relatively more "administrative" than a conventional governor's. If a state or UT has the benefit of an LG with skills and accomplishments in a certain domain, as indeed Puducherry does with Kiran Bedi, the same ought to be used for the benefit of the state and its people. Unlike inter-party or intra-party rivals, the LG and CM do not compete with each other for electoral gains. In fact, Bedi's claim to fame is due to her professional accomplishments, and herein lies an invaluable opportunity to redefine "cooperative federalism".

Beyond the technicalities of being bound by the "advice" of the Council of Ministers, the governor has to finally render his/her "advice" only after ensuring its constitutional compliance from a prism of non-partisanship; else, the import of punishing the government with a "return" or "review" of a file can only be explained in the calculus of morality. The brilliance of constitutional intervention in the democratic framework was exemplified by the late President K.R. Narayanan, who personified constitutional propriety in the most dignified, revolutionary, yet reformatory way. From "returning for reconsideration", the files pertaining to the imposition of President's rule (and succeeding in protecting the federal instincts), standing in line to exercise his franchise, to deftly working on presidential drafts, and articulating views that often reflected opinions different from that of the elected government, Narayanan was constitutionally protectionist, reformist, and action-oriented at the same time; this, without lowering the collective dignity of the will of the people that was manifested in the elected government of the day.

Certain genuinely apolitical interventions by the constitutional heads do run the risk of acquiring a political colour, given the different political dispensations in the State/UT and the Centre. However, commenting on the incumbent chief minister in one of her write-ups Bedi noted, "...and here comes the chief minister of Puducherry who decides to put a ban on use of social media in all official communications. He even threatens officers with departmental action if they do not drop out of the groups." The point is beyond the inelegance of expression or the public mainstreaming of dissent--that is the individual's prerogative. However, the tone and its public mainstreaming militates against reconciliatory options in a more civil, discreet, and mature way. Such public grandstanding could potentially discolour even genuine points of gubernatorial displeasure.

Bedi's gubernatorial assignment requires her to adapt to the role in a manner that is less confrontational, and still not "rubber-stamp". In the Indian democracy, the opposite of confrontational need not be conformist. In an era of extreme societal polarisation, divisiveness, and vitriolic politics, there is a need to soothe the frayed nerves of the electorate. Such a healing touch can only come from the "conscience-keeper" of a State/UT, who is above the humdrum of political intransigence. Bedi has the intent, capabilities, and options to deliver her stated promise to the citizens, and to her own talent, as long as she overcomes her instincts.

Conscientious Objector

(STATESMAN, 8 Aug 2016)

The 44-year-old Irom Chanu Sharmila, also known as the "Iron Lady of Manipur", has decided to end her hunger-strike, which started sixteen years ago in November 2000. Believed to be the "world's longest hunger-striker", she has been the face of dissent and debate, on the repeal of the AFSPA (Armed Forces Special Powers Act) in Manipur. Force-fed through a nasal tube in Imphal's Jawaharlal Nehru Hospital--which also serves as her prison ward--the civil rights activist has led a powerful *satyagraha,* rooted in a restive state, which has the dubious distinction of the highest number of terror groups in the country (34 of the 65 terror groups active in the country are said to be operating in Manipur).

The fractious "Seven Sister States" of the North-East are precariously perched on the other side of the narrow, 23 km wide, "Siliguri Corridor". The "land of a thousand mutinies" dates back to Independence. The Naga insurgency started in 1947. Apathetic integration post-Independence, tribal turf wars, the conflict between locals and "foreigners", and the overall lack of development have bred extensive disaffection amongst the people, against Delhi. These groups have been clamouring for statehood, regional autonomy, redrawing of borders, and secession from India. Easy availability of arms, and the presence of anti-India governments in Bangladesh, Myanmar, and China have fuelled the fire, and exacerbated the bloody insurgencies. A schizophrenic and inconsistent approach by the Centre has fluctuated between the overtly military, to piece-meal development packages, peace overtures to insurgents, surrenders, rehabilitation, and economic doles. For all that, peace has been elusive whenever the military is deployed. It is always the multi-dimensional approach of involving civil societies, tribal and religious leadership, political integration, economic initiative--along with the military--that has worked in favour of rapprochement and peace, in the restive state. Mizoram, Assam, Tripura, and Arunachal Pradesh showcase the relative success in curbing secessionist tendencies, and addressing dissenting voices by mainstreaming the popular disillusionment.

Tackling the 1966 Mizo secessionist uprising is a textbook case of success, where a multidimensional approach was followed. From a situation where the Indian Air Force was called in to bomb Aizwal (the only occasion when the IAF conducted bombing operations within the country), to the emergence of a Union Territory called Mizoram in 1972, the journey entailed a measure of give-and-take that was not bereft of the state's military might; yet, the authorities gave a patient hearing to certain socio-economic and societal concerns involving the local people. The political experiment and innovation continued thereafter, and it culminated in the unprecedented appointment of Laldenga, as the first Chief Minister of the "state" of Mizoram, in 1987. Laldenga was once the leader of the Mizo National Army (MNA), which had led the bloody secessionist war seeking independence from India. He had also stayed in exile, both in Bangladesh, and Pakistan.

This political rapprochement was preceded by the Mizoram Accord 1986, which had entailed the stepping down of Lal Thanhawla, from the office of Chief Minister to Deputy Chief Minister, so as to accommodate Laldenga as the interim CM. Basically, the secessionist overtones of the movement were subsumed in political rehabilitation, and inclusion within the framework of the Constitution.

Today, Manipur and Nagaland remain the last two bastions of active militancy, though there were signs of normalcy with the signing of the peace-agreement with the NSCN (Isak-Muivah). However, given the constant shadow of the gun, and the perennial insurgency-like situation in Manipur (six soldiers of the Assam Rifles were killed in the attack in Chandel district in May), alternative means of expressing dissent--in the manner of Irom Sharmila--ought to be appreciated, primarily, because she did not follow the usual praxis of violence or terror. A fast is inherently designed to express vulnerability, compassion, and empathy towards an issue. This template of expressing dissent is powerful, and contrary to the means deployed by the insurgents. It mocks at the futility of an armed struggle against the Indian state. Irrespective of the merits of her case against the AFSPA, her method calls for reflection, if only to ensure a political settlement towards normalcy in Manipur. Ironically, Sharmila had been continuously alluding to a "normal" life.

Certain concessions such as the vacating of Kangla fort by the Assam Rifles, and the lifting of AFSPA from certain areas of Imphal, had yielded political space and opportunity to accommodate and reassure the people; however, the little gains were frittered away amidst the overwhelming indifference, and a unidimensional approach.

Sharmila has called off her hunger-strike out of a sense of frustration over the government's failure to bring about a more favourable situation. Her future course of action offers yet another political opportunity of "mainstreaming" her voice, within the ambit of the Constitution. Her decision to contest the impending Assembly elections, as an independent candidate, should be welcomed as an effort to arrive at a political solution, as opposed to resorting to violent methods for secession, and the intervention of the army. She was awarded the Gwangju Prize for Human Rights in 2007, for, "An outstanding person or group, active in the promotion and advocacy of peace, democracy and human rights". It is this precise denominator of peace, democracy, and human rights that is rarely found in conflict zones, and one that needs to be recognised, lauded, and tapped with an inclusive political approach to address the phenomenon of dissent.

In terms of people's unrest, Jammu and Kashmir offers a parallel case-study. Of course, the Valley lacks the voice of a local stakeholder who is agreeable to a political solution for normalcy, without raking up secessionism, violence, or external influence. To be impervious to local concerns is not a solution, as the history of the North-East, J&K, Punjab, and the Maoist "Red Corridor" illustrate. Boots on the ground can yield diminishing returns, and a misconception that the AFSPA is a "privilege" of the military, sets in. AFSPA is only an operational "enabler", which is needed to carry out functional requirements. Therefore, any opportunity to incorporate political, civic, and economic imperatives and discourses in a conflict zone, along with involving the military to rein in subversive elements, is the only way forward. Political solutions to buttress the imperative of rapprochement need to be harnessed, and it is in this context that the role of Irom Sharmila as a conscientious objector--either through a hunger-strike, or as an aspiring politician--needs to be lauded.

Political Dissent

(STATESMAN, 30 Jul 2016)

Texas Senator Ted Cruz refused to endorse fellow Republican Donald Trump, as the presidential nominee, at the Republican national convention. Britain's former Prime Minister, David Cameron of the Conservative Party, was engaged in a bitter discourse with his party leaders, pre-eminently Boris Johnson and Michael Gove over the Brexit debate. In both instances, the individuals concerned held on to their personal positions, and their dissent did not translate to disloyalty to their parties. In advanced democracies, the democratic space to dissent individually, and legitimately, is both institutionalized and insulated from aspersions of insubordination towards the party. Both Ted Cruz, and David Cameron, remain committed Republican and Conservative members respectively, and are rumoured to be working towards a tactical retreat with long-term plans to return to the party centre-stage, at an appropriate time.

In India, the concept of intra-party democracy is more talked about than practised. The ultra-sensitivities, insecurities, and institutionalized intolerance of a view that is different from the party's position is frowned upon. The dissenters are immediately asked to fall in line. Rarely, is a party member allowed to take a contrarian view on a subject (even without compromising on the larger ideological fundamentals). The only choice this leaves the person with, is abandoning the party membership for another rival party that welcomes the prospect of electoral dividend.

The run-up to the 2014 General Elections saw a long list of regional satraps, who deserted their sinking ships for surer ground. The ideological conversion was almost immediate with negligible pressure from the home constituents, and a large number of those who had "converted" were rewarded with suitable ministerships, and other positions. Today, the impending state election scenario in Punjab, UP, Uttarakhand, and Manipur is witnessing its own set of high profile candidates shifting to alternative political formations, for both political, and personal reasons. The principal grouse expressed by those who have resigned is their supposed "inability" to do the needful for their states and constituents, given the indifference of their party leadership.

Hemanta Biswa Sarma, in Assam, and Vijay Bahuguna, in Uttarakhand, spearheaded revolts within the Congress in their respective states. There is speculation that Navjot Singh Sidhu in Punjab, and Poonam Azad (wife of suspended BJP MP Kirti Azad) are planning to join the Aam Aadmi Party. The AAP has its quota of turncoat MPs such as Dharamvira Gandhi, and Harinder Singh Khalsa. The Russian roulette being played by a section of the political fraternity spins unabated with no aspersions cast on the individual's change of heart, and ideologies, even after the extreme positions and language used against some of the parties that these individuals subsequently join.

It is surprising, however, that none of the turncoats could claim any ideological or issue-based difference with the stated party positions. In almost all cases of individual resignation, the reason for quitting party membership is rooted in disputes over leadership, and positions in the hierarchy.

The other deterrent of our political system is the frequent use of the concept of "Party Whips", who dictate that all party members must attend the legislature during a vote. They also insist on casting the vote according to the party line, leaving little or no scope for individual thinking, discretion, and choice. Thankfully, these "Whips" have no role to play in the Presidential election; they are not allowed to direct a Member of Parliament, or a Member of the Assembly, to toe the line.

Decentralization of the task of gathering opinion, grassroots empowerment, and a culture of inner meritocracy ensures vibrancy and innovative ideas from the party cadres, which can automatically come through the funnelled groundswell of popular pulse, if allowed a free-flow of vertical expression. This sort of an evolutionary process facilitated the emergence of "New Labour" in the United Kingdom that led to the eclipse of the "Old Labour", led by Tony Blair, and Gordon Brown. The Labour party's position on market economics was redefined, relations with trade unions restored, and a greater assertion in foreign affairs was manifest.

Critical dissent and disagreement ensures a calibrated, inclusive, and aspirational appeal for the political parties. The Democratic National Convention in the US saw Bernie Sanders stating, "It is no secret that Hillary Clinton and I disagree on a number of issues," adding, "that is what this campaign has been about. That is what democracy is about". Considering the import of the moment, occasion, and the long-term implications, he graciously hastened to add, "Any objective observer will conclude that based on her ideas and her leadership, Hillary Clinton must become the next President". This sort of institutionalised debate and dissent enables a party to be in step with the changes on the ground, and various opinions amongst the party members.

The BJP, which claims to be the "Party with a difference", is essentially of the same hierarchical construct, as the Congress, or the AAP. The coterie ruling the roost in the corridors of power is essentially made up of loyalists. It lacks the diversity of gravitas. The BJP, in the heyday of Atal Bihari Vajpayee, had a more open and congenial environment that allowed highly-opinionated individuals, pre-eminently Arun Shourie, Jaswant Singh, Bhairon Singh Shekhawat, Govindacharya and the like to co-exist, and postulate their individual opinions amidst the occasional uproar, and disagreement over certain issues. It used to be a mature and profound platform that came closest to the tag of "Party with a difference", in terms of inner democracy.

Political positions have hardened and polarized with the prevailing insecurities of leadership across the political spectrum. Lip service towards formats like *chintanbaithaks, chintinshivirs,* or *Margdarshak Mandals* are poor substitutes for the acceptance of alternative viewpoints, and intellectual disagreements. On the contrary, a pliant subservience that does not question the status quo, and toes the official line, is the best means to ensure political relevance and position. This lack of inner democracy and dissent within all political parties and classes is depriving the nation of much needed freedom, creative genius, and unstifled output.

Democracy Survives: When 'Loss' isn't 'Defeat'

(ASIAN AGE/DECCAN CHRONICLE 17 Aug, 2017)

In the backdrop of the vile and morally questionable drama entailing political machinations at their worst, in the lead-up to the Rajya Sabha polls in Gujarat, the more crucial race for the post of the vice-president was a forgotten footnote in time. For the second time in a row, the losing vice-presidential candidate, albeit from different parties, dignified, upheld, and embellished the vibrant (but threatened) democratic instincts of a wounded nation, which frequently goes numb in the face of cold electoral math and the hubris of the political classes. The Indian political system has a Machiavellian impulse which ensures that the "numerically-lesser" political coalition attempts to embarrass the "numerically-greater" political coalition, by proposing a more "compelling" candidate. This "compelling" element usually takes the form of race, religion, gender, or some other undeniable socio-economic dimension.

Sometimes, however, the "compelling" candidature takes the shape of genuine competence, giving the electoral race a semblance of moral high ground, and forces public opinion favourably towards the choice of the "numerically-lesser" coalition. In such cases, while the electoral results are a foregone conclusion (except for some embarrassing cross-voting), the collateral opportunity to reiterate, reaffirm, and celebrate the essentialities of the composite and profound "idea of India" is invaluable in the face of brute numbers.

In 2012, cavalry "officer and a gentleman" Jaswant Singh, as the NDA nominee, lost to the UPA's Hamid Ansari, a former diplomat. By 2017, the political winds and fortunes had totally reversed, and the UPA nominee, "man of letters" Gopalkrishna Gandhi, lost out to the quintessential politician M. Venkaiah Naidu, known for his quick-jab alliterations and allegories. However, the stately and intellectual queries posited and initiated, by both "defeated", allowed the critical expression and venting of the proverbial "other voice".

Today, India is a deeply polarised, fractured, and increasingly fragmented polity with an ongoing "consolidation of the fragmented". The last election ushered in a government with a thumping majority, albeit with 31 per cent of the popular votes across the nation in its favour, signalling the sensitivity of recognising and respecting the 69 per cent who may have a contrarian view of governance and national imperatives.

Jaswant Singh had famously quoted the spirit of the word "*umeed*" (hope) in the subsumed context of the larger term "*umeedvar*" (candidate), to postulate the intrinsic "hope" of his supporters that lay in his candidature, even though the electoral votes were heavily stacked against him. Then, in an expected equestrian flourish, he insisted against the futility of the contest when he resolutely stated that he was "not being put out to pasture".

Similarly, Gopalkrishna Gandhi invoked the Indian Constitution's finest pulse when he stated, "I see myself as a citizen candidate who has been asked by a large spectrum of Opposition parties to contest without party bias but with an unambiguous commitment to the cardinal tenets of the Constitution of India, and specially its guarantees in the matter of freedom of conscience, speech and expression". Interestingly, neither of these two insisted on the politically-kosher flagstaff of their naturally-expected bearings to make their respective cases. "Major" Jaswant Singh, an irrepressibly proud soldier, never invoked or stoked his military credentials to titillate the fire of hyper-nationalism; and neither did the unmatchable gene pool of Gopalkrishna Gandhi (with Mahatma Gandhi as his paternal grandfather, and C. Rajagopalachari as his maternal grandfather) figure in any posturing for suitability. Between the two, they have written over 20 books. Jaswant Singh has been a visiting professor at Oxford, and a senior fellow a

t Harvard. Gopalkrishna Gandhi has been a professor of history and arts at Ashoka University, besides a powerhouse of intellectual views which are routinely published in journals. If one is a non-political "Gandhi", the other was arguably the most "secular" figure from his party--both represented the fading profundities of liberality, inclusivity, and genteelness that has almost vanished from the political mainstream of today.

Our constitutional posts are the vanguard of apolitical and constitutional propriety that require a deep maturity, searing conscience, and intellectual independence from the clutches of partisan politics--herein, both Singh and Gandhi were eminently qualified. While Gopalkrishna Gandhi was no party cardholder, and had achieved the rare distinction of getting endorsed by both the Trinamool Congress and the Communist parties in recognition of his impeccable conduct as a governor of West Bengal, Jaswant Singh was the perennial oddity within his own ranks for having staunchly independent views (with a book aptly titled *The Audacity of Opinion*). Yet, both were consumed by the prevailing winds of neo-nationalism when their intellectual enquiries and postulations were misread (or perhaps, never read!) as unpatriotic.

Jaswant Singh's book on Mohammed Ali Jinnah was ostensibly his undoing the first time, whereas Gopalkrishna Gandhi's insistence on terming the death penalty as a medieval concept that had outlived its time, was misconstrued as unpatriotic, given the Yaqub Memon case (ignoring a similar plea by him for Kulbhushan Jadhav). Irrespective of the political calculus that determines the winning candidature, both Jaswant Singh and Gopalkrishna Gandhi lost the election but were certainly not "defeated" in the larger context of the "idea of India". They fought on principles, ideas, and wistful philosophies that are the essential oxygen of democracy; often contrarian, always enriching, and certainly never unpatriotic. With the quality of debate, perspective, and opposition on the decline, the nuanced and righteous tenor of Gopalkrishna Gandhi was a brief whiff of fresh air that added the much-needed gravitas and alternative thought to the still-air of political opposition, a celebratory feature of a thriving democracy that must always be sought.

Sadly, Jaswant Singh's health has stalled the erudite man from contributing to public discourse, but "citizen candidate" Gopalkrishna Gandhi must continue to add to the perspectives of the "argumentative Indian". The toxicity of a stalled or snubbed intellectual culture does not befit a 5,000-year-old civilisation. The dignity and poise in gracefully congratulating the duly elected vice-president only added to their individual lustre and halo.

On Federalism, just walk the talk

(ASIAN AGE & DECCAN CHRONICLE, 23 Jul 2016)

India's federal structure calls for the division and sharing of powers, on a territorial basis, between the Centre and States. After Independence, the predominance of a single party in the national narrative ensured a strong centrifugal system that was given to its own agenda, arbitrariness, and biases. It also fuelled regionalism, and gave rise to anti-Delhi sentiments.

The larger issue of a tenuous Centre-State relationship came to the forefront only in the late 1960's, when the State Assemblies saw the rapid emergence of the Opposition, and regional parties beyond the Congress. In 1969, the flag of concern was raised by three non-Congress chief ministers from Orissa, Kerala, and Andhra Pradesh. They insisted on decentralisation of power, and transparency in the financial doles meted out to the states.

Given the increasingly fragmented political landscape, and the natural impulses and instincts of all sides, constitutional appointments like governors, and the provision requiring presidential assent for bills passed in the State Assemblies, became invaluable political tools.

Often, the constitutional resources and processes were deployed to checkmate, and suppress, the States' autonomy and the federal framework--tainting the hallowed spirit of the Indian Constitution, and militating against popular sovereignty.

The frequent invoking of Article 356, through the state governors' recommendation to impose President's Rule in a state, is one such contentious Centre-State flashpoint. It was prophetically pre-empted by the chairman of the drafting committee of the Constitution, B.R. Ambedkar. He had wished that the use of Article 356 be a "dead letter", only to be used when all other means had been exhausted. The partisan behaviour by parties of all hues, denominations, and combinations has been responsible for the misuse of this provision.

The recent instances of gubernatorial overreach, in both the Arunachal Pradesh, and Uttarakhand Assemblies has given fresh ammunition to disgruntled chief ministers (belonging to Opposition parties), to voice their concerns on the mirage-like reality of the oft-quoted principle of "cooperative federalism".

With the Supreme Court indictments in sail, Bihar Chief Minister, Nitish Kumar, launched a meaningful debate that questioned the relevance, role, and conduct of those appointed as governors. The debate in the 11th Inter-State Council, saw riled Opposition chief ministers invoking several parts of the unimplemented findings of the Sarkaria Commission, and the Punchhi Commission, and alluded to the Supreme Court's guiding principle in the landmark S.R. Bommai case.

Clearly, the ruling dispensation has boxed itself into a corner with the questionable conduct of some of its new appointees, in the past couple of years. To appoint any individual as governor is the sole prerogative of the ruling party, as long as the individual meets the basic criteria of eminence, and hails from outside the state and its politics. However, what has really raised hackles is the post-appointment conduct of these individuals, including questionable political preferences, and the constitutional compromises they have made. The familiar rote and protracted quasi-purge, of removing the appointees of an earlier government, was justified on the grounds of similar behaviour by previous dispensations--an opportunity to correct a historical malaise was lost.

The demonstrated gubernatorial actions have now taken on hitherto unseen, and brazen levels of politicisation, and deep tones of ideological colours that are being projected, unconvincingly, as a "nationalistic" imperative.

Comments like "Hindustan for Hindus", or that Muslims "are free to go to Pakistan" by one governor, or such as, "whatever gave you the notion that I am secular, I am a Hindu...", by another--the list of avoidable opinions that are rooted in ideological beliefs is unfortunately long.

The popular notion of the Raj Bhavans being "old-age-homes" for party lions in the winter of their lives, or as dens of the Centre's apparatchiks, is both regrettable and true, in parts. However, given the proliferation of parties, and the accompanying mathematics of permutations and combinations of cobbling together electoral numbers--the presence of an apolitical, and constitutionally upright "wise man" cannot be overemphasized.

Given the political nature of the domain, the induction of erstwhile political warlords who have sheathed the sabre, is also kosher; it is not wrong, as a certain political understanding is required to handle the constitutional quandaries that can emerge in a multi-party coalition, or in an Assembly.

Certain border states with a strong democratic culture, and regional parties (with "soft-secessionist" tendencies) are always susceptible to testing the limits of constitutional, territorial, and sovereign frameworks--herein, the role of a Delhi-appointed governor who can rein in the political enthusiasm, to within the contours of constitutional fences, is invaluable.

Neither a "rubber-stamp" nor "politically active" governor is needed. On the contrary, "textbook" conduct, like that by the late President K.R. Narayanan (who defined himself as a "citizen President"), who had the wisdom, moral courage, and political sagacity to "return" files relating to the President's Rule, twice--once, to the United Front government trying to dismiss a BJP state government, and again to the NDA government, seeking to remove a RJD government in Bihar--in both cases, given the strict impartiality, and "textbook" adherence to the egalitarian spirit of the Constitution, no taint of individual or political bias were attributed to the constitutional conscience-keeper.

The Bihar Chief Minister, Nitish Kumar, has raised a valid point in pre-aligning chief ministers on gubernatorial appointments, purely from the perspective of healthy Centre-State ties, the dignity of the post, and the respect for decisions taken by the constitutional head of the state.

These points are in conformity with the ignored and forgotten portions of the Sarkaria Commission report. The operative words in Nitish Kumar's pitch was "transparency" and "consultation", which are reminiscent of the 1969 trust deficits in the Centre-State relationships.

Now, with judicial intervention leading to the restoration of Opposition-led governments in Dehradun, and Itanagar, the Centre has an opportunity to mend fences, and walk the talk on "cooperative federalism", and indeed on the BJP's claims to be a "party with a difference".

Lessons from Itanagar

(ASIAN AGE/DECCAN CHRONICLE, 30 Dec 2015)

Arunachal Pradesh is no ordinary state, it is a hyper-sensitive bone of diplomatic contention with China, and with the winds of local insurgency sweeping the Northeast, it is also susceptible to errors of omission and commission on the free-flowing, democratic, and constitutional impulses of the border state. History is replete with unfortunate instances of playing partisan politics, and compromising on constitutional freedom (e.g., Jammu and Kashmir in the '80s and '90s), which tend to trigger local separatist tendencies in the veritable tinderbox of any border state. Therefore, it is even more important to demonstrate our finest constitutional commitment and guarantees, as a nation, to ward of any external and internal questions on the correctness of all political, and executive actions.

The gubernatorial disquiet in Arunachal Pradesh begets a more profound inquiry than the one that often gets mired in the legalities, and technicalities, of constitutional articles and clauses. J.P. Rajkhowa was the preferred choice of the prevailing political dispensation at the Centre, and therefore chosen to replace the incumbent midterm, as the 19th governor of Arunachal Pradesh. Questions were raised at the time about an Assamese in the Itanagar Raj Bhawan, given the fractious sentiment and scepticism of the Arunachalese, with regard to Assam, and its unresolved border disputes that are felt locally to be even more important, than the ones with China on the McMahon Line.

However, every Central government is in its democratic right to select, and appoint, the person it deems most appropriate to uphold the tenets and spirit of the Indian Constitution, and rise beyond partisan politics. Thus, the filter of not selecting an incumbent from the state, or one who has participated in active politics recently, and might have ideally detached him/herself from the local politics of the state.

However, the filter is not fool proof and it allows for an incumbent who can still "manage" or "influence" local politics, whilst ticking all the points in the filter box. Each and every party since Independence has been guilty of facilitating such appointments. The incumbents toe the political line of those to whom they owe their appointment, instead of ensuring the loftiness of being the constitutional conscience keeper of politics in a state. The *impasse* in Itanagar needs to be contextualised, and evaluated from this prism of determining whether any active role was played by the governor in helping the principal Opposition party in the state--the Bharatiya Janata Party (also the ruling party at the Centre)--to foment trouble against the Congress, the ruling party in the state.

So the question begs the point: Did the governor know the import of summoning a three-day Winter Session, without the state government recommending the same or making the Deputy Speaker "chair" the "session"? Article 174 ostensibly empowers the governor to summon, and also prorogue the Assembly, and decide timing and cancellation. However, it needs to be read in context of the legally established position via various judgments, requiring the governor's conduct to be in line with the "advice" of the chief minister, and his Council of Ministers of the state (as long as they are not compromising the constitutional correctness by way of their "advice"). It would be politically naïve, and highly improbable of the governor to be unaware of stirring the political hornet's nest, when pro-actively supporting the partisan stand of Congress dissidents.

Not surprisingly, the Arunachal Pradesh Chief Minister, Nabam Tuki, took the matter to court on the constitutional validity of Mr Rajkhowa's orders, and was able to extract a "stay" on the gubernatorial "over-reach" by way of "partisan" decisions, willy-nilly establishing the questionable and overtly political moves, *prima facie*. Perhaps, the temptation of the local Arunachal Pradesh politics, and intra-party intrigues of the Congress, had opened the window of opportunity to destabilise the incumbent Congress chief minister and embarrass the grand old party. This episode should not be assessed in terms of the adequacy or legality of constitutional clauses, but the adequacy of the constitutional spirit (which mandates a certain political aloofness and sobriety).

The questions, as to the urgency of certain gubernatorial actions, which would have precipitated a political crisis remain unanswered, thereby bringing the governor's office to question, who, like the proverbial Caesar's wife ought to be above suspicion!

There is a fine difference between the "active" dispensing of a constitutional responsibility, like that of a President/governor, and a "political" role--the opposite of a "rubber-stamp" office is not necessarily, "politically active".

One of India's foremost Presidents, K.R. Narayanan was an epitome of constitutional balance and correctness, when he unfailingly acted on the aid and advice of the Union Cabinet (a Congress appointee, he served the majority of his term with the BJP at the Centre), yet expressed his mind whenever he felt the constitutional spirit was compromised, without going public or becoming an activist, which would have undermined his constitutional role and visible conformity.

He made his point politely, when refusing presidential assent, returning them for "reconsideration", the moral burden of which ensured the requisite correction or acquiescence. Recently, in the wake of the Dadri lynching, and the subsequent downplaying by the prevailing political dispensation, President Pranab Mukherjee's astute and sobering comment of "tolerance (being) core to India's survival", had the requisite impact and received acknowledgement from the government.

In the case of the crisis in Arunachal Pradesh, one does not suggest gubernatorial "inaction" or "rubber-stamp", but the need for incumbents who bring back the much needed constitutional succour, relief, and guarantee to the state constituents in an increasingly divisive, fragmented, and politically short-sighted environment. There are enough socio-economic challenges, security issues, and burdens of history for India to overcome--seeing that no one exploits the same internally or externally, requires a wise man/ woman to rise beyond political partisanship--and it must be ensured that the path to constitutional and democratic adherence remains protected.

The Road to 2019

(TRIBUNE, 7 Apr 2017)

According to all surveys, anecdotal accounts and electoral results, Prime Minister Modi currently leads the popularity stakes, even as he nears the third anniversary of the 16th Lok Sabha. The recent State Assembly results, including the billing to the proverbial "semi-final", to the general election in 2019, in the state of UP, has seen the incumbent Central government tide over the impact of demonetisation. Former CM of J&K, Omar Abdullah, went as far as to tweet, "In a nutshell, there is no leader today with a Pan-India acceptability who can take on Modi & the BJP in 2019". However, behind the ostensible success rate of anointing governments in four out of the five states that went to elections, lurks some pointers that posit an alternative enquiry; Is the approval rating for the ruling dispensation infallible or unsurmountable? Not necessarily.

Besides the statistical reality of the Congress overcoming the incumbency factor by still retaining the most number of seats in Manipur (after 15 years of continuous rule), snatching defeat from the jaws of victory in Goa, with more law-makers than the ultimately successful BJP in Panaji, and romping home in Punjab; the undisputable "tsunami" in UP has to be contextualised within the flicker of contrarian statistics, in three other states. True, the "Captain's knock" and the "Openers" sheet-anchor role in Punjab offered credible faces in popular imagination, unlike in UP, where the Congress displayed a night watchman's batting inelegance in offering a credible alternative. Ultimately, winning 419 out of the 690 seats in the electoral sweepstakes was the most decisive indicator of the prevailing Modi-BJP wave, three-fifth into their tenure.

Gallup poll indicates that it typically takes over two years in the US to reach majority disapproval: it took Bill Clinton 573 days, Ronald Reagan 727 days, Barack Obama 936 days, and surprisingly, George W. Bush 1,205 days (presumably on account of his "fight back" against terror, post 9/11). Incidentally, Donald

Trump smashed the record by reaching "majority disapproval" within eight days of assuming presidency!

Constituents give the governments the initial benefit of the doubt, and the more strident and "nationalistic" the fervour (think George W. Bush's uber-Texan drawl invoking, "you are either with us or against us"), the more long-lasting the honeymoon. The second half of the governmental tenure normally sees a more nuanced assessment, factual debate, and the onset of dispassionate conversations that are bereft of the initial hype. Hard numbers validating economic prudence, and the upswing in most of the social indicators explained the emotional call for a "third term", for both Clinton and Obama (despite the "disruptive" narrative of personal misdemeanour in the case of the former, and the perennial angularity of minority race, for the latter). Invariably, the last leg gets more real and stripped of seductive jingoism--George W. Bush ultimately slid away from public memory as the hard reality and implications of his muscular approach sunk in.

India, in 2019, will similarly do a more rigorous assessment of the various political alternatives for the next five years. The ability to window-dress figures and repeat fantastic promises are usually at their lowest towards the end of tenures--undeniably, other factors like individual personality "brands", and perception of national leadership impact the voting preferences. Yet, the political agenda and philosophy of any ruling party gets thoroughly re-tested after a patient time frame of five years, and a hard evaluation of delivery against promises.

Here, a clear governance test between UP and Punjab could emerge as an important lodestar for the national narrative. Both states have the scale and profile to postulate the two divergent and principal political alternatives (individually, or even collectively as UPA or NDA). Both have won a clear political mandate to posture as the "political pilots" for the rest of the country--neither of the states is constrained with any coalition issues. From a raja to a yogi, the personality contest is also as colourful as it gets--in Punjab, the victor was "to the manor born", who earned his literal stripes as a "Captain" in the Indian Army, whereas in UP, the "outsider" was born a commoner, but earned his right to political divinity as a "yogi". Beyond these cheeky monikers, the acid test of displayed governance would have earned its two years of invaluable and incontestable report card, which ought to be the critical deciding factor between the two principal political alternatives, more than the initial flashy moves which are designed to please the core cadres.

Both states are in dire straits of economic and social deprivation; if it is about the drugs menace in one, it is about social disintegration in the other. Opening moves from both the state leaders were expectedly cavalier, yet the long road to 2019 will be peppered with the litmus test of managing the "palace intrigues" in both Lucknow, and Chandigarh, where a lot of enemies would be within their own ranks, as indeed from outside, wishing to disrupt the "political pilots". Leaders in both states are decisive and firm, and not necessarily known to kowtow to the "high command", but herein, could emerge the true test of political philosophies and their ultimate deliverables in a diverse country like India, with its myriad socio-economic challenges.

Interim state elections in 2018 (Gujarat, Nagaland, Karnataka, Meghalaya, Tripura and Himachal) would be reflective of the topical sentiment, then. However, the time assigned to these new state governments would be too short to make cases for political preferences in the 17th Lok Sabha elections, in 2019. Political eyes are already fixated on UP and Punjab, for the promises of a truly vibrant and prosperous Punjab, or the peaceful and progressive UP, to be delivered. These would go longer than any chest-thumping, sloganeering, or bravado that is typically deployed before and after each state win, or defeat, by all parties. The land of the five rivers, and the fertile Gangetic plains will narrate their own unaided and true narratives of political deliverables emanating from two opposite political philosophies, which could hold the key to capturing the national imagination and deciding the political choices for 2019.

Where were the Millennial Issues?

(MILLENNIUM POST, 23 Mar 2017)

The generation of Millennials (born (roughly) between 1980 and 2000) are said to be redefining the world in the form of base expectations, inspirations, and actions. As a generational force, the impact of the Millennial generation is being felt in the evolving societal framework (especially in the cultural, corporate, and commercial space). Given their chronological bearing that makes them eligible for voting (18 years), the recent State elections in the five states were expected to reflect some sort of a political espousing, posturing, and issue-clustering that perhaps reflects the constituency of the Millennials. But did it? The civic idealism, pragmatism, tech-savviness, and impatience with the status quo, which defines the Millennial mind is at stark variance with the existing rigidities in the narrative of all political parties in India.

The simplistic bogey of "youth" politics is an insufficient equivalent of the more profound instincts of the Millennials, who put a premium on "new ideas" and not just the much-bandied "age" of the candidates. The recent Presidential elections in the US showed that the Millennials in the Democratic Party overwhelmingly preferred a 75-year-old Bernie Sanders to a younger, Hillary Clinton. It was not the age, but the spirit of inherent "liberality" that is associated with the politics of Bernie Sanders, which swung the choice (28 per cent of Millennials describe themselves as "liberals", as compared to 21 per cent for both the "Gen X", and the "Baby Boomers"). Even though, over 24 million Millennials voted in the final leg and the majority of them voted for Hillary Clinton instead of Donald Trump, yet the result swung in favour of the Republican nominee, perhaps explaining the current restiveness amongst the Millennials, in the American mainstream.

In India, echoes of "development" politics did find indirect cues, from Samajwadi Party's, "*Kaam bolta hai*" and, "*Vikas ka Paiya, Akhilesh Bhaiya*", to BJP's, "*Saath aayen, parivartan layen, kamal khilayen*", to BSP's, "*Betiyon ko muskurane do, Behnji ko aane do*". Yet, these were essentially insipid, personality-linked, and lacked new themes that could be considered transformative for the Millennials. Similarly, Akali Dal's, *"Raj nahi, sewa"*, or even the more contemporary AAP's, *"Saada Khwaab Navaa Punjab"*, were equally vacuous and generic for a generation that seeks fresh and vivid thoughts, and concrete plans. Unfortunately, the accompanying political discourse in these state elections was at its lowest with innuendoes and direct attacks that ensured polarisation, divisiveness, and personality vilification.

Often, the Millennials are uncharitably described as disinterested and disconnected from the political mainstream, whereas, the spirit of civic activism that is at the heart of their social disposition is knowingly, or unknowingly, intensely political; albeit, not in the conventional sense. However, it is important to realise that the Millennials don't think that the formal governmental-political structure is the only way of partaking in their civic responsibilities. So, no political party or individual spoke the Millennial language or can claim to own the Millennial heartland--it was the more familiar undertones of casteist, religious or "nationalist" credentials that were routinely invoked. Metaphors of *"suit-boot-ki-sarkar"* or, *"kabaristan-shamshaan ghaat"* or even, *"tilak-taraju-aur-talwar"* are as antiquated and retrograde, as can be.

Clearly, the Millennials in India are not a composite and bankable political constituency, as yet-- reflective of the rural and urban divide in popular aspirations-- that has not bridged the gap between "India" and "Bharat", unlike the West, where the Millennials are more homogeneous in their political thought. Transparency, responsiveness, and accountability are the leitmotifs of the conventional Millennial generation. Whereas, all our current political parties are perennially prone to palace intrigues, platitudes, and shifting-of-blame. The quintessential Indian refrain of resorting to "it's a political conspiracy or *chaal*", at the first instance of getting caught, is reflective of the yawning gap in philosophies of the mainstream political parties, and those of the Millennial mind-set. Also, the current politicos benefit from the transitory phases of Millennial emotions and concerns--if the horrific "Nirbhaya" case resulted in massive outpouring onto the streets in 2014, the stark reality of the underspent "Nirbhaya" budgets in 2016, barely warranted a Millennial outrage.

In an era of rising intolerance, the modes of communication (especially, social media) to express Millennial dissent or a contrarian view is susceptible to immediate retaliation, clamp-down, and shaming by the powers-that-be. The famed "argumentative Indian" is giving way to the hyper-nationalist-Indian, who brooks no alternative to the regimented outlooks. Even the initial "disruptive" appeal of the AAP in traditional politics (born out of a modern civic movement), which was rooted in political iconoclasm, and the unabashed celebration of "today" (e.g., promise of free Wi-Fi), as opposed to the usual optics of defending any contentious history, icons, or past actions, has over time morphed into the morass of "sameness", which hardly distinguishes AAP politics from that of most other political parties. The initial promise of "social change" that was decoded enthusiastically by the auto-drivers, housewives, slum dwellers, and the bored middle class, has become desultory with the ineffectiveness of its "street-politics", which has defined the imagery of AAP, without effecting tangible benefits or change. So, it was yet again the victory of fear and hate over free thought and new ideas.

However, the next round of national elections in 2019 will have the bulk of voters with no personal recollection of landmark events like the partition, emergency, 1984 riots, or even notions of a once-peaceful Kashmir. This history-agnosticism can be both positively transforming and dangerous, as the Millennials will be spared the memories of history, which are sometimes important to remember, and sometimes, to forget. Hopefully, the future agenda and manifestos of the political parties would have to incorporate the Millennial flavours of "today", and not one that constantly invokes the ghosts of the "past". Sadly, the recent elections were essentially a blast-from-the-past, and the Indian hinterland reverberated to the same old tunes. The more evolved concepts, ideas, and agendas of the Millennial generation were essentially missing, as they have perhaps not yet become politically meaningful, and relevant to the current politics of India.

Much more than the first Dalit President of India
(TRIBUNE, 1 July, 2017)

Amidst the ongoing clamour for "Dalit" presidential credentials, the politically symbolic tag of the "first Dalit President of India", is an inadequate and insufficient legacy for the erudite man from Kottayam district, who personified the idyllic, "Indian Dream". KR Narayanan, the 10th President of India, dignified the highest office of the land and embellished its pluralistic, inclusive, and democratic instincts, way beyond the calculus of his "Dalit" identity. The latter had realistically secured his nomination to the Rashtrapati Bhawan, and made his selection, ironically, "untouchable" (securing 95 per cent favourable votes in the Electoral College).

From being the favourite student of the legendary Professor Harold Laski at the London School of Economics, to joining the Indian Foreign Services at Jawaharlal Nehru's behest, the intrinsic genius in Narayanan saw him serve as India's Ambassador to Thailand, Turkey, and the very sensitive China. Academically inclined, he later taught at the Delhi School of Economics, and then shone as the Indian Ambassador to the US and finally, as the Vice Chancellor at Jawaharlal Nehru University. His political journey was no less impressive. Winning his moral stripes as the "clean politician", he won three consecutive Lok Sabha elections, and then got elected to the constitutional appointment of the Vice President of India. With an unmatched CV like that, arguably the most cerebral, humble, and statesman-like President of India ever, he is still popularly remembered along with the political prefix of the "First Dalit President".

The fiercely independent-minded scholar and diplomat, nuanced India's social awakening, economic emergence, and the accompanying political tumult in the restive 1990's with gentle assertion. He defied notions of a "rubber stamp" President, albeit with unwavering constitutional equanimity. He alluded to the changing atmospherics of the office when he stated, "My image of a President is a working President, not an executive President, but a working President, and working within the four corners of the Constitution." He very presciently alluded to the moral angularity that the "conscience-keeper" brought, "There is a subtle influence of the office of the President on the executive and the other arms of the government and on the public as a whole".

He exercised his discretionary powers in setting many reformatory precedents, like insisting on "letters of support" before deciding the right to form the government, voting when in chair, personally intervening in the efforts to mitigate tensions with China after the second Pokhran Test, and insisting on independently expressing views, which were sometimes contrary to that of the ruling dispensation of the day. He elevated the stature of the office from being merely ceremonial, to one befitting the first citizen of India. The depth of his comprehension of the societal, international, economic, and political landscape expectedly put a moral reign and perspective on matters which till then were expected to be parroted from the "advice" hand-outs of the government. His classic interventionist trait came forth in the speech he gave to the visiting US President Bill Clinton, when he profoundly and prophetically chided the hegemonistic attitude of the Americans. He said, "As an African statesman has observed to us, the fact that the world is a global village does not mean that it will be run by one village headman", and then called the bluff of the lecturing and alarmist US government, which had earlier suggested that Kashmir had become the "most dangerous place of earth," by stating, "It has been suggested that the Indian sub-continent is the most dangerous place in the world to-day, and Kashmir is a nuclear flash-point. These alarmist descriptions will only encourage those who want to break the peace and indulge in terrorism and violence".

No spring chicken on the topical matters of the time and their implications, Narayanan graciously chiselled and propounded the constitutional Indian stand, without any bluster, bravado, or political taint. Though the activist "spoke" his mind, often to the discomfiture of the political classes; importantly, no political party could, or ever did, complain of any political bias or favour.

The gentle colossus was acutely aware, and sensitive, to the social ignominies and tribulations that he personally, and the millions of other deprived Dalits routinely faced. He would channelize and invest his hurt and concern in the genuine hope of changing India. He believed his life journey reflected the transformation, "That the nation has found a consensus for its highest office in someone who has sprung from the grass-roots of our society and grown up in the dust and heat of this sacred land is symbolic of the fact that the concerns of the common man have now moved to the centre stage of our social and political life. It is this larger significance of my election rather than any personal sense of honour that makes me rejoice on this occasion". There was no demonstrated bitterness, violent undertones, or couched political threats implied in his "Dalit" identity. It was a matter of plain reality, and one that he disallowed to be milked politically, and morally.

Ignoring a handful of exceptions, the hallowed office of the Indian President has withstood the overtly-politicised, and polarised environment of the day. Even though, most incumbents have had a political past--their subsequent avatar as the first citizen has been credibly non-partisan, and beyond the regression and decay of the political classes, and compulsions. While the Presidential elections are a wholly political process; yet, it is amongst the very few institutions that have exemplified the sobriety, dignity, and correctness of constitutional conduct. Political and social identities like "Dalit", need not be the defining identity, constraints, or leitmotifs of Presidential tenures. The call of the day is to ensure that like the "first Dalit President", it is the constitutional spirit, wisdom, and stature that ought to define the President of India, and not just the "Dalit" identity.

Societal Commentary

The (un)social Media

(MILLENNIUM POST 30 April 2017)

Trust is the single most significant casualty in Kashmir. Trust-deficit amongst the various stakeholders is manifesting in the ongoing battle of the "online" domain. Social media is equally an instrument of empowerment, as it is, of abuse. The concept of "sousveillance" which entails the recording and the subsequent public mainstreaming of an activity, by a participant (or witness) to an activity, is the latest weapon in Kashmir to ensnare the opponent, amongst the conflicting parties. The recent "Arab Spring" saw an invaluable role of the social media in shaping the contentious street debates that facilitated the "mobilisation, empowerment, shaping opinions, and influencing change". The demonstrated ability of the social media to instigate, inflame, or activate public opinion is beyond doubt.

Moral outrage was the standard currency of exchange, when a video surfaced showing armed CRPF *jawans* maintaining utmost restraint in the face of constant heckling and extreme provocation by Kashmiri youths. Similarly, videos of a Kashmiri stone-pelter tied to an army jeep as a "human shield", against further mob frenzy, is an exact opposite optic of the ground situation. Both incidents are realities of the ground situation, which get contextualised differently depending on whose side of the argument, one is. However, in a conflict zone that has already borne an internet sensation in Burhan Wani, the expanded use and abuse of social media is inevitable. The accompanying "morality play" is the reflexive and reductive consequence of these situational posts that go "viral", and find themselves on public platforms like WhatsApp, Twitter, Facebook, and other means of "forwards" that are then given a more expanded context. Immediately, the binary of "us versus them" plays out from Kanyakumari to even Peshawar, with justifications of individual perspectives that readily invoke rationales of uber-patriotism, secessionism, or hopelessness.

However, terrorism in a "moral state" like India is a complex business that necessitates almost utopian demands on the security forces, in the face of deathly danger; whilst, suggesting a certain "accommodation" and "understanding" of the provocative and deadly acts, by the "misguided youth". That these "misguided youth" have no Geneva Convention or moral grandstanding to honour, invariably leads to a societal angst, and ire, which divides opinions on the security forces in the country. This "online battle" in the Valley is an unequal one with the scales tilted strongly in favour of the militants versus the security forces, as the soldiers have an operational code-of-conduct, national/international policies and considerations, and even certain institutional instincts that invariably ties-back one hand of the soldier in the Valley. Adding to the pent up pressure on the "Sword-Arm" of the executive (i.e., Armed Forces), is the mandated "silence" following any act, operation, or situation that leaves the institution virtually voiceless in the face of a public barrage of questions and perceptions. The political executive, especially in the Kashmir Valley is the last to stand-up for any operational consideration of the security forces; this, unfortunately leaves the field to the equally regressive hyper-nationalists to defend the Forces on social media platforms. The misplaced and politicized logic that they assume, wrongfully postures their personal opinions as the perspective of the security forces.

The reality is that the Chief of the Indian Army Staff has actively engaged in discussions with the Governor, Chief Minister of J&K, NSA, besides his own top brass to take stock of the situation. A prudent assurance to take timely action against the personnel is delicately nuanced with an unmistakable steel in his words, when he echoes the denominator principle, "The local youth should understand the security forces are showing restraint, which should not be misconstrued as weakness. Instead, the security forces are showing patience and are giving them an opportunity to shun violence". To say any less or to the contrary would have equated the Armed Forces to the "misguided youth", on human rights violations--this is a consistent and unequivocal canon of the Indian Army, to uphold the tenets of a "moral state". While the Indian Army "saved" the lives of the trapped paramilitary personnel in the "human shield" incident, they also faced the parallel ignominy of a FIR registered against the involved unit. The Army has rightfully clarified that it does not approve of the tactic deployed in the incident. It is aware of the selective umbrage expressed by the valley politicians, every time a soldier errs. If anything, the Army is paying the price for political mismanagement that goes back many decades, and accounts for political parties of all denominations, without exception.

Political engagement and rapprochement is clearly missing from the Valley--Kashmir is not a "military" creation, and neither does it have a "military" solution, solely. It is important for the state to remember that the Indian Armed Forces (unlike Pakistan) do not have an independent "will" of their own other than that of the government. The institution has a formal system of redressal and penalty whenever an act of omission or commission occurs. Contrary to the voices of jingoism, the Armed Forces do not take a political or personal stand on any issue. It is a professional body that is designed for kinetic operations, subject to already laid down conditions. In Kashmir, the Armed Forces have an extremely disadvantageous position of partaking in operations for which they are not fundamentally designed (where the administration, politicians, and police forces have already thrown in the towel), where the local politicians make ingenious commentary on the Forces, and the locals make the Indian soldier the leitmotif of their frustrations. Yet, the model conduct that warrants certain behavioural action like officers leading from the front, explains why, unlike any other Armed Forces (including US, Russia, Israel, or UK), the "officer-to-soldier" fatality ratio is the highest for the Indian Army; but, errors happen, and they are not condoned by the institution, even if there could be a contextual justification (as in the "human shield" case).

It is this unwavering and almost inhuman existence by the Indian soldier that needs recognition. "Online battles" are a new reality that will only increase, but it is not just the stone-pelter who has failed the Indian soldier--it is the local politician, the administrator, and the state police officials who have allowed the situation to deteriorate to such an extent, that the last man standing in the *Olive-Green* is expected to hold-up to the exacting standards, when everything else around him has failed. While this is how it should be, neither the "state" nor the "misguided youth" (or their benefactors on both sides of LoC) can claim a record remotely close to that of the Indian soldier, despite wrongs like the incident of the "human shield", which get more than their share of screen and mind space.

Hero Worship
(ASIAN AGE & DECCAN CHRONICLE, 27 Apr 2016)

The dustbowl districts of Bhiwani, Sonepat, and Hisar in Haryana are the inexplicable factories of fine sportswomen, and sportsmen who are rewriting conventional theories about Indians underperforming in "power" sports like boxing (think Vijender Singh, or Vikas Yadav), wrestling (Geeta Phogat, or Yogeshwar Dutt), "urban" sports like badminton (Saina Nehwal), mountaineering (Santosh Yadav), and even cerebral sports like chess (Anuradha Beniwal from a small tehsil, Meham) to name a few sports, and even fewer sportspersons.

Providentially, even the latest toast of the nation, Dipa Karmakar, attributes her success to an ex-Army physical instructor Dalip Singh, from Haryana, for training and shaping her prowess in gymnastics.

Whether it is the sweaty pugilists in India's "Little Cuba" (i.e., Bhiwani), or the ultra-disciplined, *shakti-bhakti-brahmacharya* abiding wrestlers, in dilapidated *akhadas* in the rural hinterland-- their devotion, singular focus, and commitment to sport is almost inhuman, and sacred.

Emanating from such a furnace of challenges, is the lament of Yogeshwar Dutt against the frivolous appointment of a Bollywood star, as the goodwill ambassador of the Indian contingent at Rio Olympics--a 140-character tirade does not come naturally to a sportsman who typically prefers to let medals do the talking, especially in an "unglamorous" sport like wrestling.

Yogeshwar rightfully pondered, "What is the purpose of an ambassador. Stop fooling the people of this country." This is not posturing for publicity. This comes from someone who has won the gold in Asian Games, gold in Commonwealth Games and, even rarer, an individual medal in the holy grail of sports, the Olympics. He was the Bronze winner in 2012 London Summer Olympics. The dismay of the sporting fraternity got echoed in the haunting tweet by

Yogeshwar, "Big sports stars like P.T. Usha, Milkha Singh worked hard for the country in tough conditions. What has this ambassador done for sport?"

Importantly, the point raised was beyond emotions, and rooted in facts. Salman Khan was named the brand ambassador of football in 2009 by the All India Football Federation (AIFF). Though the efficacy, commitment, and contribution of Salman is not necessarily reflected in the global ranking of India at 162, as per the latest FIFA ranking (below countries like São Tomé and Príncipe or, nearer home, Afghanistan), the grouse is about the lack of any visible efforts by Salman to popularise the game for which the ambassadorship was bestowed.

This raises questions about the choice made by the Indian Olympic Association (IOA) president N. Ramachandran, and his defence of Salman being picked as the Olympic ambassador when he said, "When he talks about it, millions of people who do not follow sport will also take note of it." History is clearly not supportive of such a simplistic hope!

India's sporting icon (sometimes *enfant* terrible for the authorities, for calling a spade a spade) Milkha empathised with Yogeshwar's stand and tweeted, "IOA has taken wrong decision. We don't need any ambassador. Sportsmen representing nation in Rio Olympics 2016 are our ambassadors. IOA shouldn't have made a Bollywood person ambassador for sports event." Coming from someone who has gone through many tribulations to emerge as a world-class athlete, Milkha's concern was brushed aside by a graceless tweet from Salim Khan in defence of his son, "Milkhaji it is not Bollywood, it is the Indian Film Industry, and that too the largest in the world-- the same industry that resurrected you, preventing a veteran athlete from fading into oblivion." This is unmistakable hubris against the sporting fraternity.

Given the dismal contribution by Salman to an earlier sporting ambassadorship, Yogeshwar alluded to the commercial aspects of the need to differentiate between truly representing and supporting sports, versus, the act of promoting impending movie launches (Salman's upcoming movie "Sultan" has him playing a wrestler). The major beneficiary of such an ambassadorial arrangement is therefore clearly the Bollywood star, and not the sport or sports people. Adding to the questionable selection are the multiple cases in which Salman is accused, some with serious charges like a hit and run case, poaching of black bucks, and many other disciplinary issues, including strange comments about Yakub Memon and 26/11, only to retract and apologise subsequently; together, they betray a sense of the lack of responsible public conduct.

There is a precedent of cross-category ambassadors with mixed results--the Indian Defence Forces too, give honorary ranks to eminent sportsmen, and others. It is both a recognition, and a responsibility that is accorded to the awardee, to dignify the uniform with a certain conduct and commitment. Someone like Mahendra Singh Dhoni personifies the ideal ambassadorship, as he wears his military uniform as a badge of honour with much aplomb and respect, and not just on ceremonial occasions. To his credit, Dhoni went the extra mile, and trained with his parent para-commando regiment in Agra.

His honesty towards the Indian Forces is clear when he says, "It's a real honour as I always wanted to be part of the Indian Army. It's (joining the Army) something that I always wanted to achieve as a kid and now that I have donned the *olive greens*, my dream has been fulfilled."

This is in sharp contrast to the other equally gifted (if not more) cricketer, who has been made a member of the Rajya Sabha. His contribution (even in the limited domain of sports or youth affairs) remains negligible with low attendance, treating the responsibility and honour like membership in an elite private club.

It is this inconsistency of behaviour, and lack of commitment by an individual towards an institution or a cause, which rankles as their suitability to be an "ambassador".

The reaction to Salman being made the Indian Olympic contingent's goodwill ambassador has little to do with the practice of cross-category nominations, though there is merit in Milkha's line of "sportspersons only for sports", especially in a country like India where assorted politicians, and corporates are known to have treated sports bodies like personal fiefdoms; therefore, the need to purge out elements that have nothing to do with sports.

The film industry has a distinct role, responsibility, and unquestionable mass appeal in the Indian context. However, this does not lend it automatic legitimacy and credentials for being ambassador-worthy only on the basis of stardom. A certain qualitative aspect, and moral optics pertaining to institutional sensitivities, need to be considered before extending ambassadorship; therefore, the angst and ire from our real heroes.

90 Votes of Conscience

(THE CITIZEN, 17 Mar 2017)

The Malom Makha Leikai incident on November 2, 2000, resulted in 10 deaths. It was followed by the "world's longest hunger strike" by an individual, in protest against the Armed Forces Special Powers Act (AFPSA), from November 5, 2000, till July 26, 2016.

Irom Sharmila or the "Iron Lady of Manipur", launched a Gandhian *satyagraha* seeking the revocation of the AFSPA, instead of choosing the usual Manipuri narrative of launching yet another armed group (till date, over half of the 60 banned terror groups in India, are Manipur-centric).

The fast-unto-death that lasted nearly 16 years saw Irom Sharmila getting force-fed, and arrested, multiple number of times under IPC Section 309, wherein "attempt to commit suicide" is punishable, "with simple imprisonment for a term which may extend to one year (or with fine, or with both)".

The fiery cauldron of Manipur is the wounded legacy of local perceptions, which reminisce the "forcible annexation" of Manipur in 1949! This lingering perception, coupled with myriad ethnicities living cheek-by-jowl in an impermanent truce, is always susceptible to flare ups and bloodbaths.

Ethnic militias clamouring for "independence", also claim forcible space and bounty, from amongst the people, and each other; resulting in frequent violence that is equally directed against the Defence Forces, as indeed amongst themselves. The AFSPA, which grants special powers to the Defence Forces in "disturbed areas", has become the emotive signpost of local protests against the Armed Forces, and the sovereign.

The "Prisoner of Conscience", as Irom Sharmila has been described by Amnesty International, was already involved in many peace movements prior to the Malom Makha incident, and it was only natural for a peacenik like her to idolize and subsequently, invoke Mahatma Gandhi, at the Raj Ghat.

During her over-500 weeks of fasting, she routinely met and courted social activists, and politicians, in order to muster public pressure against the AFSPA--her self-denials included not combing her hair, looking in the mirror, going to her home or even meeting her mother, before the AFSPA got repealed. Her unique form of protest led to national and international recognition, besides pricking the conscience of New Delhi to address the larger and the real issue of neglect, and integration of the North Eastern states and causes, economically, socially, and even morally. The AFSPA had acquired the most visible symbolism of stated and unstated angst.

The embers of insurgency in the North East have ebbed. Arunachal, Mizoram, Meghalaya and Tripura are almost completely peaceful, and a relative normalcy has returned to Assam from the ULFA perspective. There have been some green-shoots of hope in the state of Nagaland with the signing of the peace treaty (albeit, the composite issue of Naga insurgency is still unsettled and it often slips into Manipur, where the Tangkhul Nagas of the Ukhrul hill district add another angularity, to the ongoing struggles in Manipur).

However, Manipur has remained insurgency prone and Irom Sharmila's parallel efforts ensured that she was deified in the popular imagination, both in Manipur and outside, for her valiant and noble form of struggle and commitment, towards her cause.

However, her sudden decision to end the hunger-fast, and a simultaneous announcement of wanting to pursue a political career, was met with a collective sense of disillusionment by her supporters in Manipur, as there were whispers of her having "deviated from the goal" and of "abandoning the cause".

The father of one of the victims in the infamous Malom Makha incident said, "by choosing a political path, she has come down from the highest Himalayan peak to a hillock".

Yet, the political pundits in Delhi did not share the same sense of irrelevance for Irom Sharmila, in her new avatar, and given the impending state elections, furiously courted her to join mainstream political parties. Even though Sharmila's claim of being offered Rs

36 crores by the BJP were summarily rejected by the party, it is a fact that even the Congress Party President had sought her, "We know she is a very determined and committed person. Once she takes a decision she will stand by it. Her becoming a part of the Congress is a decision of the election committee. We will welcome her if she wishes to join our party".

Perhaps, carried away by the heady maelstrom of political headwinds, Irom Sharmila went solo and launched her own party, "Peoples' Resurgence and Justice Alliance".

In a completely unexpected come-down, she garnered only 90 votes against the winner Ibobi Singh who secured 18,649 votes. Not only was she behind the runner-up BJP candidate, who bagged 8,179 votes, and even the TMC candidate from the constituency--in a cruel twist of fate, even the NOTA ("None of the above") category got 143 votes!

Sharmila was notionally supported by the Left Democratic Front (LDF) comprising six parties including CPI, CPI(M), JD(U) and AAP, yet her decision to lead a "normal" life and join the bandwagon of the electoral process, made her constituents more irate than their supposed dissatisfaction and disgust with the existing candidates, and their political parties--somewhere, something was terribly amiss and unsurprisingly, the disheartened Irom Sharmila immediately announced her decision to quit politics.

The tragedy is not in her electoral defeat, or even in the magnitude of the loss--it is the failure of the people (both the constituents and the rest of the country) to appreciate the spirit, nature, and means of her protest.

As a military man who has served extensively in the North East, I do not agree with Irom Sharmila's deciphering of the AFSPA--this is not to condone, or brush aside any violation that may have happened. However, to state that the AFSPA is basically a "privilege" or a "perk" that is routinely abused is as untrue, as perhaps stating that acts of dereliction never happen.

Nevertheless, the Iron Lady's unwavering choice of the methods of protesting her point of view were extremely brave, commendable, and spirited--it takes a very large heart to stand up against public pressure for assuming more belligerent and violent postures, especially in Manipur.

Her civic transformation, which saw her adopting an even more conventional route of participative democracy is reminiscent of similar rapprochements, which were successfully encouraged, and yielded the much-needed peace in Mizoram and Punjab, with some who had gone so far as taking up the gun, against India.

At a fundamental level, it is the loss of a potential template for many frustrated Indians, who unfortunately transit from genuine socio-economic protests to acquiring more hostile and violent tangents. Her political success could have re-endorsed the magical formula for integration and inclusivity (e.g., for the Maoists). The fickle public charm for a tireless protester is only until sacrifice and pain is publicly endured.

Ultimately, 16 years of almost inhuman renunciation could yield only 90 votes of conscience, with nearly 30,000 other votes swaying towards the familiar appeals, and promises, of the political classes.

How "Republic" is the Day?

(MILLENNIUM POST, 24 Jan 2017)

While the definitive imagery of the Republic Day is the impressive march-past, and muscularity of the Indian Armed Forces, colourful state tableaus, and the cultural showcasing of the country, the exact reason to celebrate the Republic Day of India remains a bit nebulous. Increasingly, the critical conversations veer around the relevance of the ordained pomp and show, as indeed of the construct, costs, participants, and the length of the proceedings. However, the real question about celebrating "Republic" Day (one of the only two national holidays that are singularly ascribed to the nation and not to an individual, religion, or culture), pertains to the candid assessment of what defines a "Republic", worth celebrating in India, and where we stand on that lodestar. India's tryst as a "Republic" started on Jan 26, 1950, when the Indian Constitution came into effect (it was adopted earlier on 26 November 1949).

The term "Republic" is multi-dimensional, varied, and expansive--from mandating a democratic framework of participative democracy, to the exclusion of vassalage or monarchist denominations, to even necessitating the character of inclusivity, and the universality of the rule of law. In India, the symbolism of Republic Day is in celebrating the unifying and enabling soul of the Indian Constitution, which seeks to address the challenges of diversities and disparities. It is tantamount to defining the destiny that India aspires and works towards; in essence, the supreme and inviolable codes to be honoured. Various guiding principles, statues, structures, procedures, powers, responsibilities, rights and duties of the individual, and the state, were etched out to protect our future from any potential deviations. Even the supposed collective will of the people, as manifesting in the Parliament of the country, is not allowed to tinker with the national agenda and character, as envisaged in the definitive spirit of the Constitution. It ring-fences the Indian imperatives and characteristics of secularity, democracy, equality, liberty, fraternity, and sovereignty that cannot be tempered with; even by the most puritanical offshoot of democracy (i.e., majoritarianism).

This chosen path has defined and distinguished the Indian narrative from most other nations, where the absence of a similar rigour (the Indian Constitution is the world's longest) of a national document has made their evolution susceptible to the moods, and agendas, of the various ruling dispensations of the day. While the contours of conscience of the Indian "way to be", are generally outlined and protected, it retains its dynamism and breathing space to capture the specificities, interpretations, and expansions of the times that be; ensuring the unambiguous, and uninterrupted working journey of India. The "rights and duties" clearly spell out the compelling impulses and expectations for, and from, the individual, the state, the executive (various arms within), and the judiciary. Despite the multitude of unhealed wounds on the Indian journey, like internal insurgencies, historical injustices, continuing economic challenges, societal inequities, and political crises to name a few, the country has held its course, trajectory, and democratic instincts (the 1975 Emergency was an unfortunate interlude), only due to the sheet-anchor provided by the Indian Constitution. It is the intrinsic genius of the Indian Constitution, and its chosen form of destiny that we celebrate.

Therefore, in the Republic Day parade, the gallantry ceremonies, ramrod-straight marching contingents, and the roaring fighter jets are to be seen as the contextual symbols of the "Sword-Arm" of the nation, which shields this land and its onward journey "as is", from any external exigencies, and the cultural *razzmatazz* signifies the hallowed "Unity in Diversity", wherein we cherish and take pride in the innate diversity as a strength, and not seek to work in accordance of a stock template, and aim at uniformity, as is done in some governmental models across the world. Given that we subconsciously take our Constitutional promises for granted, it becomes the base prism to evaluate the performance of the various political dispensations, and allows making informed choices towards the one, which delivers and personifies the soul of the Constitution.

The election results of the General Elections, in 1977, reflected the collective angst of the electorate against the compromising of Constitutional "normalcy". Similarly, the unfulfilled rights, opportunities, and privileges of certain sections of society have manifested in the change of the electoral landscapes, parties, and outlooks. At the same time, perceptions of walking the talk, of the mandated Constitutional promises, duties and responsibilities, have ensured the repeat of certain governments (defeating the "incumbency factor"). Democratic systems enable the auto-correcting, adapting, and choosing from the various political dispensations towards the one that best promises to deliver a constitutionally safeguarded journey, and destiny.

Today, we must continuously assess our prevailing status *vis-à-vis* the benchmarks of the constitutionally ordained spirit of liberality, inclusivity, and empowerment to all. Any subjugation or selectivity of rights, privileges, and expressions vitiate and militate against the soul of the Constitution, and by that extension, the nation. In many ways, the Constitution lays a reformist agenda that breaks the historical shackles of perceptions, and glaring inequities in society--as Dr BR Ambedkar noted presciently, "Indians today are governed by two different ideologies. Their political ideal set in the Preamble of the Constitution affirms a life of liberty, equality and fraternity. Their social ideal embodied in their religion denies them". These accommodative and flexible contours of the constitution have enabled progressive and encompassing solutions, to address the various wounds and challenges, for the welfare and sovereignty of the nation. Often, short-term compromises to the Constitutional spirit are knowingly undertaken, entertained, or overlooked. However, the young history of Independent India shows that no political dispensation can milk such violations, forever.

Speaking at the joint meeting of the US Congress, Prime Minister Narendra Modi, remarked loftily, "For my government, the Constitution is its real holy book. And, in that holy book, freedom of faith, speech and franchise, and equality of all citizens, regardless of background, are enshrined as fundamental rights". Recognising this special day on which we truly embraced our destiny, and the accompanying means, we affixed the term "Republic" to India. The Republic Day parade is a powerful symbol, reiteration, and celebration of the inviolability of that sacred covenant, internally, and externally.

Walls of Distrust and Hate Threatens
the Global Village

(THE CITIZEN, 3 Nov 2016)

Marshall McLuhan's seminal concept of the "Global Village" got a fillip in the early 1990's, with the utopian innocence that followed the end of the cold war, and the boom of the internet that threatened a certain cultural, commercial, and societal morphology that could make borders irrelevant.

The fall of the Berlin Wall typified the euphoric spirit of eliminating man-made hurdles, and celebrated the triumph of collectivism, inclusivity, and interdependence. In the "us-versus-them" slugfest till then, "them" had been squarely defeated, and was on a self-destruct mode with the subsequent implosions in the vast tracts of the Caucus; the new mutations of "them" had yet to arrive.

The 1990's saw the emergence of political leadership "reaching-out" internationally, like the poet-dissenter in Vaclav Havel in Czech Republic, the "opening-up" of the economy in India by then Prime Minister, PV Narasimha Rao, the return of the democrats after 12 years in the USA, with Bill Clinton promising, "It's time to change America". Even the supposedly "rogue" nations, like Iran, saw the advent of a pragmatist-reformist in Akbar Hashemi Rafsanjani--suddenly, the days of international "Statesmanship" loomed large with the brewing prospects of a "Nehru-Tito-Nasser", on the political horizon.

The fire in the Middle East was against putative dictators and not against "Islam", as yet, and terms like "Global Highway" were eliminating commercial intermediaries, and bureaucracies; blocs like EU and ASEAN were replacing the security-treaty-led ghosts of NATO and WARSAW, with an incestuous inter-mingling that promised better days. Even in India, the reign of the principal opposition party, in the form of the right-wing and nationalistic BJP, was swerving towards the pacifism and inclusive leadership of Atal Bihari Vajpayee, as opposed to the alternative of the "Iron Man", LK Advani.

Cut to 2016--on 27 July 2016, the RCP Poll in the USA tracked a 45.7 to 44.6 lead in favour of the Republican, Donald Trump, versus the Democrat, Hillary Clinton, in the race to the most important office in the world, POTUSA. This stark reality in the ostensible "land of the free" is that it has dangerously swerved towards a man who infamously said, "I will build a great wall –and nobody builds walls better than me, believe me – and I'll build them very inexpensively. I will build a great, great wall on our southern border, and I will make Mexico pay for that wall. Mark my words". Horrifically, even today more than 40% of American populace prefers his ideology, thoughts, and approach to make America great!

This spirit of exclusivism and protectionism is sweeping across continental Europe too--growing economic disillusionment, migrant concerns, and constraints imposed by EU (e.g., Brexit) have resulted in the sudden rise of the populist, right-wing, and neo-fascist parties. Donald Trump's "America First" finds echoes in Austria's anti-immigrant and uber-nationalistic, Freedom Party that beseeches, "Austria First"!

The top 5 countries in the "Democracy Ranking" in the world that tracks the "quality" of democracy with progressive parameters are in Europe: Norway, Switzerland, Sweden, Finland, and Denmark. Without exception, all these five countries have seen a sharp turn to the extreme-right in politics, and a growing preference for the same. Even Germany's Angela Merkel vowed not to make the same "mistake" of her open door immigration policy, in a desperate bid to win back fleeing electorates. Whereas, in France, the rising star, Marine Le Pen, could potentially translate into the country's first far-right President, who promises "Frexit" and had stated that it was not possible for French-born Muslims to be "truly French", since they did not share France's Christian "traditions and values". Clearly, protectionism, xenophobia, and authoritarianism are gaining currency and empathy.

Similarly, Asia's tryst with political and cultural illiberalism is on a quagmire of unprecedented regression. From the iron-hand treatment of dissent in Turkey, religious fanaticism spanning Israel to Aceh in Malaysia, continued belligerence by the Chinese, intolerance in the Central Asian countries, to even the blatant reneging of the "special friendship" between the US, and the Philippines, where the incumbent President, Rodrigo Duterte felt it appropriate to say, "Son of a whore. I will curse you in the forum", to the US President--the winds of populism and extremity are sweeping the globe (incidentally, the approval ratings for the Filipino President is in the vicinity of 90% approval, domestically!).

This spirit is also consuming the economic realm, with the G-20 summit calling on the world community to enhance access and end protectionism, and isolationism--suddenly the populist walls of divisiveness and fearful rhetoric are choking the arteries, which lead up to the promised "Global Village".

The lines between jingoism and nationalism have blurred with secularism, intellectualism, and liberalism perceived to be political weaknesses that need to be overcome. A deep sense of insecurity and potential deprivation is giving rise to religion, exclusive protectionism, and populist policies that promise a "quick-fix" to fundamental problems.

The "left" is a dying political position, and the "centrist" is perceived to be an apologetic, meek, and irresolute philosophy--so, the need to sound confident and muscular to "deal with situations" is forcing the political leadership towards hard-right (whereas, the dispossessed often retaliate with an equally dangerous and utopian extreme-left, as in the case of the "red corridor" that runs through nearly 150 districts in the heart of India).

A latent fear of cultural, religious, and national domination is resulting in the violent reassertion of "identities" that works against the assumed "enrichment with diversity", as envisaged in a "Global Village". In such an environment even progressive cultural necessities like a "*Swadeshi*" movement, acquires a protectionist dimension instead of a celebratory or a revivalist undertone.

If communication and information were the bedrock of an integrated and inclusive "Global Village", it is the disinformation (and the rapid dissemination of the same) that is threatening the applecart of a "Global Village". Ironically, it is the very features of a participative democracy with its tenure-based outlook, which is fanning the fire of populism, and "quick fixes"--statesmanship is *passé*, and a new strain of illiberal protectionists are winning the popularity stakes; again, the walls of distrust and hatred are coming up, and the "Village" is coming apart.

Amjad Sabri Assassination – *Sabse Pak Saaf Kaun*
(THE CITIZEN, 24 June 2016)

When Choudhary Rahmat Ali published his famous pamphlet, "Now or Never", in 1933--he cleverly arranged the acronym PAKISTAN (from the first letter of the Muslim dominated regions of Punjab, Afghan region, Kashmir, Sindh and Baluchistan), which in its composite form also translated into a lofty concept, "The land of the pure", with "Pak" translating into "Pure" in both Persian and Urdu.

Today, competitive-religiosity for ascertaining the "purest of the pure" is consuming and combusting the nation with extreme strains of sectarianism and puritanism to establish the Tawhid (pure monotheistic worship).

The brazen gunning down of the famous *Arifana Kalam* (mystic poetry) *Qawwal*, Amjad Sabri, in Karachi, is the latest wound in Pakistan's continued project of denial of factual history, and the ongoing attempt at rewriting its genealogical narrative.

The new history sought is a marked departure from Jinnah's syncretic instincts, when he urged Pakistanis in his famous constituent assembly speech in 1947 to feel free, "to go to your temples...mosques or any other places of worship in the State of Pakistan. You may belong to any religion or caste or creed-that has nothing to do with the business of the State".

Since then, the Pakistani landscape has regressed into an angry and extremist society, aided earlier by General Zia-ul-Haq's "Sharia-ization", Af-Pak region's "Talibanisation" and the aggressive pumping of petro-dollars from the Gulf Sheikhdoms with Wahhabi or Salafist infusions, to challenge the region's equilibrium, which was once nuanced by pacifist and mystical Sufi traditions, and are now on an accelerated retreat.

Invoking *hadiths* (questioned on authenticity by some scholars), the extreme elements declare music to be *haram* (forbidden) as,

"Those who listen to music and songs in this world, on the Day of Judgment molten lead will be poured into their ears", thus justifying violent actions on *qawwals*, Sufi shrines and Urs festivals (over 30 terrorist attacks killing over 200 people, have occurred in the last 10 years).

Even though, Amjad Sabri's murder motive has not been conclusively established as yet, *Tehreek-e-Taliban Pakistan* (TTP), the Pakistani Taliban group led by Hakimullah Mehsud, has accepted the responsibility. Giving credence to this theory is the fact that in 2014, Amjad Sabri was slapped with blasphemy charges for playing *qawwali* in a morning TV show, and mentioning some religious figures, which afforded the group a high-visibility opportunity to target a national cultural icon, with allegations of religious disrespect.

Ironically, Amjad Sabri was not a "heretic", in the Salafist sense--he was a mainstream Sunni adherent and did not belong to any of the minority sects like the Shias, Ahmediyas, Ismailis etc.

The Sabri brothers were known to be quite austere and conservative--the signature style of interspersing the *qawwali* with repeated usage of *"Allah"*, belonged uniquely to the Sabri brothers--with strong adherence and reverence to Islamic principles, and a guarded avoidance of intoxicants. *Qawwals* like Aziz Mian, were inspired by the legendary verse-play against Shia theology *(Aziz Mian's Main Sharabi was countered by (the) Sabri Brother's O Sharabi chor dey peena)*. However, even in its increasingly virulent and extremist dimension, this form of Islamic adherence was still not considered good enough, and often invited censure by the growing clout of the *Mullahs*.

The political project of the 1970's and 1980's to tactically "Arabize" the basic liberal culture of the land, mutated into a hapless and freefall retrogression, as a consequence of the *"Chaadar aur Char deewari"* (veiled behind high brick walls) dream, of Zia-ul-Haq's Pakistan. So, in a land where only 1% of the population spoke Arabic, Article 31/2 (a) of the Pakistani Constitution, now states, "The State shall endeavor, as respects the Muslims of Pakistan to make the teaching of the Holy Quran and Islamiat compulsory, to encourage and facilitate the learning of Arabic language", encouraging the replacement of the Indo-Persian influenced "Khuda Hafiz", with "Allah Hafiz". Codes and cultures of the Arabian Peninsula have been gleefully injected into the Pakistani mainstream to create an empirically false, but utopian narrative (the Hindu-Buddhist past is not even mentioned).

A similar incident occurred in 2014, when the pop star-turned-televangelist, Junaid Jamshed, of the *Tableeghi Jamaat* order, had to face blasphemy charges and publicly atone for his offensive remarks--a growing trend that often leads to vigilante justice (as in the case of the murder of the Punjab Governor, Salman Taseer by his bodyguard), or mob retribution (as in the case of Junaid Jamshed himself, who was assaulted in Islamabad airport in March this year, after onlookers discounted his earlier apology and called him *Ghustakh-e-Rasool*).

The providential sub-contracting of the cold war to Pakistan, and the Gulf-sponsored *madrassas,* often bear the sole brunt of the blame for the current societal breakdown, as postured by the Director-General Inter-Services Public Relations (ISPR), Lt. Gen. Asim Bajwa, who stated incredulously, "Pakistan has wiped out the roots of terrorists, planted by others, and we have fought the entire world's war in this region. The world then abandoned Pakistan to handle, manage and face the terrorists in the region all by itself", symptomatic of the prevailing martyr syndrome, and a nation in systemic denial.

However, Rubina Saigol, an educationalist has a more prescient and profound observation on the overall institutional failure of Pakistan, "Our state system is the biggest *madrassa*. We keep blaming *madrassas* for everything and, of course, they are doing a lot of things I would disagree with. But the state ideologies of hate and a violent, negative nationalism are getting out there where *madrassas* cannot hope to reach", therein lies the curse of all that afflicts Pakistan today. A nation that is hell-bent on rewriting a false history, and ultimately, paying the price for what that change actually entails.

The hypnotic, sonorous and soulful voice of Amjad Sabri has been muted forever, but the echoes of, "*Hai mukhaalif zamaana kidhar jaaein ham. Haalat-e-bekasi kis ko dikhlaaein ham. Ham tumhaare bhikaari hain ya Mustafa. Kis ke aage bhala haath phailaaein ham. Bhar do jholi meri Sarkaar-e-Madeena* ... (The times are against me, where should I go. To whom should I show my state of helplessness? I am your beggar, O Mustafa. In front of whom else shall I spread my hands. Fill my bag, Lord of Medina...)", are a haunting and pertinent lament of Pakistan's tryst with itself.

Regressive Phenomenon of Cults

(MILLENNIUM POST, 17 Jun 2016)

Political correctness in the West necessitates the term "New Religious Movements" (NRM) instead of "cults" to define movements that are rooted in beliefs that are contrary, or foreign, to the prevailing codes of culture. *Swadhin Bharat Vidhik Satyagrah* (Free India Legal Struggle), the Mathura-based cult which propounded the abolition of the post of President and Prime Minister, replacement of the Indian Rupee with Azad Hind Bank currency, and a host of economic illogicality's, was a mumbo-jumbo movement that mandated strict adherence to the *diktats* of faith (though, not necessarily religious).

The Indian subcontinent contributed the English term, "thugs"-- the genealogical successor of "Thugees" (Sanskrit for concealment). This cult was, arguably, the first form of professional assassins, a fanatical group that undertook ritualistic killings, ostensibly to appease Goddess Kali. For nearly six centuries (13th to 19th), this group had codified rituals and superstitions that defined their language, rules, and conduct.

Societal fault-lines, extreme poverty, and illiteracy are a potent combination to indoctrinate the vulnerable masses into a socio-spiritual-economic nirvana that invariably comes through "enlightenment" (read, blind adherence), and often, a salvation-motivated apocalyptic end. The fact that these cults have unwavering members running into millions, make them hot-currency politically, as they have the ability to decide electoral results; hence, overtly and covertly, they are tolerated and encouraged for electoral gratification

Even the cults gleefully slip into the political domain to establish their space and relevance--as Prabhat Ranjan Sarkar (or "Anandamurti" of the freakish Ananda Marg) noted, religion encompasses politics, since the state of "Ananda" (or bliss) would require a corresponding government system supporting the faith.

Hence, given in its core area of Bihar and West Bengal regions, the political spiel was understandably anti-Marxist and anti-capitalist. The patterns are eerily similar, globally--usually a "camp" of believers is led by a leader who defines the contours of the day-to-day living, and the belief system. The faith requirements soon translate into actions that put it at automatic variance with the laws of the land, and then a violent confrontation ensues between the believers, and the state apparatus. The Branch Davidian Seventh, a sect that separated from Davidian Seventh-day Adventist Church in Waco Texas, the Movement for the Restoration of the Ten Commandments of God in Uganda, and the Aum Shinrikyo in Japan are symptomatic of the doomsday cults with "salvation" as an integral promise.

The Mathura confrontation which led to 27 deaths (including an SP and an SHO), was reminiscent of the earlier Satlok Ashram infamy at Hisar (of self-styled "Godman" Rampal) who pitted his private army of "commandos" (termed, Rashtriya Samaj Sewa Samiti), armed with guns, walkie-talkies, and crude bombs against the state machinery. In Mathura, too, the police recovered 47 pistols, 184 cartridges, 178 hand grenades, and 1,000 LPG cylinders as the "commandos" prepared to take on the police. In both the cases, the infrastructure of terror was slowly but surely built up, the area around the compound was booby-trapped, and the training professional enough to cause the resultant casualties, and mayhem.

Another feature of these cults and sects is the bloody end which may or may not be completely voluntary for many adherents. The Waco stand-up between the Federal agents, and the Davidians resulted in a devastating fire inside the camp that led to 80 deaths; the "salvation" promised on the "Judgement Day" in Uganda, led to the self-immolation and poisoning of nearly 1000 followers.

Post the Mathura and Hisar clearing raids, a lot of adherents subsequently complained of being confined to the premises by the aides, and reported of multiple abuse and coercions to comply. More than 20,000 security personnel were deployed to force their way into the ashram in Hisar, and at Mathura, the police remarked, "…we did not expect such a violent reception". It is estimated that there are nearly 10,000 *deras* in the state of Punjab itself--a lot of them are implicitly peaceful, pacifist, and conform to the laws of the land. However, a few have agendas and beliefs that posit them at crossroads with the prevailing societal equilibrium, thus evolving into strident positions and electoral clusters--an attractive opportunity for political parties of all hues to pander, and perpetuate the cult's idiosyncrasies.

With the impending state elections in 2017, a beeline for blessings in favour of a particular party or candidate is priceless. Therefore, the cults and its blind followers are often brazen and oblivious to the laws, smug in the ostensible "goodness towards society" that they propound, which automatically elevates them in their own eyes, and hearts, to pedestals beyond societal concern or reproach from the mainstream or the statutes. The extremists, disgruntled elements, and the fringes of all races and religions are prone to such occults and groupings that are inherently regressive, and revanchist.

While the Constitution guarantees freedom of speech and expression (Article 19, 20, 21, and 22), it is not absolute, and there are caveats against the misuse of the same when there are risks to the security of state, public order, incitement to offence, and contempt of court. The acts of the cults like occupying governmental lands illegally, procuring arms, and with questionable acts of decency and morality (not to mention, sovereignty and integrity of the state, and its apparatus e.g., police and court judgements) are tantamount to violation of the Constitutional spirit, and expected public conduct--the court of law cannot be subservient to any other recourse, or faith. Inordinate delays that facilitate explosive situations, like Mathura, raise questions of political complicity. The Indian state has to stay visibly and perceptibly clear, and agnostic, to state benevolence or promotion of the mushrooming phenomenon of the myriad empires of the Godmen/Gurus/Clergies, and cults; this, in strict observance of the 42nd amendment of the Constitution of India (enacted in 1976), wherein the Preamble to the Constitution asserts India's secularism. The tinkering or liberties with the same lead to deadly procrastination, and fatal tolerance that ultimately manifest in the avoidable Mathura-like situations.

As India faces the Demons of Racism
(DAILY EXCELSIOR, 18 June 2016)

India is constitutionally and institutionally, liberal and democratic. Often, this is at variance with the basic instincts that emanate from a wounded civilization. Home to varied ethnicities, races, regions and a complex caste system, societal fault-lines like: racism, misogyny, bigotry etc., are irrefutable complexes, which exist subconsciously, and flare up unwantedly. Our founding fathers had the vision and humility to accept the reality of inherent diversities, thereby, pedestalling the lofty "Unity in Diversity" as an emotive lodestar. Thus, the architects of the Indian Constitution, insisted on an extraordinary spirit of national synthesis, by way of the unambiguous language of Article 14 of the constitution, which is about the "Right to Equality", where, "The State shall not deny to any person equality before the law or the equal protection of the laws within the territory of India". Even more specifically, Article 15 (1) states, "The State shall not discriminate against any citizen on grounds only of religion, race, caste, sex, place of birth or any of them". Clearly, the import of language was only for Indian citizens, but the definitive national spirit, instinct, and outlook was sought to be defined.

Unsurprisingly, our national heroes always stood up against racism--Mahatma Gandhi against the ingrained racism against "untouchables", and Nehru against political racism via the "Non-Aligned Movement". Ambedkar sowed the constitutional protection laws, while Tagore castigated the duplicity and hypocrisy of European imperialism in Africa, via literature and poetry. All the national founders stood up against racism in one form or the other. It is in this backdrop that the recent murder of a Congolese national, in the national capital, has re-triggered debate on the existence of this virulent strain of racism. The uncomfortable questions challenged our officially declared status, and sensibilities, personally and politically--ironically, for a nation that is usually at the vanguard of the fight against global racism.

Africa has had a unique place in our historical narrative, and evolution as a nation--we share the empathetic burden of a colonial past and subjugation by imperial powers. It is the land from where Malik Amber, an African Siddhi slave became the popular Prime Minister of Ahmadnagar Sultanate, where Gandhi came into his spiritual-political own, and where Ghana's Kwame Nkrumah and Egypt's Gamal Nasser jointly conceived NAM with Nehru. It is a land where Nelson Mandela and Jomo Kenyata got inspired by India's "non-violence", as a political tool. Therefore, with such a rich tapestry of joint struggles and dreams, the broken "Indian dream" for the African expatriates is a harsh reality that needs to be recognized, albeit, sensitively and in a nuanced manner.

Racism in India exists per se--it is not something that we need to live in denial of. With frequent cases of discrimination against the "other", it plays out for each minority profile in the land of majority. An Indian from the North East gets castigated as a "*Chinky*" on the streets of Delhi, whereas a North Indian is addressed as a "*Mayang*" ("outsider") in Imphal, caste panchayats routinely dole out shameful verdicts against the "others", while the tribals and religious minorities have their own trysts with the inequities of the past and present. Our xenophobia is unrestricted geographically, Indians are racist against Indians. But, importantly, racism in any form ought to be shamed and penalised by the statutes of the constitution and the law of the land. So, in that sense, India has made its choice of societal direction and preference, clear--therefore, we need to craft and present our reaction to the recent allegations of "Afro-phobia" contextually, and not with jingoism.

The External Affairs Minister, Mrs. Sushma Swaraj did well to give a sense of urgency, purpose, and importance to the incident with a decisive tone, "I have spoken to Shri Raj Nath Singhji and Lt. Governor Delhi regarding the attack on African nationals in South Delhi yesterday. They assured me that the culprits will be arrested soon and sensitization campaign will be launched in areas where African nationals reside". However, this was in sharp contrast to the line of competitive racism by the irrepressible Cultural Minister, Mahesh Sharma's, "Even Africa is not safe", an unnecessary and inelegant affront, which vitiates a healing moment. This incident follows an earlier *note verbale* from the Tanzanian High

Commission on the beating and stripping of a student in Bengaluru, in February this year, and earlier still, the infamous midnight raid in Khirki Extension, by the-then Law Minister of Delhi, Somnath Bharti, in which two Nigerian, and two Ugandan women were mobbed. This is reflective of the backdrop, and is indicative of the joint concern, and position of "Afro-phobia", taken by the Group of African Heads of Missions. Thankfully, the mature statement by the Foreign Secretary, S Jaishankar, in which he stated that the safety and security of the African community was an "article of faith", is the kind of governmental assurance that is needed at the moment, and not an unnecessary playing down of the issue, competitive racism, or outright denial. The police have swung into action and made arrests, pushing for a speedy trial and conviction, to establish a racist angle or a purely a situational angle, which will aid and build credibility of governmental action and sincerity.

More importantly, India has had a chequered history in Congo--the ONUC (*Organisation des Nations Unies au Congo*) operations in 1960-64, saw the gallant participation of two Indian infantry brigades, and six Canberra bombers of the Indian Air Force. 39 Indian soldiers died, including Captain G. S. Salaria, who was posthumously awarded the Param Vir Chakra. Even today, MONUSCO (United Nations Organization Stabilization Mission in the Democratic Republic of the Congo) has an Indian contingent, the single largest contributor to the UN peace keeping mission in Congo. Such historical precedent and historical links to the African sub-continent, led the acting High Commissioner of South Africa, Melrose William Mogale to conclude, "It's racist attacks. But it is not government policy", and further, "We have firm belief in the capacity of Indian government to deal with these incidents", thus putting balm on frayed nerves and tempers.

Even diplomatically, India has "invested" in Africa, by hosting the "Africa Summit", amongst many other initiatives--a key recognition of the 54 seats in the UN General Assembly, which could hold the key to India's global ambitions of a permanent seat in the UN Security Council. While governmental outreach, historical ties, and diplomatic positions have been aligned to further the obvious Indo-African equation, the people-to-people connect has been missing, and the complex societal moorings and intrigues, in both the multi-plural African and Indian societies, often gives way to ultra-regressive and racist tendencies (in the 70's, the Ugandan dictator Idi Amin Dada had similarly expelled the Indian community) that mar the inherent potential of the economies, people, and emerging aspirations of both the lands. Sadly, and often, the historical victims of racism, unfortunately, end up victimizing each other, as indeed practice discrimination amongst themselves. In such situations, we must accept our reality of the demons of racism, boldly, and assert corrective action with utmost sensitivity--our constitutional morality and the future of the two lands, insists that we do so.

Aya Ram, Gaya Ram Redux

(MILLENNIUM POST, 11 June 2016)

Hassanpur is a nondescript state constituency in Haryana's Vidhan Sabha, which has the notoriety of adding a deliciously nimble-footed term in Indian democracy, *"Aya Ram, Gaya Ram"* (literally, Ram comes, Ram goes!). This sneaky phrase owes it origins to the famous MLA of Hassanpur, Gaya Lal, who, in 1967, changed his political party three times in a fortnight--from the Indian National Congress to the United Front, back to the INC, and then unbelievably, in nine hours, back to the United Front!

Gaya Lal's feat did not go unrecognised, and Rao Birendra Singh, on re-inducting Gaya Lal to Congress yet again, immortalised the flighty legislator by announcing to the press, *"Gaya Ram* was now *Aya Ram"*. Interestingly, the current MLA of Hassanpur too faced anti-defection law charges, for hopping across to Congress in 2004--he is the son of Gaya Lal, Udai Bhan! Later, the trio of "Lal's" in Haryana (Bhajan, Devi, and Bansi) would oversee multiple cases of permutation and combination of legislators, to evolve the jokes on government formation to a fine art that would spread its springy practice across the country, and across all political parties. Harsher Anglo-Saxon terms like "turncoats", "rebels", and "defectors" lacks the earthy grime of Indian politics that an *"Aya Ram, Gaya Ram"* captures in its assumed gratification-inspired subtext, and tonality.

This gave birth to resultant practices like herding party MLA's to an iron-clad hotel/resort, or whisking away the flock to an undisclosed location to, "decide the future course of action" (read, avoid horse-trading). On the anointed day of voting for and against a government, the banal and ritualistic pretence of the "debate", following the crucial vote motion, is accompanied by tense moments for the respective "Whips" of the political parties, who keep shifty-eyes on any potential bolting of a *"Gaya Ram"*, from their stables.

Ideological considerations suffer temporary amnesia, as the reward for shifting sides makes the legislator and his/her constituency forgive the enthusiastic action, and a fatalistic and philosophical reasoning in the form of, "everything is fair in love, war, and politics" is rationalised. Similarly, a comic-tragedy played out in the recent vote of confidence in the Uttarakhand Assembly, where a curious case of "*Aya Arya, Gaya Arya*" levelled the score of namesakes, for the two competing political blocks. Dissident BJP MLA, Bhim Lal Arya, joined Harish Rawat's ranks in the Congress, while Rekha Arya, from the Congress, joined the BJP. Rekha Arya had gone "missing" a few days back. However, the Congress did not bat too many eyelids on her resurfacing with the BJP legislators, as her tactical disappearance was presumably accounted for, in the Congress calculus.

Unfortunately, for the BJP, the Supreme Court upheld the High Court's decision on the disqualification of the nine rebel Congress MLA's, and barred them from participating in the trust vote--a crucial move that could have swung the decision the other way. Interestingly, in the 2012 Uttarakhand Legislative Assembly elections, when Congress denied Rekha Arya the ticket from Someshwar, she stood as an independent candidate, and later joined the BJP. A few days ahead of bypoll to the three vacant seats in 2014, Rekha Arya again switched over to Congress, as she felt let down by the BJP, and said, "BJP leaders are again trying to deceive me and give ticket to the brother of BJP MP from Almora or another contestant", only to do another *volte-face* yet again, in 2016.

To counter the menace of "*jod-tod ki rajniti*" (politics of make and break) owing to any dubious considerations, the landmark Tenth schedule (Anti-Defection Act) was included in the Constitution, in 1985, by the Rajiv Gandhi government. Only a "defection" by one-third of the elected members, of a political party, was allowed to be considered a legitimate "merger"-- later, pursuant to the recommendations of the Dinesh Goswami Committee on Electoral Reforms and the National Commission to Review the Working of the Constitution, the 91st Constitutional Amendment Act, 2003, made the "merger" qualification more stringent, with two-third members of a party required, to establish a constitutionally claimable change of heart and vote. This has reduced the phenomenon of "*Aya Ram, Gaya Ram*" considerably, though constitutional technicalities and systemic processes still allow for the entrepreneurial swinging of crucial votes, in whichever direction the carrot lies for the legislator.

The most famous no-confidence motion in the Indian Parliament was on April 17, 1999. The BJP government was on the mat, after BSP retracted from an earlier commitment to support the BJP. However, the most decisive vote was cast by Saifuddin Soz who defied his party, the National Conference, and voted against the BJP (former Orissa Chief Minister of BJP, Giridhar Gamang too would vote against). The incumbent government of India lost by a solitary vote!

By itself, holding a contrarian view, and voting against a party position can be a sign of a mature, confident, and vibrant internal democracy. However, in Indian politics, the reality is that the decision to vote for or against a motion invariably happens at the proverbial last minute, and is usually followed by the rebelling legislator's seamless entry, into the opposition party. Such issueless and transactional party-hopping should be publically discouraged, and penalised on both the defecting legislator, and the accommodating party. However, there are serving examples of such jumpy legislators "accommodated", as high as Cabinet Ministers and Chief Ministers, by all political parties (the leftists are usually a notable exception). Until such time, the jumping jacks are here to stay, and in a very perverse manner, entertain.

Sedition and Blasphemy

(STATESMAN, Mar 11, 2016)

Etymologically, both sedition and blasphemy are rooted in sinister utterances--the former against the State, and as provocative as to incite a public revolt, and the latter against God or any other sacred issue, and inciting religious sentiments. Born of the same womb, both India and Pakistan chose different paths towards defining public discourse. While the Secular Republic of India posited the "State" over everything else, the Islamic Republic of Pakistan ensured the supremacy of the Islamic tenets and symbols, and regarded them to be beyond reproach. Therefore, while sedition in India is an offence defined in Section 124 A, of the IPC; blasphemy, in Pakistan, is covered in the Pakistan Penal Code's sections 295, and 298. Sedition could lead to life imprisonment in India; in Pakistan it can be a lot more severe with blasphemy violations under Section 295C, which attracts the death penalty. Questions of what constitutes sedition or blasphemy are rife in both countries, given the conflicting interpretations, possible abuse of the laws, and relevance in a modern democratic society.

Both the Indian and Pakistani societies are passionately debating the appropriateness of sedition laws for India, with the JNU unrest as a backdrop. The Pakistani parallel, for blasphemy, has been sharpened with the news of the execution of Mumtaz Qadri, the police commando convicted of gunning down the former Governor of Punjab, Salman Taseer. Like the sedition narrative in India, the spirit and relevance of the blasphemy laws divides Pakistani society. By default, the supporters of the sedition act, and the blasphemy act, in the respective countries derive the logic to support their positions, as part of an integral and essential component of their interpretation of nationalism. Therefore, doing away with the Act completely, or relaxing the terms of punishment would be construed as compromising with the integrity and soul of the nation. The environment on both sides of the border is emotionally surcharged, with various political parties taking varying stands to secure their respective constituencies, by invoking doomsday implications for the past, present, and future of the nation.

If the ruling political dispensation in India alluded to "conspiracies" to unsettle them, and their government, to explain the prevailing acrimony and polarisation in society, the blasphemy debate in Pakistan can stretch even further than the perceived "Zionist conspiracies", said to be working against the welfare of that country. However, unlike India where the political contours of the issue are clearer, and defined in terms of support (and against the interpretation of sedition), Pakistan's political position on blasphemy is more complicated.

Pakistan is in the midst of an ongoing tryst with its own destiny, with sectarian tendencies that are steering the nation towards chaos, and strife against itself. Blasphemy laws are symptomatic of the former President, Zia-ul-Haq's drive towards concerted Islamisation of the laws and society, as a means to tighten his grip over governance. The serendipity of the prevailing geopolitics in Afghanistan ensured international support. His regressive internal policies were overlooked as long as he did the bidding of the Western powers. However, this resulted in long-term damage to Pakistan's intrinsic fabric and instincts. Fundamentalism has seeped in irreversibly, and drifted into the space beyond the mosques. It has influenced legislation, political power, and even the security establishment--a worrisome reality for a nation with nuclear arms.

The dichotomy of Pakistan is exemplified by the fact that it is the PML (N) government of Nawaz Sharif, which is ostensibly responsible for sending Mumtaz Qadri to the gallows. It is important to remember that the Prime Minister is the *protégé* of Zia-ul-Haq, and was handpicked because of the ideological persuasions of the Sharif bothers. Zia's conservative outlook is at the root of Pakistan being a failed state.

The slain Governor, Salman Taseer, had courageously taken a public stand against the blasphemy laws, and had termed it as a piece of "black legislation" that had been imposed against a Christian woman named Aisa Bibi. This stand, on a matter of law, had infuriated his personal security staff member belonging to the elite police commando force. In a fit of rage, he had pumped in 27 bullets into Salman Taseer. More than 500 clerics spoke in favour of Mumtaz's action; 300 lawyers offered their services to Mumtaz for free, and showered him with rose petals when he appeared in court. What added salt to the wound was the last-minute disappearance of the chief cleric of Badshahi Mosque, to avoid conducting the burial ceremonies for Salman Taseer.

Pakistan's inbuilt reluctance to review the blasphemy laws, was quite apparent. Less than two months later, Pakistan's Federal Minister of Minorities Affairs, Shahbaz Bhatti, a Roman Catholic and a vocal opponent of the blasphemy laws, was killed after his vehicle was sprayed with bullets. Clearly, blasphemy laws are not open to review, which has been opposed by a very large section of Pakistani society. There are 1300 trials, mainly relating to minorities, under the blasphemy laws. As many as 60 under-trials have been murdered before the award of the verdict. The intelligentsia, middle and upper sections of society, and the military are broadly in favour of firmly containing the fundamentalist strains in Pakistani society that were manifest in the uproar on the streets, following the execution of Mumtaz Qadri.

The fact is that the Pakistan Supreme Court had upheld the death sentence twice, and the Pakistan President had rejected his plea for clemency. Given the overall political consensus across party lines-- with proactive military courts pronouncing verdicts against militants--it was inevitable that the Pakistani establishment would carry out the execution. The Supreme Court has observed that appeals for "improvements" in blasphemy laws are not objectionable as they seek to provide protection against misuse. Yet, an initiative to change the blasphemy act will not be easy given the societal fault-lines, and hardened positions of the various groups. However, the National Action Plan (NAP) that was devised following the massacre in a school in Peshawar offers a ray of hope, as it seeks to crack down on terrorism, irrespective of its implications.

Thankfully, the sedition debate in India is a lot more civil and nuanced, with enough scope to ensure an outcome that reflects India's inherent plurality and freedom. The struggle in India is to remain true to its lofty constitutional spirit of freedom. The reverse struggle, for freedom, confronts Pakistan which seeks to correct the constitutional tenets of its laws on blasphemy.

Personal Musings

Either way, there is nothing "Rajput" about it!

(THE CITIZEN, 3 Feb 2017)

I was born in a Rajput family, and consequently brought up on the notion of "living up" to being one.

My father was a commissioned officer in the British Army, and his military travails took him to far-flung outposts. Consequently, I was brought up by my grandparents. My grandfather was a progressive educationist, who believed that education was the only way out of society's regressive tendencies and "cultures". While he was a proud Rajput, he was unsparing of the community's retrograde rigidities, and empty posturing that needed to be shed and contemporise, without letting go of the "spirit" (befittingly, he started a Rajput Student's Aid Society to propagate the community's educational needs). He would repeatedly say, "A Rajput is made by *Karma* and not just by *Dharma,* or *Janama*".

Education made perfect sense, India had recently attained Independence, and we were "Indians" before any other denomination, albeit, proud (not supremacist) of our family's, and community's history.

My ode to my forefathers, and my own dreams took me to the imposing steps of the Jodhpur-stone building of the NDA, at the age of fifteen. At the time, I thought, soldiering was the only way to answer the call to honour (I am wiser today), and my grandfather gently acquiesced.

I joined the "Rajput Regiment" at the age of nineteen, and for the next forty-one years, wore the Rajput lanyard with much aplomb, and justifiable pride. We were baptized with the 1965 Indo-Pak war, and like any subaltern, hero-worshipped my Commanding Officer. He was a fatherly figure with an imposing personality, reckless bravado, and a provincial heart that bled for his soldiers, Colonel "Baba" Gill--a strapping Sikh, quintessentially "Rajput".

Irrespective of the casteist nomenclature, it is a "mixed" Regiment with India's myriad diversities that proudly call themselves, "Rajput soldiers". So, Kamal Ram, our Regiment's Victoria Cross winner is a *Gujjar* by caste, and the pride of my unit, Field Marshall Cariappa, a Coorgi--for us, they are as much "Rajputs", as our PVC winner, Yadunath Singh.

Being a "Rajput" is an idea, and not a caste--part historical, part mythical, and the exact veracity of our stories, irrelevant. The Indian Army has an inexplicable "Indian" formulation that belies the obvious--the current Chief of Indian Army, ostensibly a Rajput by caste, a Garhwali by regional definition, is neither a "Rajput Officer" nor a "Garhwali Officer"--He is a very proud "Gorkha Officer"!

Our regiment stoically insists, "Victory or death in battle has been the religion of the Rajput from time immemorial. It is his character that he knows no fear", this ingrained "spirit" drove a fearless "Rajput" in Major B.K. Pant to exhort his men, with his last dying words to defend the indefensible, during the 1962 Indo-Chinese war, "Men of the Rajput Regiment, you were born to die for your country. God has selected this small river for which you must die. Stand up and fight like true Rajputs". Although, 282 gallant soldiers of the 2nd Rajput were massacred in the attack, no blow could dissolve our "spirit" and resolve. The roll of honour, of the martyrs, included all castes, regional, ethnic and religious divisions--we are proud of them as "Rajput soldiers".

I, therefore, struggle to comprehend the absurdity that surrounds the Jaipur "Rajput" drama. Like all communities, Rajputs are a reality, who, much like other communities, have evolved their own narratives, values, and mythologies that they choose to remain invested in--faith is illogical, and not necessarily factual, and that is fine. But "values", and not antiquated rituals and grandstanding, should matter.

Maharana Pratap is lesser known for his territorial conquests, and more for his nobility, and resolve to "never accept defeat". He was aided in that by the indomitable tribals of the region (i.e., Bhils), who shared the same sense of honour; as their beloved Mewar.

Beyond fearlessness, the other two equally definitive Rajput "values" are chivalry, and civility. This "spirit" supposedly made Prithiviraj Chauhan release Muhammad Ghori, after capturing him, in the spirit of magnanimity that we celebrate. What the mob did in Jaipur does not qualify as gallant, civil, or chivalrous.

Likewise, it is true, Bollywood is guilty of perpetuating stereotypical impressions about many communities, including the Rajputs, such as, the *"Thakur"*, who is portrayed as a villainous character. In a 1990's potboiler, *"Joh Jeeta Wohi Sikander"*, the two competing colleges were named "Modern" and "Rajput"-- shockingly, the goons and villains belonged to the "Rajput" college, while the hero's college, "Modern", symbolised opposite values of contemporaneity, in direct contrast to the "Rajput" college. Bollywood typecasts some communities to bring comic relief, portrays some as the flag-bearers of nationalism, and makes villains out of others.

I, unequivocally, disagree with this oversimplification, but I choose not to express dissent with violence. Often, I squirm at the screen allusions that run contrary to my belief-system, and I try to put my contrarian point across, as much as I can, in as civil a manner, as I can. My violent streak is reserved for my country's enemies on the LOC, not within (like it did for of the brave-heart from Rajasthan, Major Shaitan Singh, PVC). There too, the mandate is to conduct oneself in a manner befitting the nobility of a soldier, and not the ignobility of a terrorist, or a mercenary.

Therefore, I reserve my equal displeasure at some young talented artistes, who choose to express their justifiable anger at the condemnable act of a few in Jaipur, by either dropping "family names", or expressing "shame" on belonging to the community. By being "ashamed", or dropping family names, you closet the entire community as the exclusive preserve of the retrogrades, which derides all.

To each his/her own, but I am saddened to see the alacrity and selective sense of outrage, as the foolishness of some is given a sweeping and collective condemnation. Dropping their name is an insult of unimaginable import and symbolism, to this community and its modern renditions, like the Rajput regiment, where regimental soldiers lay down their lives, to uphold the "Rajput" name. On the contrary, the successful amongst the community need to guide, inspire, enlighten, and not surrender to shame on social media, which is an easy outlet--but, it is your choice, and I choose to differ with you, in the same way as I do wholeheartedly, with the elements of the Jaipur mob.

My own unit, 17th Rajput has a suffix, *"Barhe Chalo"*-- militarily, it connotes the unstoppable. However, socially, it can be decoded as an inspiration to continuously evolve, and enlighten oneself to meet the challenges of the 21st century. Being a "Rajput" is beyond caste based identity politics, it is a concept that my grandfather taught me to "live up" to, wherein, the "State", with all its elements was above all else(from Mewar and Marwar then, to India now), and where "values" mattered.

I am a proud "Rajput", without its narrow, ignorable, or pejorative context, although I remain concerned about a few community members, who bring disrepute by uncivil acts, or abject surrender, which is unbecoming of the "Rajput" spirit.

Politics of Houbara Hunting

(MILLENNIUM POST, 23 Dec 2016)

Modern Pakistani narratives owe their financial sustenance, religious credentials, and diplomatic beneficence to the various Gulf Sheikhdoms who have generously doled out irreplaceable petrodollars to harness the "Islamisation" drive, which started in earnest, with the puritanical rule of General Zia-ul-Haq, in the 1980's. This absolute clientelism drove Pakistan away from Jinnah's secular moorings towards retrogressive extremism, Hudood ordinances, and the crippling "Kalashnikov culture". The Sheikhdoms have supported Pakistan during 1965, and 1971, in dealing with sanctions following the Pakistani nuclear test, and in a reciprocal gesture the Pakistanis have steadfastly provided the much needed security (both conventional, e.g., 11,000 Pakistani troops were sent to Saudi Arabia to defend the monarchy in the Gulf war of 1990-91, and with the ostensible security cover and pride of the only "Islamic nuclear bomb"). Crucially, remittances of hard currency from its diaspora of over 4 million Pakistanis in the Arabian Gulf (majority of 2.2 million in Saudi Arabia itself), accounts for a substantial economic rationale beyond the multiple bilateral and multilateral agreements with the Sheikhdoms, which virtually ensure the control of the economic windpipe of Pakistan.

Across the trilogy of the institutional power centres of the Pakistani establishment (politicos, military, and clergy), all three hold the Gulf Sheikhdoms with a special reverence. While the Gulf money has successfully injected the alien Wahhabi strains in the Pakistani mainstream, the life-saving bailout to the Nawaz Sharif family (after the coup by General Pervez Musharraf, in 1999) by Saudi Arabia, and the most recent optics of the "first foreign visit" of the new Pakistani Chief of Army Staff, General Qamar Javed Bajwa to meet King Salman of Saudi Arabia (to promise, "complete security for the holy places in Saudi Arabia along with its regional sovereignty"), is reflective of the obsequious hold of the Sheikhdoms over the Pakistani establishment. One of the regressive privileges that the Gulf Sheikhs routinely extract out of the overenthusiastic Pakistani establishment is the "special hunting permits", to poach the endangered pheasant species, Houbara Bustard (also known as MacQueen's Bustard, or Asian Bustard), in unashamed violation of the Pakistani Wildlife Laws.

Hunted by both guns and the more traditional Arab method of Falconry--these rare birds with black and white cravat make their annual breeding journeys from the Central Asian region to the arid wastelands of Pakistan, in winters. For decades these migrations have attracted the Arab princelings to Pakistan, to indulge in their wanton hunting sprees that have dangerously depleted the numbers of these Houbara birds. These "special permits" help circumvent the protectionist laws that ostensibly ban the hunting of the same, in Pakistan. A wide estimate suggests that only 50,000 to 100,000 birds are left, less than a third of what existed 50 years back. The Houbara hunting parties itself are a throwback to the feudal times, with advance parties that set up the camps near the nesting sites, replete with an array of glistening SUV's, well-fed falcons, local guides, and retainers--till the arrival of the principal hunting retinue, usually in private jets that land in makeshift airstrips, maintained essentially for the annual Houbara hunts.

In an ode to the Arab Bedouin culture, hunting falcons are frequently used to unleash themselves, and swoop down on the hapless Houbaras (Falconry was included, by UNESCO, to its "Representative List of Intangible Cultural Heritage", of the Middle East). With mythical aphrodisiac properties, these Houbara hunts have acquired magnetic charm for hordes of Arab royalty. The winter season (December to January) witnesses the hunting mayhem with the issuance of these contentious "special permits". A couple of years back, public outrage broke out over the news of over 2,100 Houbaras that were killed in a hunting spree in Baluchistan (i.e., over 20 times more than the official limit of a 100 Houbaras, per permit!) Clearly, Houbara Bustards have been an integral part of Pakistan's "soft diplomacy", to ingratiate itself with the Gulf Sheikhdoms, and nature is seen as a small price to pay for the Arab largesse. So much so, that the Pakistan government requested, and successfully overturned, the ban issued by the Supreme Court to hunt Houbaras as it shockingly noted, "Inviting Arabs to hunt is a pillar of foreign policy".

The Ministry of Foreign Affairs had blatantly pleaded in review, "The petition involved a question of fundamental importance having a direct bearing upon foreign relations of the federation with the Gulf States". Recently the farmers in Baluchistan's Kachhi District had protested in anticipation of the "special permits" to the Qatari princes, to hunt down the Houbara Bustards. Besides disrupting the cropping season, and daily life, because of the accompanying humdrum of hunting paraphernalia, it is increasingly seen as a political symbol of the Pakistan government's sovereign infirmity, and pusillanimity. This has recently woken up the Pakistani Supreme Court to uphold a petition to seek a ban on these "special permits". However, despite loud protests from conservationists, affected locals, and even some political parties (Imran Khan's PTI-ruled, Khyber Pakhtunkhwa province has refused permission to the Gulf princes to hunt in their area of jurisdiction), permissions were granted in the provinces of Baluchistan, and Punjab, to the Governor of Tabuk province in Saudi Arabia (in Awaran district), and to the two sons of the former King of Saudi Arabia (in Layyah district in Punjab).

While the official permission is supposedly for a 100 Houbara Bustards per permit, the Governor of Tabuk is the same person who had infamously hunted down 2100 Houbaras in 2014-15. The language of the recent "special permit" issued is an unequivocal testimony to the obsequious relationship that belies all international agreements, towards protecting endangered species, "The Ministry of Foreign Affairs of the Islamic Republic of Pakistan presents its compliments to the Royal Embassy of Saudi Arabia in Islamabad and has the honour to state that the government of Pakistan has conveyed its recommendations to the authorities in the provinces concerned for allocation of following areas to the dignitaries of the Kingdom of Saudi Arabia for Houbara bustard for the season 2016-2017".The servile mentality of the Pakistani establishment allows the sovereign pride to be conveniently swallowed, and to remain bound to such archaic and shameful surrender to their Arab benefactors.

In the face of the desperate economic situation at home, international isolation for its famed double-standards on terrorism, and the looming prospects of further tightening of the noose with the impending Donald Trump government--Pakistan is desperately latching on to its few remaining supporters, even at the cost of depleting its natural resources, disrupting the lives of its vulnerable rural folk, and worse, compromising on its sovereign pride, when it acts like a vassal state that still prepares for royal hunts in the twenty-first century.

The Forgotten Dogras

(MILLENNIUM POST, 16 Sep 2016)

Armed militancy, growing religious extremism, and cross-border firing have hijacked the headlines of the state of Jammu & Kashmir, since the early 1990's. Today, this region is amongst the most militarised zones in the world, with the nuclear-tipped armies of India (in the state of J&K), Pakistan (in Pakistan occupied Kashmir), and China (in *Aksai Chin*) facing each other in a hostile standoff that often sparks with blazing intensity. The wounds of Kashmir were inflicted during the birth of the nation itself, in 1947, with the Pakistanis initiating the first of the four wars to be formally fought between Pakistan and India--armed Afridi Lashkars, along with Pakistani irregulars threatened to take over the state, leading to the Dogra ruler, Maharaja Hari Singh, to sign the treaty of accession, and merge his state with the Union of India. Since then, the narrative and history of the fractured state has varied on both sides of the Line-of-Control. However, Pakistan has steadily chosen to ignore the terms and conditions set forth as part of the much-bandied plebiscite, in 1948. It has conveniently chosen to disown the subsequent Shimla Treaty and its mandated bilateralism, and finally, Kargil was a frightening testimony to the Pakistani adventurism, belligerence, and dangerous misreading of the ground situation that continues till date, in the misplaced hope that India will eventually let go of Kashmir.

Irrespective of the reality, the externally stoked fire in the Kashmiri insurgency has led to the unnecessary spilling of blood and precious lives, besides the slow decay of the syncretic culture of *Kashmiriyat* in favour of the wholly imported strains of the puritanical and alien Islam, (i.e., Wahhabism). Amidst this tragic saga of external interference, regressive religiosity, and misplaced distrusts--the story of the non-Kashmiri population of the state emerges as a mere footnote, with nearly 30 percent of the population residing in the Jammu, and Ladakh regions. The largest "minority" of Jammu and Kashmir are the indefatigable Dogras, whose glorious history of ruling the state of Jammu and Kashmir aside, have an unparalleled (and unsung) role in the sacrifices made for the security, and safety, of the nation-building process in modern India. Hidden from the principal frame and telecasts that beam regularly out of the troubled J&K mess, is the genteel, yet ultra-gallant people of the erstwhile Duggar lands, who are tucked between the Pir Panjal mountain range in the North, the plains of Punjab to the South, the LoC in the West, and the Ladakh region in the East; composing nearly 28 percent of the state's population. According to caste and religion, the Dogras are predominantly Hindus, although there are Sikh and Muslim Dogras as well.

However, public memory and modern perceptions do not do justice to the multiple legends of this race who famously include, "India's Napoleon", General Zorawar Singh, whose legendary conquests include Tibet, Baltistan, and vast swathes of Ladakh. The unfinished narratives of the post-Independence saga and the subsequent state rules, predominantly by the Nehru-Sheikh Abdullah imprints, have given an almost pejorative twist to perceptions about Dogra rule, fuelled by their own individual and political outlooks. A statistical "minority" existence within the state has ensured that no major state leader emerges in the arithmetic of electoral democracy, with Kashmiris ruling the state predominantly, whilst, even at the national level, no significant leader was allowed to flower and occupy a prominent place in the public imagination (Dr. Karan Singh, a titular inheritor of the ruling Dogra family, was never a mass leader in the political sense). Strictly speaking, the Dogra population spills over into the adjoining mountains of Himachal Pradesh, and the fertile plains of Punjab.

This lesser-known race is also home to an unprecedented four Regiments of the Indian Army that essentially take their manpower from the Dogra catchment areas: Dogra Regiment, Jammu and Kashmir Rifles, Jammu and Kashmir Light Infantry (which has a half-half composition of the Dogras, and Valley-based stock), and even Punjab Regiment (nearly half of its manpower are the Punjabi Dogras). The combined gallantry awards to the Dogras in the Indian Armed Forces could shame any other race or region in the country--with military heroes like Brigadier Rajender Singh Jamwal (the savior of J&K in 1947-8 whose gazette notification reads, "Brigadier Rajender Singh, and his band of soldiers carried out the orders of the Maharaja to the letter and spirit. Fighting bravely for every inch of land, they delayed enemy advance by two crucial days during which important decisions were made. The Indian Army joined the fight, and the J&K State was thus saved for India by Brigadier Rajender Singh..."), Major Som Nath Sharma (India's first Param Veer Chakra), Captain GS Salaria (India's first Param Veer Chakra for gallantry outside India, in Congo), to more recent PVC winners like Honorary Captain Bana Singh (for action in Siachen), to Kargil's immortal, "*Yeh Dil Maangey More*", Captain Vikram Batra, the list is endless and unmatched.

For these simple yet battle-hardy folks, soldiering comes as a natural instinct and their locational geography, martial history, and sensitivities of state politics have afforded them an inherent sense of patriotic dignity that is bereft of any political colour, chest-thumping shenanigans, or touristy trumpeting. Jammu, as the historical, provincial, and emotional "capital" of the Dogras is reflective of the neglect and ignominy of Dogras, in modern India. A forgotten city that has grown shapeless, unplanned, and without the trappings of modern amenities that define urban development; it is the proverbial "other" city in the J&K dynamics. Forever considered for necessary attention "after the valley"--the nondescript existence of Jammu cannot boast of any substantial industry, commerce, or infrastructural wonder.

The muted response to including "Dogri" in the list of official languages, ensured that although it got recognised as one of the 22 scheduled national languages, this happened as late as 2003, with the 92nd Constitutional Amendment. The delay ensured the virtual disappearance of the unique Takri script, a sad price to pay for silently waiting on the side-lines of other regional movements that often deployed aggression against the nation. This oasis of calm since Independence has seen the historical ravages of Alexander, Babur, Ghazni to the more recent tumult in neighbouring Punjab in the 1980's, Kashmir from 1990's onwards, and a perennially hostile Pakistan that fires brazenly into the long border stretches that run through the Dogra lands. Today, the Dogras need to be acknowledged and recognised for the invaluable role that they have played (and continue to play), in rendering their services to the nation; the region is forever devoid of largesses in the form of the grandiose "J&K Packages", which are essentially directed at the Valley. Providentially, a Jammu/Dogra representative in the form of a Deputy Chief Minister of J&K is there (Dr. Nirmal Singh), and two important ministers in the Central government including Dr. Jitendra Singh and JP Nadda (he is a Dogra from Himachal Pradesh).

Technically, the ruling dispensation in the J&K state and the Centre are also aligned, and therefore should be in a position to push through the much-needed development and upliftment of the Dogras. From the heyday of the Dogra rule in the region, to the current status as a forgotten people, the Dogras have typically punched above their weight in other fields like arts, culture, and sports but have never gotten their due of recognition and support. Planned development in these areas will usher in much needed opportunities for the Dogras, as indeed for the Kashmiris and Ladakhis who often have to venture far into the hinterland to partake of education, medical care, and other job opportunities--the madness that has consumed the valley, and has polarised its soul, can be healed with the balm of national integration and opportunities, in its nearest area of calm and order.

Tiger Tiger not Burning Bright

(DAILY EXCELSIOR, 11 May 2016)

The "Tyger", in the *Songs of Experience* collection, is an immortal poetic ode by the English poet, William Blake, published in 1794. It philosophically ponders over the Almighty's Divine will and craftsmanship (akin to a blacksmith), to create a magnificent beast capable of horrifically destructive powers--an intriguing and luring image that has shocked and awed, simultaneously. Giving rise to the subsequent characterization in popular culture as Sher Khan, the perennial enemy of Mowgli in Rudyard Kipling's *Jungle Book*, as Richard Parker, the Bengal Tiger, on the boat in Yann Martel's *Life of Pi*, or even factually; as depicted in Jim Corbett's 1944 classic, *Man-Eaters of Kumaon*. This sense of fear and fascination has led to the inert human desire to assert supremacy over the tiger by hunting down the biggest cats, as trophies and mementoes of individual triumph and manhood; as also in the form of *Shikaars* by the royalty, nobility, and the later day colonial aristocrats.

At the beginning of the 20th century, over 100,000 tigers roamed across the vast swathes of the Caucus to the South Eastern tip of Asia in Java, and the Bali Islands--today, apparently 3890 abound (supposedly up from a figure of approx. 3200 in 2010), as released by WWF- International and Global Tiger Forum, in New Delhi, recently. Overall, it is indeed a sobering and sad reality of the decline in tiger numbers within a 100 years, irrespective of the premature and questionable celebratory pitch of the "rise in numbers for the first time in the century". Basically, in the last 10 years itself, the tiger has completely disappeared from nearly 40% of the forest cover where they existed with an "extinct" status afforded to tigers, in countries like China, Vietnam, Laos, and Cambodia (an experiment to reintroduce the now "functionally extinct" tigers, 2 male and 5 to 6 female tigers in the Eastern Plains from India, has been mooted). In these South Eastern countries, the use of tiger bones and almost all body parts in traditional Chinese/ East Asian medicines, as pain killers and aphrodisiacs, has led to fatal poaching and rampant black marketing of body parts and fur. The numbers in Bangladesh (where it is the national animal) and Malaysia (home to the Malayan tiger), which ironically is on the insignia of the gallant Dogra Regiment of the Indian Army (in recognition of the Regiment's fine battle record in the Malayan Campaign), has been declining steadily--including, in the so called period of "tiger population revival" in the last 5 years.

It is only in India, Bhutan, and Russia where the statistical numbers have gone up since 2010. India recognised the formal criticality of tiger conservation via "Project Tiger", in 1972, by establishing tiger reserves and setting up a tiger protection force to take on poachers, amongst many other habitat protection measures. This was given more teeth by the successive National Tiger Conservation Authority, in

2005, for more scientific tracking, protection, and strengthening of laws to improve the ecosystem within which the tigers resided. It also benefitted from an active and high voltage campaign by many private organisations, NGO's, and corporates towards the conservation cause.

However, conservation and industrial "development" invariably cross paths wherein the single-window clearance approach for "development", often results in the tapering down of the conservation parameters, to enable the "development" imperatives, which overrule tiger conservation means. Therefore, given the advancement in tracking and irrefutable decline in the dedicated forest covers, sceptics question the veracity of claims suggesting "increase in numbers", even in India. Recently, 2 tigers were reported to have died at Kanha Tiger Reserve, taking the death toll to 20, for tigers in Madhya Pradesh itself, since May last year--with some deaths indicating clear tell-tale signs of active poaching, even in India, and in a state with arguably, the most effective tiger conservation and management approach. Still, with 2226 of the 3890 tigers globally residing in India, the success of India in conservation of tigers is pivotal to the survival of the magnificent animal. The days of *Shikaars* with nobility hunting on horsebacks or elephant backs with reckless machismo and abandon, is behind us; it is said that King George V on ascending the throne, slayed 39 tigers in 10 days.

The Maharaja of Surguja is supposed to have told the wildlife biologist George Schaller that by 1965, he had bagged 1,150 tigers. Tiger hunting started as a passion for the Mughal emperors, with Babur (whose name incidentally means tiger, in Persian) vividly describing tiger hunts in his memoirs to eventually, Emperor Akbar, who elevated the game hunt to an exclusive sport for the royalty. The same sentiment is glorified in the miniature paintings of the Rajput, Afghan, and Turk nobility as well, who indulged in the same as an integral ritual of kingship. However, it was technology in the form of easily available hunting guns by the British colonisers or Sahibs that truly mainstreamed the game hunt to an easily accessible "gentlemanly sport", which led to the debilitating tiger hunting purges, pre-Independence. Tiger conservation is complex, multi-dimensional, and expensive; this, because besides the expected stringency and manpower to take on poaching, smuggling, and black marketing, it needs adequate habitation landmass (already under immense pressure with invariable crisscross of roads and deforestation, already impacting the quality of tiger ecosystems). It also needs the requisite quantum of prey hunting for survival which is also facing similar depletion issues, for the same and multiple other causes.

Ultimately in an era of scarcity of resources, it will be the fight of conservation against the ostensible "development" that will be the most fatal, as the government of the day and the corporates will expectedly close ranks in one direction. The stated goal of a 50% increase in the global population to 5890 by 2022 will call for a renewed commitment and concerted efforts, as the current bonhomie of "increased numbers" is not truly reflective of the deterioration and increasing challenges to the tiger ecosystems, or to the actual extinction rate of tigers from various habitats and countries--clearly, it is still not a case of "Tiger Tiger burning bright...", at least in the sense of conservation.

US Honchos Quit Trumps Advisory Council, Where Is The 'Searing' Conscience of Indian Corporates?

(THE CITIZEN, 19ᵗʰ Sep 2017)

Reverse optics were at play in the corporate boardrooms of the land of karma (i.e., India), versus those in the land of brazen capitalism (i.e., USA). One of India's most idealized and celebrated "garage (house in Matunga) to NSE" success-stories, headquartered in our very own Silicon Valley of Bengaluru was embroiled in murky accusations and talks of a "coup" that runs contrary to its historical image of a conscience-conscious and value-based organisation. As the dust settles and the warring sides lick their wounds in a seemingly acceptable rapprochement formula, questions abound about the man who famously stated, "A clear conscience is the softest pillow in the world."

Meanwhile in the land described by Oscar Wilde as, "unmatched in vitality and vulgarity", and where the corporate culture was stereo-typified by Tom Scholz as, "sometimes I actually start to think human life is just as cheap to corporate America as animal life, so long as there are profits to be made", a complete antithesis of the popular perception and an unthinkable movement was afoot with five senior executives of some of the world's largest companies, acquiescing to their inner conscience and quitting the prized membership of President Donald Trump's Business Advisory Council. The handling of the Charlottesville incident was the latest in the series of gaffes made by Donald Trump, who yet again demonstrated his natural proclivity, inclination, and tolerance for bigotry and racism.

Presidential dilly-dallying and the deliberately ambiguous (criticizing violence "on many sides") and obviously wasted opportunity to come down hard on race-supremacism, infuriated the sane-minded Americans into registering their disgust. In a pleasantly surprising move, either out of their own sense of moral outrage or by getting compelled to take a stand by their employees, the galaxy of CEO's either quit the high-tables of advisory boards or stopped just short. For instance, Walmart CEO, Doug McMillon, who rued Trumps' inaction on, "a critical opportunity to help bring our country together by unequivocally rejecting the appalling actions of white supremacists", simultaneously declined to quit the Strategic and Policy Forum platform (a powerhouse of corporate glitterati with CEO's of Pepsi, General Motors, and JP Morgan), as he ostensibly wanted Walmart to, "stay engaged to try to influence decisions in a positive way and help bring people together".

However, people like Richard Trumka, the president of the American Federation of Labor and Congress of Industrial Organizations (representing 12 million workers and retirees), was unequivocally brazen in quitting immediately from the advisory council and bluntly stated, "We cannot sit on a council for a president who tolerates bigotry and domestic terrorism". Not one to take a contrarian view lying down, Donald Trump hit back at the "grandstanders" when he inelegantly tweeted, "For every CEO that drops out of the Manufacturing Council, I have many to take their place. Grandstanders should not have gone on". Expectedly, he lambasted the media for being "truly dishonest" yet again, and incredulously suggested that it was the media that was dividing the country. He branded journalists as those who, "do not like our country".

Unfortunately, Trump's Jekyll and Hyde performances and utterances do resonate amongst a sizable section of the mainstream, and the pugnacious counter-attacks, mocks, and personalised jeers by none-less-than-the serving President of USA, has its own set of illiberal believers and fanatics. Corporates profess to walk the talk on "values" and have embedded "vision statements" in their public documents like annual reports and memorandum of associations. These obligatory bedrock-responsibilities reflect a seemingly civic and socially-conscious face, beyond the goods and services that they offer.

Often the wordsmithing captures the necessary compulsions and tensions of the times that be, which potentially leaves almost all corporates stating the same banalities on their moral compasses, for instance, the infamous Enron postured itself as the "Global Corporate Citizen" that aspired to conduct business by four values--Respect,

Integrity, Communication, and Excellence! The poster boys of the 2008 recession trail, Lehman Brothers, saw themselves as amongst other drivel, "ensuring the highest risk management standards"!

Walking the talk is never easy, but there is silent revolution afoot and it is being led, ironically, by the younger workforce, or the Millennials, who are driven by a genuine sense of purpose in everything that they do. As per the Deloitte Millennial Survey 2017, 59% feel accountable "towards protecting the environment", 53% towards "social equality" and 40% towards "direction of the country". Backlash against Donald Trump's pusillanimity, and de facto encouragement of the regressive elements in the Charlottesville episode, has stirred a nationwide call for boycotts, protests, active lobbying for more resignations, and condemnations from the corporate Tsars. Clearly, the taint of abdicating moral responsibility is weighing heavily on the CEO's, whose credibility and reputation is getting interlinked with Donald Trumps', as they get declared guilty by silence, when the onus is on standing up and getting counted!

In India as well, the chickens are coming home to roost on many corporate houses who built their name and fame because of their proximity to various political parties of all denominations (perhaps with the singular exception of the Communist parties). However, providential business circumstances, competitive ambitions, and changing power dispensations are more responsible for the corporate shake-up or financial belly-up, as opposed to any searing conscience amongst the board members or shareholders. While there are growing whispers alluding to the unhealthy proximity of certain corporations to the corridors-of-power, there is no similar groundswell compelling the board members to any conscience issues, as yet.

The vulnerabilities of the Indian environment are said to be very dominant and overarching, which ensures "practicality" over the "values" and "ethics" that get printed in very small fonts in annual reports. However, increasingly the consumers and the common man on the street is prefixing corporations with "good", "bad" and even "irresponsible", herein the pressure on invoking the corporate conscience is inevitable.

Shaktiman Triggers a Debate
(DAILY EXCELSIOR, 25 Mar, 2016)

As the white Kathiawari mare Shaktiman backed away in self-defence from the alleged assaults, by a BJP law-maker and his associates, in Dehradun, one of his hind legs tragically caught the railing, resulting in a horrific injury that might ensure it never recovers. Therein, ensued a politics of blame-game and "brownie-point visits", to see the injured animal, and the absurdity hit a new low with the law-maker naïvely suggesting that he only "snatched" a stick from the policemen on duty, and had not physically hit the animal. However, the consequences and the apparent spirit displayed, in taking the law into your own hands, never crossed the mind of the law-maker (imagine the audio-visuals of the same incident, had it been a regulation gun instead of the regulation *danda* that the law-maker had snatched). The incident also showcased the hollowness of the actual implementation of the law that mandates having the Society for the Prevention of Cruelty to Animals (SPCAs) in every district; SPCA exists in Delhi only. However, a parallel narrative questioning the logic of mounted police (with allusions to the practice as a colonial-era legacy), merits debate and defence.

The link between soldiers and horses goes back to the pre-Iron Age period. The trust, mobility, and distance afforded by the mount has been immortalized in history from our own Chetak, to the fearless horsemanship of the marauding Cossacks. Even the fabled Cavalry owe their origin to the French cavallerie ("Cheval", horse). However, with the advent of technology, the armies abandoned their sabres, and started conversion of its horsed regiments to mechanized/tank cavalry. In fact, the 61st Cavalry Regiment of the Indian Army is the largest non-ceremonial horse-mounted cavalry unit remaining in the world--it did undertake mounted patrol tasks in the Indo-Pak war of 1971.

Within the DNA of the 61st Cavalry is the ancestry of the Jodhpur Lancers, who in 1918, led possibly the finest cavalry charge in history with just lances and swords. These cavaliers decimated the heavily armed and fortified Turks. Counted amongst the greatest cavalry charges in history, it is celebrated annually as the "Haifa Day". Today, the role and relevance of the horses and mules in the Army is redefined, and limited to doing yeoman service of hauling loads and critical provisions in inaccessible high mountain areas, besides the ceremonial roles, and contribution to equestrian sports by regiments like the 61st Cavalry, and the President's Bodyguards. The Remount Veterinary Corps (RVC) is the 236-year-old service that is responsible for the breeding and training of the Indian Army's equine and canine resources. The relevance of the horse for the Army is reduced, but still very relevant and irreplaceable at many fronts.

Similarly, in Police functions, while the roles of horses have reduced, and the costs of maintenance have made it difficult to sustain the earlier scale, the sight of mounted police in places like New York City, London, and Sydney is ubiquitous the world over. As in the Dehradun incident, the mounted police are primarily deployed for crowd control situations like protests. Empirical data points to high efficacy of the same, with minimum damage to either the assemblage of people or the horses, as raised by some concerned activists, and the law-maker concerned in Dehradun. It is believed that in such crowd control situations, a mounted policeman is as effective as 7 to 10 policeman on ground. However, on a day to day basis, high-visibility patrols in areas that are inaccessible to motorized transportation like parks, narrow lanes, and unlevelled areas makes mounted police effective for policing purposes. It is a scientifically proven fact that their highly visible presence can deter urban crimes, and have a reassuring presence for the public. Rand Europe, in partnership with Oxford University, conducted an extensive study to assess the qualitative and quantitative indicators of the value of mounted police in various scenarios, and the same study confirmed higher levels of visibility, trust, and confidence in neighbourhood settings that were patrolled with mounted police. Critically, mounted police was said to evince six times more casual public engagements and interactions in equivalent time, versus foot patrols, alluding to the sensitive empathy and connect that is invaluable in a public-police relationship.

That said, constraints like the inability to respond swiftly to basic policing requirements, like emergency calls, and the inherent danger of inadvertently causing injury to the masses in front has often led to the half-truth of "show horses", which are used only for ceremonial purposes. Actually, the New York mounted force is an elite and much sought after unit that is actively, and very usefully deployed for daily policing operations. These "10-feet-tall cops" afford a preventive outcome with the added height and visibility, allowing the mounted policemen to assess the situation better, in terms of crowd-control, as also conversely positing the presence of the law enforcers in a *mêlée* of a large gathering. With proper training, requisite equipment, and established charge procedures, the incidents of collateral damage have been negligible, and in fact figures suggest higher crowd control ability by the mounted police as opposed to policemen on foot.

Any concerns about the work conditions and the health of the horses, used either in the Army or the Police, is allayed by the apparent physicality and the institutionalized ration, care, and upkeep procedures that are part of the operational norms in such institutions--as opposed to horses and mules that are seen to be working as transportation carriers, draught animals, or even for marriage purposes, where the exploitative conditions are borne out by the apparent sight of the animal's health. There are estimated to be 1000 horses in the mounted police across India (with overall numbers for horses sharply declining by 24% as compared to 20 years back, in India). Besides invaluable policing service, these bastions are keeping alive Indian breeds like the Marwari, Kathiawari etc., which have seen a worrying trend of decline in numbers, with the advent of mechanization of transportation.

The real question in the Dehradun incident is one of identifying the perpetrator of the brutal attack on Shaktiman, and the final verdict on the same is still out there--irrespective of the name, party or political allegiance, the age old adage about a horse, "Let the horse teach you about yourself, for you may be at the age where no one else can", rings so true for the perpetrator!

As Captain Ram Pratap Sheaths his Saber

(DNA, 3 Jan 2016)

Tepid tea in a white mug brings temporary relief to Captain Ram Pratap's scraggy, frozen face as he squats on a bunker atop a 17,000ft. picket, overlooking the LoC. There's a shortage of nearly 12,000 army officers, and not surprisingly--given his battalion's deployment on the active border--his and many of his platoon boys' leaves were cancelled.

Hopefully the old warhorse of a helicopter, *Cheetah*, will continue belying its service age of over 40 years and drop some "fresh greens", to usher in much-needed cheer to these hardy men from the Thar desert, sick of canned food. He thought to himself, "why complain about the flying bird, when even the weaponry and equipment can do with upgrading". There's only so much that spit-polish and old-fashioned scrubbing can do, to retain the glint on the bayonet. He wonders if the civilian *babus* around Rajpath really understand the conditions in which the *fauj* operates, yet get to decide everything for them.

With snow covering the passes, they had hoped cross border infiltrations would cease, but no such luck. Down in the valley, Colonel MN Rai had been shot dead while leading an attack against terrorists. "Thank god for such heroes", he quietly reflected. Word had spread in the *paltan*, and they all felt honoured to be part of an outfit where officers still led from the front.

Later, Colonel Mahadik, the spirited Maratha, had put himself in the line of fire. Despite all organisational cribs, it was stories like these that kept the *Olive-Green* chins up. All the thundering braggadocio by pot-bellied politicians, about bringing enemies to their knees, hadn't helped on these pickets; infiltrations by terrorists and "friendly cover-fire" by enemies still continued. Suddenly, his mind raced to the super-awesome, real-time action in Myanmar, where they had been sent to settle some scores, by his Para Commando buddy, Captain Shyam, the "devil's-very-own", and his band of toughies, which had inadvertently helped further inflate the chests of the *kurta-pyjama* folks in Lutyen's Delhi.

"Shouldn't be complaining about these *civvies*", he thought, "maybe things aren't as bad as they seem". Previous battalions who thought they were getting out from this hellhole to more salubrious "peace stations", like Chennai and Rishikesh, didn't enjoy "peace" much. One was drawn into rescue operations in the Chennai floods, and the other was up and running doing flag marches in out-of-control, riot-stricken Saharanpur and Muzzafarnagar.

Maybe this minus 15 degree Celsius (-15 °C) temperature, with canned food, was a better option. It was best to stay back and do what one had joined the army to do, not be running errands for *sarkari chappies*, who are supposed to handle situations but never do, and invariably throw in their towels to call in the Forces to do their bidding!

Whatever happened to the much-promised appointment of Chief of Defence Staff, even after so many years? Surely his position in the warrant of precedence must have made a few *dhotiwalas* nervous? Interestingly, even they had questioned the organisational perception, "Respect for army is diminishing as the army hasn't fought a war". That wasn't fair. What did they think this active LoC was? What was Manipur then, where we had lost 20 men? What was Kargil all about? Captain Pratap remembered that his village of grand old soldiers had voted *en masse* to bring in what they thought was a more nationalistic, pro-military party. He looked forlornly at the men earnestly cocking their weapons for the evening drill. Such innocence. We were taught about honouring a given word. But did the nation really care about these spirited *faujis*?

He remembered his dad, a second-generation soldier and battle-decorated Infantarian, who had oscillated from sadness to confusion at Jantar Mantar for another failed promise: OROP. Captain Pratap had initially told him to go easy, but thinking that he too would be a veteran in a few years, and with TV screens blaring the need for veterans to "adjust", it had made his blood boil as well. We never "adjust", "compromise" or "bargain", whatever be the conditions, or the danger to our lives.

His father had dug in his heels even more after an imperious statement--that most veterans had agreed to the government's watered-down version of OROP, and only a minority were "holding out". This was a commitment to people who had given their lives and limbs. Ram's dad had moist eyes whenever he narrated the story of the 86-year-old whose shirt, emblazoned with war medals, was torn apart while he was protesting peacefully. No one had apologised. There was no mention in rallies or on Twitter. Maybe that was because OROP was a less important issue, than say, the national day of Mozambique. His old man was further saddened when told about the "double-whammy"--seems Defence Forces had been "done-in" yet again, this time in the Seventh Pay Commission.

Suddenly, Ram heard the call for the "evening stand-to", and dropped his now-cold mug, standing ramrod straight in solemn deference. He made a sharp turn, walking on the swampy, white blanket of snow to the platoon bunkers where the weekly snail-mail was to come, and saw that the irrepressible Rajasthani men had unusually-broad smiles on their fiercely-mustachioed faces. It was that time of the week when one desperately wanted to hear from home, via the "duty runner" who would soon arrive at the lonely picket.

www.ingramcontent.com/pod-product-compliance
Lightning Source LLC
Chambersburg PA
CBHW051721260326
41914CB00031B/1677/J